HARPERCOLLINS
PUBLISHERS LTD
A PHYLLIS BRUCE BOOK

GRASS,
SKY,
SONG

Promise and Peril in the World of Grassland Birds

TREVOR
HERRIOT

Grass, Sky, Song
© 2009 by Trevor Herriot.
All rights reserved.

A Phyllis Bruce Book, published by
HarperCollins Publishers Ltd

First Edition

HarperCollins books may be purchased for
educational, business, or sales promotional
use through our Special Markets
Department.

HarperCollins Publishers Ltd
2 Bloor Street East, 20th Floor
Toronto, Ontario, Canada
M4W 1A8

www.harpercollins.ca

Library and Archives Canada Cataloguing
in Publication

Herriot, Trevor
Grass, sky, song : promise and peril in the
world of grassland birds /Trevor Herriot.

A Phyllis Bruce book. Includes
bibliographical references and index.

ISBN 978-1-55468-038-2

1. Grassland birds.
2. Grassland birds—Ecology.
I. Title.

QL681.H46 2009   598.174   C2008-907107-7

DWF 9 8 7 6 5 4 3 2 1

Printed and bound in Canada

Grass, Sky, Song is printed on Ancient
Forest Friendly paper, made with 100%
post-consumer waste.

Pen-and-ink illustrations by Trevor Herriot
Interior design by Sharon Kish

For Karen

For a bird of the air
Shall carry the voice;
And that which hath wings
Shall tell the matter.

ECCLESIASTES 10:20

CONTENTS

Preface

A Way Home

How do you know but that ev'ry bird that cuts the airy way
Is an immense world of delight clos'd by your senses five?
William Blake

On warm, clear nights near the end of April, a barely notice-
able movement begins in the skies over the grasslands of
Montana, North Dakota, Saskatchewan, Alberta, and Manitoba. For
three weeks or more, snow geese have passed by in the milky light
of the moon, yelping excitedly of arctic pastures ahead of them, but
now there are softer notes falling from the night air, voices easily
lost in the clamour of a prairie spring. These are the contact calls
of Sprague's pipits and chestnut-collared longspurs returning to the
northern Great Plains, where they will spend the summer. As day
breaks, they will look at the land below and compare its patterns of
colour, light, and shadow with patterns they carry in their genes or in
their memories. If they see the monotone of cropland or the longer
shadows of bush and shrubs, they will fly on.

Within a day or two the pipits will choose an upland site with
longer, thicker grass and some thatch left over from the year before,
while the longspurs will settle for shorter, grazed-down pastures. They

will join the horned larks and western meadowlarks already on their nesting grounds. The males will sing over their piece of prairie; the females will accept or reject them. Bonds will be made, nests will be stitched out of grass, eggs will be laid. The summer-long winnowing down through the perils of weather and predators will begin. Some eggs will survive to hatch, some nestlings will survive to fledge, and some fledglings will survive to disperse and migrate south in fall.

Biologists place these birds in a group they call "grassland obligate," meaning that they are among the species that depend on grassy habitats. In North America, the term is often applied to the pipits, prairie hawks, longspurs, and other birds that breed only on the high plains of the west, but in its broadest sense it includes the bobolinks and field sparrows found in small hay meadows from Ontario to Florida, the wrens and sparrows that use wetter grasslands, and the shorebirds, hawks, and owls that nest in grassy places from coast to coast. As a group, birds that need grass are declining faster than any others on the continent—more than birds that nest in forest, wetlands, mountains, urban areas, tundra, or desert. Some of these species will vanish from large portions of their breeding ranges in the next twenty to thirty years; many already have.

In the triage that determines which environmental issues receive attention, something like the decline of grassland birds barely makes the waiting room. Amidst the din of the ecological emergencies that gain public attention by threatening discomfort and extinction—changing climate, collapsing fisheries, looming pandemics, vanishing aquifers—an alarm set off by a few small brown birds in the middle of nowhere has little chance of being heard. People try to make economic arguments for the protection of grassland birds, but the argument always bears the strained tone of a lawyer defending a client he knows to be doomed. The damnable truth is that if ten or fifteen species went extinct tomorrow we would have trouble detecting any significant ecological or economic consequences. The water and nitrogen cycles would carry on in their absence. The soil would continue to grow crops. The ecology of grassland places might shift, but few of us would be able to discern any change. Farm production and its attendant economies on the Great Plains would make a slight adjustment to account for the loss of some natural weed and insect control and then get back to business as usual. Tourism publications and marketing plans might need some revising, but any shortfall in tourists would be minor and easily managed with new campaigns. A few birdwatchers, some rural people, and environmentalists would kick up a fuss, but the majority of people would not notice or care.

It's a fool's dream, but a part of me can't stop imagining that if enough people would discover all that is good and holy in these birds, we might be able to turn things around before it's too late. Every spring the wish comes back even if the birds do not. I drive out to a local pasture in early May, open the car door and listen. I try to enjoy the air, the light, and the birdsong, but I'm holding my breath. A sense of dread creeps in as I realize that the song is not what it was last year: one longspur is singing where there once were six. No upland sandpipers, no Baird's sparrows. Burrowing owls gone for a decade. The exaltation of a prairie spring reduced to a few meadowlarks and savannah sparrows holding their own. I drive back to the city wishing things were different, wishing I didn't know how the pasture used to sound, and wishing I could get others to see the spirit made flesh in such birds.

For a naturalist, this is a dangerous kind of desire. It begs for more than pure natural history can provide, and then takes its questions to the narrow and treacherous terrain that runs between faith and reason. You stumble back and forth between the testable statements of science and the untestable impressions of experience, looking for ways to locate in words something of the lyric and resonance of living mysteries. Both sides tempt the mind with a lofty roost from which it can pronounce philosophies, reasons, and solutions, as though we

3

might think our way to the grace of living in a just relationship with the other-than-human world. Prairie people, I believe, are more susceptible than most. The simple act of standing upright on the high plains is enough to foster delusions of dominion and knowledge.

Navigating that terrain between the knowable and the unknowable, this book follows obscure and diminishing birds into the shadow of a wounded land. Each story, argument, species profile, and drawing was conceived within a longing to reclaim the original spirit of grassland that survives yet in its birds. Beneath that longing lie the deeper human wish we all share: to find out how we might belong to a place, to find a way home. Precise directions are hard to come by, but for those of us who live on the Great Plains I have an idea of where we might at least take our bearings. It's that place at the edge of town where a large patch of wild grass grows, the little field that no one mows. Try going there sometime. Walk into the middle and lie down. Press your back against the earth and let the exhalations of the soil enter your body breath by breath. With grass blades waving overhead and the sky beyond, the human spirit has half a chance to come to its senses. If there are birds singing in the air, all the better. They will tell you where you are and, if you listen long enough, they may tell you who you are in the bargain.

Growing up in prairie towns and cities, I never once considered the grassy places beyond the ball diamond or the unploughed land at the edges of my grandfather's fields to be anything but ordinary. If there were birds in the grass, no one paid any attention to them. The exception was the sharp-tailed grouse. "Chickens" my father called them as we walked the field edges on fall afternoons, killing time and a few grouse between morning and evening duck shoots. The long walks in rubber boots seemed like some kind of penitential trial by boredom, so I would daydream most of the way in the drowsy warmth of my parka, my feet finding places between the clods of summerfallow or stubble. Small birds would sometimes fly up from swaths of grain, but their chittering cries were nothing more than the ambience of an October chicken hunt, the sounds that accompanied a plodding reverie.

I was twelve, fourteen, sixteen, eighteen years old, each fall hunting the birds with my father and my brother, until a growing ambivalence disturbed my daydreams. I never made a conscious decision to stop hunting and I've tried it several times in the past twenty-five years, but the unease always returns. It began, I believe, with a reading assignment in my third year of university.

American Lit classes at the University of Saskatchewan were taught by a gentle and endearing alcoholic who could resuscitate a Thomas Paine treatise until it seemed like it had been written for our own generation. As he read Whitman's "Body Electric" or Thoreau's "Economy," his lips and spindly fingers would tremble, as much from his passion for the writing as from anything in his blood.

For Thanksgiving, he asked us to read "The Bear," Faulkner's novella of men and boys hunting in the bottomlands of Mississippi. This suited me fine because Thanksgiving weekend has always been mixed up with hunting in my mind. I was born on Thanksgiving Day, and my mother never let my father forget that he was hunting geese at the time. Until I was old enough to join him, Thanksgiving was the weekend when my father was away from home looking for something that he could not find in his job at the potash mine.

I wasn't keen on the others seeing me reading on our annual Thanksgiving trip, but I'm a slow reader at best so I knew I would have to take the book with me. That year, we drove to the autumn goose staging grounds in Saskatchewan's southwest, and camped in the town of Eston: my father, two hunting buddies of his, a couple of older cousins, my brother, and I. We were a far cry from the McCaslins, Boon, and Sam Fathers hunting deer in the big woods, but in the lamplight of our tent trailer, with the October wind rattling the canvas, Faulkner's story made sense of the succession of feelings

I experienced in hunting: the sustained excitement and innocence of pursuit giving way to brief moments of awe and then remorse; and beneath it all the silent, brooding presence of a land that has borne more respectful hunters.

There was young Ike McCaslin all alone in a clearing without his gun, and Old Ben, the slewfoot bear, rearing up before him, near enough for him to make out a tick on the inside of his leg. Sam Fathers, half-Indian, half-Negro, had placed him there, prepared him for the sacrament that would initiate him properly into the primordial truth of the woods.

There I was digging goose pits in wheat stubble with elders whose hunting rituals depended heavily on garlic sausage, cheese, cheap wine, and voluntary flatulence. Each morning, we crawled into our foxholes before dawn, surrounded by swathed grain and cardboard decoys. As the sun rose, the ducks and then the first flocks of geese came in and we stood to blast them with number 2 shot. At the end of the morning shoot, we collected the birds we'd killed, made another sweep to find the wounded ones, wrung their necks, and then hauled our gear and birds off to the cars.

I continued to hunt for a few years afterward, but the regret I first experienced that weekend soon grew into a strong sense of unworthiness I could not shake. I'd latched onto a romantic ideal against which I compared the reality of blasting ducks and grouse out of the air without any gestures of respect or rites of passage that might earn me the privilege of taking their lives. It's not that I suddenly came to believe that hunting is wrong. Within proper constraints, killing a wild animal is one of the healthiest and most responsible ways to include meat in your diet. In autumn the urge to be out on the land looking for something hidden and wild always returns. I go out walking with binoculars around my neck, and between the *ha-ronk*ing of geese overhead, the scent of barley in swath, and the feel of the stubble underfoot, I'm back to those days in field and slough that first embedded me in this landscape. But the body remembers things that are missing too, and my hands feel the shotgun that is no longer there.

Locked away in a corner of our garage, I still keep a single-shot 12-gauge I received for my fourteenth birthday. It has been joined recently by a Lee Enfield .303, an heirloom my father passed on to me a couple of years ago. The shotgun—a single barrel attached to a trigger, hammer, and unadorned stock—has a plainness and simplicity about it that in any other sort of tool might be taken for beauty. The rifle, a worn and battered veteran of the Boer War, is its opposite. To me, it has always been an artifact of the colonial enterprise that conquered new lands the world over and sent my ancestors out west and onto the prairie. My father tells me that the four notches on its butt represent pronghorns shot here on the plains, but its first duty was on my great-uncle's shoulder in 1900, when his regiment marched into Pretoria in defence of Queen and empire.

Eight years later, the Lee Enfield was on this side of the globe and in my grandfather's hands as he arrived on the parcel of wild prairie he would eventually homestead on the edge of the Great Sand Hills, north and west of where Swift Current is today. The grass he walked upon was long and shaggy from lack of grazing and, through the melting snow of a February chinook, he could see bleached buffalo skulls—the remains of some of the last wild bison killed on the plains, likely shot for the fee their hides would bring. The only animal in sight was a single pronghorn. He shot it with the rifle and carved the first of the four X's on the butt. That day he ate its liver for breakfast, some steak for dinner, and a stew for supper before heading back to the city, where he would file his land claim.

Over the next sixty years, the rifle, with my grandfather and his sons pulling the trigger, dispatched a good many pronghorns, mule deer, white-tailed deer, bears, elks, and moose. Beginning in an era when there were old men who could tell stories of hunting bison, it has traced a succession from subsistence hunting in the

7

hands of settlers to the weekend hunting of my father's generation. Somewhere in that line from buffalo hunters to recreational hunters there is a fall from grace that we cannot reckon with merely by giving up our firearms.

Hunting and eating were once sacraments that mediated relationships between people and other living things. Sometime before farmer-settlers like my grandfather arrived on these plains, rifles in other hands were the first to violate the indigenous ethos of reciprocity and reverence that bound together economy and ecology in a single flow. Though both gift and weapon, the colonizer's most powerful tool merely initiated the disintegration of the hunters' circle of giving and taking.

Two hundred years later, most plains dwellers live in cities where hunting is regarded as a crude and outdated pastime. There are still people who will shoot coyotes from their snowmobiles, there are the weekend trophy hunters, and there are a scant few who hunt so that at least some of the food that crosses their table integrates their household into the life of the land. Today's conservationists, meanwhile, look wistfully back upon the good old days when you could save a species merely by educating and controlling hunters. When the Audubon Society began in the late nineteenth century, and when prairie naturalist groups like the Saskatchewan Natural History Society formed in the mid-twentieth century, the main thrust of their conservation work was to protect birds from unregulated shooting. The passenger pigeon and the Eskimo curlew had been lost to market gunners in the preceding decades, but others, including the whooping crane and the upland sandpiper, survived the onslaught of armed settlers in numbers sufficient to allow prairie conservationists to keep them back from the brink. During that same period, however, we developed other tools for extracting the bounty of the land that have proven to be far more damaging to the wild prairie than anything that might come from the barrel of a gun.

The realization that we have so much more than guns to set aside has, strangely enough, made it hard for me to let mine go. I keep them in the garage, half dreaming of the day when the encumbrances of this unsustainable life will fall away and I will finally feel rooted here, known by the places I walk in the way my grandfather was once known by the places he walked.

It would be easy to say that once I stopped hunting in my twenties I right away started noticing the glory of grassland and the music of its birds. The truth is, the route I took was nowhere near that direct. I wonder now if my senses had been so dulled from television and urban living that I had to start with creatures exotic and grand enough to open my eyes. Or maybe I was unconsciously looking for an encounter with something large and powerful without a gun in my hand. Whatever the reason, it was watching whales that awakened me to the possibility of wildness in grassland.

After university I moved from Saskatoon to Regina to take a job as a technical writer. When I wasn't at work or trying to convince a girl named Karen that she should stop dating other men and dedicate herself full-time to me, I was reading about whales or planning trips to see whales. During those years, Karen and I watched whales in the Sea of Cortez and the breeding lagoons of the Baja, hiring local fishermen to take us out in small boats. Then, a year before we married, we decided to sign up for an eight-day sea kayak trip through Johnstone Strait between the northeastern shores of Vancouver Island and the mainland, where several pods of orca whales spend the summer.

During our week of paddling, we crossed from Robson Bight to the mainland side, camping on small islands and visiting the abandoned coastal villages of the Kwakwaka'wakw people. We saw orcas and minke whales on most days, but always in the distance. The last morning of the trip brought a heavy mist down from the mountains, and as we launched our kayaks into a mercury-coloured sea we could already hear a pod of orcas blowing ahead of us. Visibility was down to a few yards, but it was the kind of calm sea where every sound seems amplified: the patter of invisible water birds, the passage of fishing boats across the strait.

Not wanting to lose what might be our last chance to get a good look at the whales, Karen and I slowly paddled our double kayak toward the sound of their puffing. In the quiet we listened to the breathing of behemoths that we trusted would not chomp our vessel in two. Orcas on the move tend to dive and emerge as a group, so when we were near enough and the mists ahead of us went silent I paddled into the middle of where I guessed they might come up for the next breath. A minute or more passed soundlessly. With each swell we could feel the sea lift our kayak, pressing through its rubber skin against the bottom of our legs. Then the water to the front and one side rose even higher, as ten feet off our port bow a large orca broke the surface and emptied its lungs, filling the air above us with moist, fishy breath. There was a small bite in the very tip of its dorsal fin, which loomed over us as it cruised away into the mist. It was the largest bull in the group, a whale the local biologists had named Top Notch.

We finished that trip knowing that we had been in the presence of the particular animus of the Pacific Northwest. Back home, the only "sea" we had was metaphorical, a picturesque phrase used to describe a landscape that had been robbed of its presiding spirit, the bison, a century ago. If I gave any thought to the matter at all in those days, I would have said that very little worth paying attention to remained on the prairie. With the bison, the plains wolf, and plains grizzly gone, grassland ecology was a lost cause.

Prairie people, though, are accustomed to lost causes. Fighting against the odds is a cultural obligation: part survival tactic, part spiritual discipline. The ethic is present on both sides of our populist politics, holding together the tension between the ranch-country myth of the lone cowman and the farm-country utility of the co-operative. Destroying the natural prairie hasn't completely erased its influence on our souls. Enormity of sky and expansiveness of landscape make us all into the little guy who won't give up no matter how bad the odds. This is a place where just staying put is an obstinate act of resistance against the lure of temperate winters and prosperity elsewhere. We hang on, believing that if we strike deep enough roots good things may yet come from the seeds our ancestors planted here.

If I had to locate the place and time I first began to believe that grassland, though ravaged in body, might still retain some of its spirit, I would say it was Canada Day weekend, 1984, at Buffalo Pound Provincial Park in Saskatchewan. The kayak trip had left me with a residue of restlessness, a longing to be in places where the role of the human was reduced to taking delight in other beings whose own roles seemed so intricately bound up with one another. Not expecting much — it was only a piece of prairie after all — Karen and I headed to the nearest provincial park to join a short guided hike at a place called Nicolle Flats.

Our guide, a soft-spoken woman in her mid-twenties, took us by the park's herd of bison, looking domestic and haggard in their paddock, and then on through a gate to begin our walk along the grassy hillsides. She stopped to point out the songs of sparrows and other birds. A flicker of black and white passed over the willows and she called it a kingbird. Then she bent low to the grass and began pointing at small things that grew close to the earth. She named club mosses, lichens, and ground algae, enlarging each humble presence with soft incantations of Latin. She showed us a pincushion cactus coming into bloom and then let us taste a bit of its flesh, which she had prepared ahead of time. It was cool on the tongue, a green, tart jelly that tasted like kiwi fruit.

I felt myself being drawn toward a world I wanted to know more about. Here was someone in my own native landscape who was inviting wonderment in the revealed truth of hidden lives under-foot and songs overhead. Later that week I bought my first two field guides: *Wildflowers Across the Prairies* by Fenton Vance and Jim Jowsey, and Roger Tory Peterson's *Guide to the Western Birds*. After looking up some of the coastal birds I remembered from the kayak trip, I began paging through the range maps at the back of the Peterson guide to see which birds bred where I lived. There were more than a hundred, but most species showed breeding ranges that extended over large pieces of the continent. Eventually I found a few that seemed to breed only on the northern Great Plains. Not the ducks or the grouse I had hunted, but smaller birds with names like "Sprague's pipit," "Baird's sparrow," and "chestnut-collared longspur." These had the most restricted ranges and, if Roger Tory could be believed, they lived where I lived. The guide indicated that there were others—hawks, owls, shorebirds, and sparrows—that bred only in prairie landscapes. The thought of creatures being endemic to the place I lived stirred something to life in my brain. I began to see that learning the names of things mattered, not so much in the possession it afforded as in its capacity to call things forth from generality into a particularity that allowed for admiration, familiarity, even wonder.

Not long after that, I went on a field trip with the local natural history society to a place just out of the city that birdwatchers called the "pony farm." It was a beaten-down horse pasture, perhaps one hundred acres of unploughed land with a shack in the middle, a farm I recognized from having come there to purchase manure for my garden a year or two earlier. The city, a five-minute drive away, sat on the northwest horizon like a stranded ship, and grain fields ran on indefinitely in every other direction.

But there they were—the birds in Peterson's field guide, long-spurs and several kinds of grassland sparrows, two burrowing owls, a loggerhead shrike, upland sandpipers. Their ecology in tatters, they lived in an island of habitat surrounded by monoculture, but they were making a go of it. The sandpipers flew above us on stiff wings, spreading their bubbling wolf-whistle song over the grass; the owls bobbed at the mouth of their den; and the air sizzled with birdsong: the fading trills of several Baird's sparrows, the rapid chiming of chestnut-collared longspurs in flightsong, and the high-pitched *pit-up zeeeeeeeeeeeeeeee* of a grasshopper sparrow on a rose bush.

Today, twenty years later, these species have all disappeared from the pony farm, but in that interval I came to believe in grassland birds as more than just another lost cause. They are for me the presiding genius of the northern Great Plains, as powerful as Old Ben in the big woods or an orca in the kelp beds of Johnstone Strait; a presence that animates the grass and sky in the absence of the bison, the embodiment of a spirit I first sensed as an almost imperceptible tug on those long walks hunting chickens with my father.

True grassland birds—species that cannot tolerate trees or cropland—bear witness to the world in their own particular way. It is a testimony as worthy of our best efforts to listen, dream, and imagine as any other in Creation; not loud enough to attract busloads of tourists, perhaps, but all the more rewarding for the attention it cultivates in any who try. These small creatures make their stand in the face of great powers transforming their prairie world, living out a yearly drama, a freedom and fidelity to the wind that may escape our awareness even as they sing out to any soul within earshot. The influence of beings as unprepossessing and elusive as grassland birds is something like gravity, a weak though persistent mystery that holds us in place. The heart recognizes such a gentle force, knows that in simply becoming aware of its pull we take a small step toward belonging here ourselves.

Part One

THE DREAM OF GRASSLAND

Chapter One

Out of the Trees

People love trees. Geographers have proven it with tests; realtors could have saved them the bother. We like the look of trees and the feeling of being near trees. Not deep woods, mind you; just a small copse or a few well-placed trees in a meadow. A lake or a stream nearby completes the picture, but without trees water has little appeal. Landscape art, calendars, postcards, urban parks, golf courses, resorts—all honour the tree. In between and around the elms and pines, of course, there is always grass, another vital part of the landscape ideal but only in a secondary role and in proportion to the trees. Grass has to be short and it can't fill the frame. There must be some trees in little clumps here and there and placed just so.

The treeless prairie that greeted our settler ancestors a century ago now has its share of picturesque wooded clumps. We call them "bluffs," a usage you will not find in Webster's. Etymologists say that prairie people started using the word when we noticed that copses of aspen look much like cliffs on a distant coastline.

I live in one of the only prairie cities built upon utterly treeless grassland. Most cities on the northern Great Plains were founded on large rivers, where ravines sheltered a few poplars and willows, but the stretch of Wascana Creek where Regina sprang up did not incise deeply enough into the tableland of its glacial lake bed to allow woody growth of any kind. Photos taken in the 1880s show Wascana's narrow channel in the foreground with Regina's first buildings sticking up from a landscape in which the highest vegetation is an exuberant patch of spear grass. Today there are 350,000 trees within a five-mile radius of that spot, every one of them planted. Our house is a stone's throw from the creek, now flanked by large elms and willows in a neighbourhood where seventy-foot-high white spruce host red-breasted nuthatches and red crossbills year round. These birds think they are in a forest and they are right. To see the prairie and its birds I have to get out of town.

A moment ago I thought I heard the windblown song of a mountain bluebird coming from the aspen trees on the slope that runs down to the lake. I scanned the bush for something the colour of the sky, but couldn't make it out. We now think of it as a prairie bird, and a lovely one at that, but the mountain bluebird is an emblem of the changes that favour woody growth over grassland on this edge of the Great Plains. There were no bluebirds here before settlement. They first showed up in the region in the early twentieth century as fence posts, aspen bush, and other protuberances made their way out onto the prairie.

I can't blame the bluebird for choosing land with a mix of grass and trees. I've done the same thing myself, twice. The expansiveness and freedom of grassland are what draw me out of the city, but both times I've gone looking to buy rural property I've opted for valley land with wooded coulees and native grass on the hillsides—a blend that gives some shelter but keeps the feel of prairie close at hand.

In 1994 we bought seventy acres of the Qu'Appelle Valley just downstream from Katepwa Lake, a popular summer resort. The next summer we moved a small farmhouse onto a grassy meadow with trees on three sides recessed into coulees. One June morning I heard a Sprague's pipit singing high overhead, scouting for the right kind of prairie to spend the summer in. I was thrilled and hopeful that it would stay, but the next day it was gone. The patches of native grass were too small and there was too much woodland and scrubland on the hillsides. The Qu'Appelle is a long east-west corridor of native grass, but over the years I discovered that the balance of vegetation in our part of the valley had shifted too far toward woody growth to host true grassland ecosystems. To see the birds that stir my spirit I always had to drive south to larger upland pastures.

Then, in the late summer of 2004, a friend told us of some land for sale in a tributary of the Qu'Appelle next to a large community pasture. I knew the place he was talking about because I had been there several times to look for birds. It was on a dead-end road in the bottom of a valley with a small wooded pond called Cherry Lake and a creek on the property, but just north and south of it on the uplands there were remnant populations of grassland birds. The property near Katepwa Lake had served us well as a private family retreat, but, like a lot of urban people of our generation, we'd never really let go of the "share the land" dream. Long before we ever owned property, the idea would come up from time to time in conversation with friends: wouldn't it be great to share a piece of land in the country, you know, grow a garden, maybe get some sheep, provide entertainment for the real farmers. When we bought the place in the valley I think we half-believed others would eventually join us, but it wasn't the right kind of land. It was too close to a resort area and did not have the kind of biodiversity and ecological integrity that we had hoped for.

The day after we heard the place by the community pasture was for sale, Karen and I were walking the property. Two days later we were showing it to our closest friends, Michelle and John and Sylvie and Rob, to see if we could talk them into joining us. I was nervous, but the land did its part. With the sun angling low from the west deepening the green all around us, the beauty of the grass and hills conspired against any doubts we might have had, any blindness to the truth that we might never find a place like this again: high native pastures overlooking three lakes, a wooded creek valley and beaver ponds; the road dead-ending in the yard; the diversity of plant communities; the potential for gardens and orchards in the yard site. In the story my memory has brewed up from its scant residue of fact mixed with photographs, I have an image of the exact moment when the decision happened. We were walking together on the hilltop above the yard. We had all stopped and were looking off into the distance across the yard site and a small field of barley cut and lying in windrows. Ducks and cormorants were moving between the lakes. The spear grass in the pasture was shining in spiky tufts all around us. I looked at the others and could see that it was going to happen.

Within a week, we had an agreement among the three families to put an offer on the place. By Christmas we had sold our old acreage and bought the new one as a community. I spent the rest of the winter dreaming of the prairie birds I would find in spring.

As I write this, with one eye out for the bluebird, I'm at a table on the front porch of an eighteen-by-twenty-foot cabin. With the help of the two other families and the construction midwifery of a carpenter named Denise, we framed and sheathed the structure during a long weekend in May. Rich food, shared labour, and hammering noises—it was a barn-raising diminished only by my ineptitude as a carpenter. Over the summer months, I have been working on the siding and trims, trying to finish the exterior before the snow comes, and before I lose any more fingernails on my left hand.

I can smell the cedar of the posts supporting the porch and the spruce of the bare plywood behind me. At my feet are two Manitoba maple seedlings in pots, which I've been having trouble finding the time to plant, but when I do it will be amongst the elms and maples in the shelterbelt where the hummingbirds are nesting and where my youngest daughter wants me to install a tire swing.

We situated the cabin to take in one of our favourite views. The porch looks across Cherry Lake to eight well-spaced balsam poplars on the far shore, their oval crowns reflecting a different shade of green against the grassy slope that the neighbour's cattle keep short-cropped. The poplars foreground the hills in a way that appeals to something deep in the European landscape sensibility, evoking a pastoral scene that would not be out of place in Yorkshire or Austria. When this valley was settled, in the late 1800s, the view from this spot would have been different. There might have been some brush in the ravines, but the lakeside flats and hills behind would have been nothing but grass. Bison and wildfire made it so. Today, the shelter of trees—in planted rows, in aspen bluffs, and in the two-by-four construction of farmsteads—allows rural people to survive year-round in landscapes where the original inhabitants might have once camped for short periods in warmer months and then moved on.

I find flakes of chert and Knife River flint regularly on the lower field near Cherry Lake, where people once impounded and processed bison. On top of a pocket gopher mound last year I found a corner-notched arrowhead—a reminder that for thousands of years, this land had a different skin, a short-haired hide that showed every ripple in the underlying musculature formed by the advance and retreat of ice.

A longing to touch something of this untreed past is part of what draws me out to the open grassland and its birds. I used to wonder what it would be like to live in a prairie observatory exposed to all the forces that reign over native grass. Reading *The Outermost House* by American naturalist Henry Beston, I began to dream about building my own prairie version of the "Fo'castle"—which is what Beston called the sixteen-by-twenty-foot structure where he lived for a year in the mid-1920s on Cape Cod's storm-lashed finger poking into the Atlantic. The Fo'castle was swept away in a winter hurricane in 1978 and was last seen headed for the Sargasso Sea. Our cabin is similar in

size and design, but when Karen and I talked about potential building sites, we never even considered the uplands. It was just a question
of deep, shaded woods or nestled up against a shelterbelt of trees.

The bluebird slipped away unseen, but I am surrounded by the
sounds of birds that live in tree and shrubland: house wrens, flickers,
least flycatchers, orioles. These are all wonderful creatures worthy
of anyone's attention, but they are the common woodland species
you can find almost anywhere in the populated regions of North
America. The birds that are distinctive in this part of the continent,
having come to their place in the sun along with the buffalo and the
grasshopper, are out of earshot, but not far away on the benchland
above this little valley outpost.

The unparalleled destruction that has come to their world in a
century and a half is difficult to hold in the mind. When I am on a
jet flying over the prairie, I search for fragments of grassland below
and try to extrapolate them into the original horizon-to-horizon
world of grass that once covered the plains. I wish away all the scars
and uniformity of the drawn-and-quartered farm landscape and try
to imagine flying north like a hawk in spring over the whole of the
Great Plains in their pre-settlement splendour. High enough to view
thousands of square miles at a glimpse, the journey begins above the
Gulf Coast grasslands of Texas, then takes in the oak savannah of hill
country north of San Antonio. Next comes the tallgrass of Oklahoma
and Kansas, the bisected plateaus of Nebraska, the drier plains and
badlands of the Dakotas, the vast wheat grass and June grass prairie
drained by the Missouri, the Oldman, the Saskatchewan, and the
Qu'Appelle rivers, and, finally, the northern fescue prairie on the
flanks of the Peace River Valley. The vista below unfurls in softly
shaded wrinkles, folds, and dimples that shift without visible boundaries from one texture or colour to another in an impossibly complex

and subtly brocaded fabric. But more than fabric, the earth shim-
mers and vibrates like something lit from the inside, as erotic and
radiant as any living thing.

Of this grassland that makes up the midriff of North America,
somewhere between 75 and 99 percent has been ploughed under,
depending on the kind of prairie under consideration. The largest
fragments are south and west of here, in big ranches, community pastures, and conservation land. By comparison, our 160 acres are just a
speck, but they join onto one of the larger remnants here on the northeastern limits of the Great Plains. Engulfed by cropland and aspen
bluffs, patches of native grass are rare in this part of Saskatchewan,
where geographers and soil scientists mark the edge of two prairie
eco-regions: aspen parkland and moist mixed-grass prairie.

Time has shifted the boundary between these two eco-regions
southward, but for now a single lobe in the crenellated edge of the
mixed-grass prairie reaches up to include the pastures south of our
property. North of here, woody growth increases with changes in soil
and precipitation, climaxing in the boreal forest, and then trailing off
again on its way to arctic tundra. South from here to the Gulf Coast
is the soil that was made by the long dominion of grass.

In the borderland between two eco-regions, on the rim of the
Great Plains, with its blend of wooded and grassland landscapes, transitions from one ecological community to the next can happen in a
matter of a few feet of elevation, or in passing from one side of a hill to
the other. The mingling of forest and grassland species here throws up
some odd juxtapositions. Last week, in the height of breeding season,
I was sitting on a grassy slope, watching a Mormon cricket thread its
way through spear grass and milk vetch. A Swainson's hawk, the common prairie buteo, wheeled on the wind overhead. Then a bird sang
from the creek valley that runs into our lake, but it was a song that
belongs in the spruce and poplar of canoe country: a white-throated
sparrow singing out its *Ohhhh, sweet Canada, Canada, Canada.*

An old settler trail in the valley bottom leads up onto the plains to the south where the community pasture offers several thousand acres of grassland. It's weedy, overgrazed, and invaded by shrubs, yet for now it is holding onto a small population of native grassland birds. There on a good June morning I can usually find Sprague's pipits, Baird's sparrows, grasshopper sparrows, upland sandpipers, bobolinks, a Swainson's hawk, and a sharp-tailed grouse or two.

Last September, after most of these birds had left for the winter, I camped at the edge of that prairie in the hollow of a deer bed formed in spear grass and sage. In the morning I planned to walk south onto the largest remnant of native grass, crossing soft boundaries from aspen parkland to moist mixed-grass prairie and back again.

I sat in my sleeping bag on a groundsheet, with snowberry and wolf willow casting their shadows on the deer bed from its western edge. The temperature and the wind fell as a vesper sparrow sang in half-hearted tribute to urges left over from the other side of summer. The minutes of silence weighed themselves against gathering dark. Flights of duck, canvasbacks and redheads whistled overhead in the presence of the first stars, their black strings and vees sliding across the sky's indigo. The moon, orange and almost full, nudged above the horizon directly opposite the place the sun had gone down.

After the procession of ducks, a great horned owl hooted from an aspen-filled coulee; after that, coyotes yipped on three hilltops, some near, others distant. Through it all, a grasshopper and cricket chorus played to a rhythm slowed by the cooling air. Within their soft chanting and the touch of the day's last breezes, transitions and boundaries faded and I felt myself arriving. This, I thought, is a good place to be: in the shifting, indeterminate territory that eases us out of the trees and into the dream of a grassland that is all but forgotten, and awaiting its chance to return.

Sharp-tailed Grouse

With the last drifts of winter melting away from the prairie, groups of sharp-tailed grouse gather to dance before sunrise. On low hilltops, anywhere from ten to sixty birds come to enact the ritual that decides whose genes get passed on during the season ahead. The females, who do the choosing, stand at the edge of the dancing circle or "lek." Inside the lek, the males whirr and jump and spin their way to centre stage, where the one who holds his position best is likeliest to win the favour of the most hens. Their feathers are fluffed out, with wings held stiffly and purple neck sacs inflated, body aligned parallel to the earth, tail at right angles and pointing skyward. The whole bird is engorged with the eros of a prairie spring and all of its possibility. A low cooing, clucking sound mixes with the rattle of pinions as they shake and stamp the grass, chasing one another away from the middle of the lek. At the height of things, a fight will erupt between two cocks. They leap into the air and reach out with their feet to make contact. Feathers fly for a moment and then the dance resumes. When the sun rises high enough, they disperse in ones and twos until dusk, when they will gather again.

Sharp-tailed grouse use the same piece of prairie for decades, or at least until the land is ploughed up. Older farmers tell stories of the birds returning each spring to dance on land ploughed and seeded to grain, trampling the wheat stubble flat for ten or fifteen years before giving it up.

The species was said to be abundant in 1857, when Captain John Palliser came west to assess the suitability of the Canadian prairie for agriculture and settlement. Thomas Blakiston, the expedition's magnetic observer and naturalist, made some notes on birds he saw around Fort Carlton, north of where Saskatoon is today: "During my stay in the Indian Country, I could not but have constant opportunities of observing the habits of the sharp-tailed grouse at all seasons of the year where I shot hundreds of them; in fact, when hard pressed for food, I often existed for days together on no other fare."[1] Blakiston would cut open the crops of the grouse, sometimes finding up to half a pint of berries and rosehips, and in birds found on burnt prairie, the roasted bodies of caterpillars.

A hardy bird that burrows under the snow in the worst weather and will raise as many as twelve young each summer, the sharp-tailed grouse has a great potential for recovery, which has been tested throughout the last 130 years. It has declined significantly from its pre-settlement abundance, but is still a game species because the fish and game departments in most prairie states and provinces believe its populations to be stable. Experienced bird observers say its numbers have dropped sharply from the 1960s onward. Lorne Scott, a farmer and naturalist who sits on the Nature Conservancy of Canada's national board, has watched sharp-tailed leks in his home terrain around Indian Head, Saskatchewan, dwindle and disappear in the last forty years. In 1977 there were still five active leks within a few miles south of Indian Head. Today, Lorne says, only one remains. The story is the same over most of the northern Great Plains.

Chapter Two

Prairie Dance

O ver time, the boundaries from one plant community to another
shift in any kind of ecosystem, but grassland boundaries are
particularly mobile. If you could watch the changes over thousands
of square miles of grass during even a twenty-year period it would
look something like a time-lapse film of a tapestry being spun by
an invisible weaver in irregularly shaped and multi-hued fields of
green. Here and there, patches of black would appear and disappear rapidly amidst the greens, showing the brief effects of fire. The
areas of green and black would change size and shape and move
across the whole of the tapestry as the weaver played with a range
of materials—hundreds of species of grasses, sedges, and forbs—and
four primary tools: soil variability, climate, grazing, and fire.

Soil quality varies from location to location, according to geological history, drainage, elevation, parent material, and so on, but it takes
centuries to change significantly in any one location. Precipitation
and temperature move up and down within a certain range that
includes long and short cycles affected by the Rocky Mountain
rain shadow and by oceanic currents. In the pre-settlement era, the
remaining two factors—grazing and fire—responded to opportunities presented by weather and soil by creating brief disturbances at

random intervals. Fire and grazing events in turn fostered a complex mosaic of irregularly shaped patches of various grassland habitats—each of which recovered from disturbance on schedules set by intensity, duration, and subsequent weather. These four dynamics—in concert with the slower, longer processes of genetic variation and natural selection—shaped ecological niches in large and small patches, determining which creatures would live where for this or that season. Fire, weather, grazers, people, birds, and other organisms moved across vast distances from one kind of grassland to another.

The bison showed up at burnt plains that were flushing with new growth after fires that had been lit either by lightning or by Indians hoping to improve the hunt. In their turn, certain bird species and other organisms that prefer shortgrass would arrive in spring to reproduce. As the grass recovered from grazing and fire, any insects or other creatures that prefer longer grass and therefore disappeared during the disturbance could easily recolonize from neighbouring patches of unburnt and ungrazed prairie. At rates determined by soil and climate, the grass would grow and build up biomass between years of grazing and fire, changing the structure of the vegetation and in turn attracting a different set of organisms. The spirit of the plains, its air of motion and freedom, has always depended upon this dance choreographed by the rhythms of earth, weather, fire, and buffalo.

On that September afternoon, as I hiked out of our valley and up onto the pasture land toward my campsite, I was stopped by a grass I seldom see, a living relic of the tallgrass prairie, a type of grassland that is all but gone from the continent. Coming across these small stands of big bluestem is one of the autumn blessings of this place. In the cooler weather we go for longer hikes, and the late season grasses like big and little bluestem put on their show. Big bluestem can be hard to find earlier in the summer, but by the last days of

August, its waist-high purple stalks and bird's-foot flowerheads stand out against the shorter and now-yellowing grasses more typical of mixed-grass prairie.

Perhaps because we never really had a chance to experience the tallgrass prairie—it was on the most fertile land and therefore sacrificed first—grassland naturalists cannot help but romanticize the lost world of big bluestem. From Willa Cather's novels to William Least Heat-Moon's *PrairyErth*, the prairie imagination has elevated tallgrass to mythic status, where it mingles with our regrets for everything else that we have lost in settling the land. The remaining shreds of tallgrass, comprising a mere one-tenth of 1 percent of the original range, survive along the railways that delivered the ploughmen west and between the headstones of the cemeteries that hold their bones. No one can say exactly how far to the north and west the boundaries of its former range extended, nor how it intermingled with the moist mixed-grass prairie.

The fall our little community formed and the three couples signed the purchase agreement, we would often gather up our younger children and drive out to the property to go for walks. As we walked we spoke about plans. We would restore the vegetation alongside the lake and the creek, which had been damaged by cattle lounging near their corral and the water's edge. We would change the fencing and use grazing to improve the health of the prairie, and we would set aside space in the yard site to grow fruit trees and vegetables. Grander schemes were mentioned, ways of engaging the local community to help protect the valley and the surrounding plains.

It was a time of utter infatuation with the place, with our ideals, and with one another. We could not believe our good fortune at having found such an ecologically diverse and healthy piece of land, and at our having come together almost overnight to become a community of its stewards. The honeymoon phase has not ended yet, but for me it began the moment we found a ten-yard-long patch of big bluestem growing on one of the hillsides. I'd seen it rarely in the Qu'Appelle farther north and east, but it was a surprise to find it thriving in this tributary twenty miles to the south, so I took it as a small blessing upon our dreams.

As much as I would like to think that we have scraps of relict tallgrass prairie on our land, big bluestem grass alone is not enough to prove it. On the other hand, a new study looking for the traces of the long-lost prairie's northwestern limits suggests that isolated patches might exist in our vicinity. A couple of years ago, two federal biologists came from Ottawa to search for evidence that tallgrass once reached farther into Saskatchewan than previously thought.[1] Their work was inspired by an entomologist who published a paper in *Bioscience* postulating an extension of the range based on the presence of certain bugs that are linked to tallgrass indicator grasses. Walking river valley slopes, ditches, and railway easements, the researchers found small (less than .01 acres) patches of big bluestem, sideoats grama, and other tallgrass species in several locations near the town of Whitewood, which is more than an hour's drive due east of our land. In their report, the biologists show a range map positing the pre-settlement extent of tallgrass into the north and west along the Qu'Appelle as far west as Buffalo Pound Lake. They speculate that near the valley, tallgrass may have occurred in small, isolated patches.

Their description of the plant composition on lower slope sites of tallgrass communities sounds like what we see on the lower slope sites in our valley: a blend of typical mixed-grass species joined by some of the plants seen in true tallgrass, including big bluestem and sideoats grama grass, Great Plains Indian paintbrush, Missouri milk vetch, large Indian breadroot, early yellow locoweed, and others. The line that affected me most in their report, though, was in their results, where they said that most tallgrass sites they found were "developing into woodland." That certainly appears to be the story for the tallgrass plants we have found on and around our land in the Indian Head Creek Valley. Most of them are within a few paces of aspen woodland that is suckering out onto the plains.

While even a low grass fire will kill aspen trees, tallgrass is the prairie made to burn. Growing in the moister climate zone far enough east to escape the Rocky Mountain rain shadow, tallgrass can produce sufficient fuel for a prairie fire in one or two growing seasons. Even today, in Kansas's Flint Hills, where the largest tallgrass pastures survive, ranchers use fire to sustain the health of their grazing lands.

Up here, though, where tallgrass may have once stretched a finger into the northeastern edge of the moist mixed-grass zone, we have been suppressing fire since the 1890s, and the results are seen in every aspen bluff: woodland birds instead of prairie birds; trees and shrubby growth where once there might have been grass high enough to hide a heifer. The grassland's dancing mosaic of life seems to require that everything in its circle be free and mobile, or widespread enough to survive sudden disturbances in any one piece of landscape. Prairie conservationists have no trouble talking about the need for disturbances like fire, until we put a cabin next to grassland. Once we get attached to a particular place, the notion of surrendering to the primal impulses of prairie loses some of its allure.

The only fires we have lit so far on our piece of prairie have been for toasting marshmallows or burning piles of unusable wood. Whenever someone in our group mentions the subject of lighting a controlled or "prescribed" burn on the property, I think of the cabin we just built, the power poles, trees, and other things we are not willing to offer up to the windblown will of the prairie. And I think about Aldo Leopold. In the 1930s, Leopold, an American biologist and writer, established the very first tallgrass prairie restoration project. Leopold is perhaps most famous for his notion of a "land ethic," in which he argued that we must come to see the natural world as "a community to which we belong."

From his small cabin in the woods near the Wisconsin River, he made forays out onto the Sand County land that had once been tallgrass prairie, searching for the upland sandpiper—in his era known as the "upland plover."

In *Sand County Almanac*, he speaks eloquently and bitterly of the reign of tallgrass lost to settlement and farming, a process Leopold called "wheating the land to death." Then, one week after he received word that his almanac would be published, he rushed to help a neighbour fight a grass fire that was threatening his own property. He had a heart attack and died on the spot, sixty-one years of age, never seeing a printed copy of the book that went on to launch generations of environmentalists and an entire movement for prairie conservation. An ironic death for a grassland naturalist, perhaps, but he died amidst grass and its ancient desire to renew itself in the wild freedom of fire.

UPLAND
SANDPIPER

A typical encounter with an upland sandpiper: on a prairie trail through a
cow pasture, the windows rolled down, you hear a strange, bubbling wolf
whistle come in on the breeze. Up ahead there's a funny-looking bird on a
fence post: neck too skinny for a meadowlark, and the legs way too long,
not to mention the bony head and short stick of a bill. This is not a showy
bird, but a close look through binoculars brings out its better points: rich
tones of brown on the back, sharply etched chevrons in lines down the
breast against a pale wash of buff yellow. It's the beer-bottle brown eye
in that pigeon head, though, that appeals, like a shiny button on a child's
toy. Disturbed from its perch, it flies to the grass on quivering wings and
then stands with its wings pointing at the sky for several moments before
folding them with surprising elegance.

"Whoever invented the word 'grace,'" said Aldo Leopold, "must've seen the wing-folding of the plover." And what wings. They are made for long flying, for passing over mountain ranges, forests, deserts to reach the grass at the centre of two continents.

After spending its summer on native pasture on the northern plains or on the edge of an airport in the eastern states, the upland sandpiper climbs into the sky of a late July evening and begins an odyssey of six thousand miles. Within a few weeks it will reach its wintering grounds on the pampas of southern Argentina, where it will be joined by the bobolinks and Swainson's hawks that also begin their lives in North American grassland.

Once the most numerous shorebird species on the prairie, the upland sandpiper has gone through fire to survive. Fred Langstaff, who settled in east-central Saskatchewan in the 1890s, recalled eating upland sandpipers and their eggs.[2] Hunters nearly took the species to extinction in the late nineteenth century, after the passenger pigeon became too difficult to find. Its flesh was thought by some to be an aphrodisiac, and "plover on toast" was served in the best dining rooms of New England. The bird is still rare in most American states, and habitat destruction on the northern Great Plains has reduced its numbers to a fraction of what they once were.

Perhaps the most terrestrial of all North American shorebirds, the upland sandpiper lives for most of its life far from any shores. On its breeding grounds it will form loose colonies in which the females may synchronize the hatching of their broods. In some areas, upland sandpipers will nest on tame pasture, on hay land, or even on cropland—an adaptation that may help it to survive the habitat loss that has reduced its numbers on the plains.

Chapter Three

BIRDS OF PROMISE

I am standing next to a pile of lichen-covered boulders on a little knoll on the neighbour's pasture south of our place. The pile is almost covered by soil that has blown in over the years and by the grasses and wild roses that grow between the rocks. Facing the next rise, and the one after that, I can see similar piles. They look like fallen cairns and line up pointing toward the edge of a coulee where local arrowhead hunters once located a kill site. The cairns, I'm told, are remnants of buffalo drive lanes. As hunters drove the buffalo toward the pound down in the bottom of the coulee, people hiding behind the cairns would jump out and wave skins to keep the herd moving in the right direction.

The drive lanes run along a strip of upland grass between two coulees. None of it has ever been ploughed, but without the disturbance patterns that buffalo and fire provide, weeds and brushy vegetation have moved in and are taking over large patches. I stop here sometimes when I walk out toward the pipit fields farther south, always hoping I will hear a Baird's sparrow or even a meadowlark, but I never do. I have another mile to go before I get to larger pastures where I will hear the first songs of grassland birds.

While it is sadly diminished and more difficult to see today without the roaming herds and wildfire, the life of grasslands from season to season and from macro-habitat to micro-habitat retains something of its original spirit, the old dance of grass and earth, vagrant and free as the clouds passing overhead. It moves through the air in the flight and song of the birds that still dwell within the graces of whatever comes on the wind.

Plains hunters once called them the "tribes of the air," and while they are not the only creatures whose lives follow the shifting tapestry of the plains, they are certainly the ones most available to our senses.

Think of the most recognized prairie bird: the western meadowlark. If you ever lived in a prairie town or on a farm you will remember it—the egg-yolk yellow of its breast, the black bib on its chest, the small dagger of a bill. You saw one on the backstop of the ball diamond or near the highway on the sign that tells passersby which hockey player your town is "Home of." On your walk to school in April, meadowlark song stirred something in your chromosomes, lending music to the wind that bore with it all the prairie could promise in spring: the gurgle of snowmelt, the hard clarity of the sun, the surprise of things that hatch and bloom.

Sometimes it sounded like words, as though the bird was speaking. You listened a little harder, or maybe your grandma told you what it said, but you knew that birds don't really say anything, at least not to farm kids.

A woman who grew up on the plains east of Regina in the German colonies of that region once asked me why the meadowlarks are disappearing from the fields her family used to farm. Then she sang the western meadowlark song for me in phrases of Low German. When I asked her for a translation, she laughed and said, "It means 'you are such a lazy boy.'"

Depending on how you look at things, our laziness may have

something to do with the trends that are making the land unfit for meadowlarks. As we spoke, it became clear that she blamed modern farming practices for their disappearance. We talked about methods of cultivation, the size of machinery these days, pesticides, and the economic forces behind it all, but she wanted a consolation I could not offer. The concern and regret in her voice stayed with me for days afterward, and set me to wondering about the quality of our listening.

If the meadowlark is not telling us we should work harder, then what is it saying to us? Have we ever really listened? We have taken the meadowlark and made it into an icon of agrarian rootedness and loyalty to the farm. Singing from the fence posts that enclose the remains of the family farm, such a prominent and visible bird is easily co-opted into our nostalgia, recruited into our myths of a golden age, its songs taken as endorsement for a culture that lasted but a few decades.

Not long ago, the western meadowlark said other things to people. I have a long out-of-print book published in the early twentieth century that gives a surprisingly enlightened account of Great Plains cosmologies. It is called *Prairie Smoke*, after the prairie crocus or pasque flower, which lends our hillsides a bluish haze in spring. The author, Melvin Gilmore, was an ethnologist who travelled in the late nineteenth century with the Dakota Sioux and other nations on the northern Great Plains, during their transition from the nomadic hunting life to reservation survival. The blessing of Gilmore is that he saw something of the truth and validity of plains cultures and could write about them without the usual romanticizing clichés.

He tells of hearing a ten-year-old Dakota girl teach other children the role of the meadowlark. She drew a large diagram in the dust of a trail, showing their tipis encircling the camp, dogs moving here and there, and ponies grazing just beyond the lodges. Farther out she drew buffalo, and farthest of all she drew the image of a meadowlark in flight. Around it she traced a faint circle and then she connected the bird to the circle of tipis with a long zigzagging line from sky to earth.

She used the traditional Dakota name for the bird, which Gilmore translates as "bird of promise." She said that it was their friend. She said the meadowlark takes delight in being near their camps and flies all around the prairie world observing the people and other creatures. It spirals upward into the sky when the sun rises and gives its light to the grass and prairie flowers. From this height it tells the Creator what each living thing needs on that particular day.[1]

For the people who made the stone flakes I find on our land, who buried their loved ones on our hillsides—and for their descendants living today—the meadowlark has never been a symbol of human ownership and entitlement. Its "promise" is in its role as an agent of the Creator's giving, helping others remain mindful of the way of the holy, which for the Siouan people (Lakota, Dakota, Nakota) is the air flowing within and around all living things. As masters of the realm that is the source of spirit and the medium of all spiritual transactions, all birds are spiritual teachers and messengers, but the meadowlark's habits of singing in air and nesting on the earth beneath a dome of grass make it a perfect messenger between creature and Creator.

That indigenous regard for the tribes of the air may persist in the practice of some ceremonialists and elders, but for most of us it is hidden away in a language and culture our ancestors assumed would die away. A distant relative I met in Manitoba two years ago mailed me a bundle of documents about my great-grandparents, James and Mary Herriot, who came west from Ontario in 1881. Amid the photocopies of census excerpts, a page from the family Bible, and their marriage certificate, I found a newspaper article published in the *Winnipeg Tribune* in 1940 on the occasion of my great-grandfather's eighty-seventh birthday. It was in a column called "Oldtimer Talks," written by a Colonel G.C. Porter. The prose lacquers James's life with a thick layer of glorifying adjectives and exaggerated tales, making him out to be a giant in body and spirit, the kind of man who came to the Wild West and tamed it with his muscle and ingenuity.

Varnish or not, the article is the only surviving description of the man who brought our clan out onto the northern Great Plains. Leaving Galt, Ontario, James and Mary travelled west to settle in Dakota Sioux country near a village that was called Plum Creek, soon to become Souris, Manitoba. The year was 1881, and Sitting Bull was still on this side of the Medicine Line, hiding out from the U.S. Cavalry after routing Custer. Settlers were nervous about Indian people in general, but regarded the Sioux nations with a heightened fear as stories of Little Big Horn and other battles drifted across the border from the States. I was surprised then to read in the colonel's tribute to my great-grandfather that he was known as a friend of the Dakota people in the area, and could speak "several dialects."

Linguistic facility is easily overestimated by those who have none, and his "friendship" might well have been entirely a job requirement. He was the town blacksmith, and Indian people, still very much on the move in those days, would have had wagons cobbled together out of wood and iron scraps, as well as pots and metal tools that needed mending from time to time. The story says that James was known as "Musakowha," which the colonel translated as simply "blacksmith." "It was not unusual," he wrote, "for a hundred tepees to be pitched around the village, all supplying business for 'Musakowha.'"

After this statement, the colonel recounts an episode meant to demonstrate how thrifty pioneers could turn the most meagre of investments into profit. "An aged squaw wanted a dollar's worth of [blacksmith] work done. All she had to trade were three wild goose eggs. Good naturedly the smith made the trade. Then his wife, equally resourceful, set them under an old hen. From this experiment the finest flock of wild geese on the prairies was produced."

A Paul Bunyan yarn like that may not have the slightest basis in reality, yet I am enough of a dreamer to imagine the opportunity that slipped away in such an interchange. Here's my grandfather's father receiving three goose eggs from an old woman who only ten or twenty years earlier had been processing the flesh of some of the last wild buffalo to be killed on the plains. What she must have seen in her life. What she must have known of the prairie, of the meadowlark and other birds. To have been there in that moment and asked questions: What do these birds mean? What do they say to us? How do we learn to listen?

In the end, the story is like the hammer stone on my bookshelf or the drive lane cairns—enough to stir longings, but more a reminder of how little we know than a way to knowing.

I look out toward the pipit fields where a male is aloft marking circles above the grass with sky-filling song. Somewhere in the circumference of prairie beneath his flight, a female incubates her eggs in long grass. A tussock of spear grass arcs over her, making her nest into the shape of an oven. Was this pair here last year? Will they succeed this year in adding one or two fledglings to the population? Will they return next year? These questions are of a different order: on the surface less about meaning and listening, and more about science with its customary distinction between spirit and matter. But from this pasture, with pipit song pouring down like sunlight given a voice, I struggle to see the boundary between a bird's physical presence and what we think of as spirit.

Perhaps that line is meant to be blurred, and if it is then nothing overflows the boundary better than a songbird—a creature covered in appendages that gather and refract light like prisms, bringing more of its invisible spectrum to our eyes; that lives upon the air while the rest of us escape gravity only in dreams; that takes the wind into its throat and returns it as the signature music of the land.

Western Meadowlark

Some of the first words written about the western meadowlark on the northern plains came from the pen of Dr. John Richardson, surgeon-naturalist on the two overland Franklin expeditions—two decades before Franklin's disastrous attempt to find the Northwest Passage by sea. Finding meadowlarks on the prairie near Fort Carlton in 1827, Richardson wrote, "This beautiful bird arrives about the first of May on the Saskatchewan [River], beyond which it was not seen by us. In the fur countries, it frequents open plains and meadows, hiding itself in the grass.... It often perches on the top of a low bush, and utters a loud, mellow and plaintive whistle, which its Cree appellation (*peesteh-atchewusson*) is intended to express."[2]

Like its eastern counterpart, the western meadowlark will nest in ditches and hay pastures and along rural easements where hay machines often destroy its nests. Not actually a lark, but a member of the black-bird family, the western meadowlark was for many years overlooked as a species distinctive from the eastern meadowlark. When Audubon finally came to name it, nearly twenty years after Richardson's encounter, he gave it the Latin species name *neglecta* to reflect the oversight.

Male western meadowlarks usually have two partners and two nests going at once. In fact, the chase display the species uses during pair forma-tion will sometimes involve all three birds, with the two females setting the pace of the chase and the male pursuing. Observers have detected a single male singing as many as forty-eight different songs.

Though it is still one of the most abundant of our prairie songbirds, the western meadowlark is now declining at a steady 2 percent per year.[3] The economic pressure to cultivate field edges and road allowances may be partly to blame. When Lawrence Beckie, a farmer-naturalist from Bladworth, Saskatchewan, sowed ten-yard-wide strips back to grass in the ditches where roads join his land, he soon noticed an increase in meadowlarks on the edges of his fields.[4]

If more farmers do not take steps to preserve or restore grassy mar-gins on their land, the meadowlark singing from the fence line will one day fade from the working landscape to become merely another piece of settler nostalgia on the Great Plains.

Chapter Four

BIRDLINE

With no telephone, television, or Internet access at the cabin, we're happily out of touch while we are there, but if we climb up on a hay bale on the high side of the yard site we can call out on a cellphone to check in on our older children back in the city. When they join us at the cabin, the poor cell coverage in our creek valley gives them an opportunity to experience the privation their parents survived in the days before we figured out how to send one another badly written messages about nothing of any consequence. On the drive home, as we crest the hill and roll out onto the plains, their cellphones give out a chorus of chirps as they are impregnated with the text messages that have been scanning around the ether, looking for them all weekend long. It feels like a small electronic assault from the digitized world, but it serves as one more reminder of why I come to the prairie. Sometimes while we are there, Karen will be expecting a call at home about a birth she is attending, so we use the phone bale to check for voice-mail messages. This morning there was one about birds.

"Don Miller from Mossbank here. We've had a bird sighting thought you might like to know about. There are two dickcissels singing in an alfalfa field south of town. Been watching them for a few days now."

Dispatches like this one have been coming my way for more than ten years now, since I started as the guest naturalist on a monthly CBC radio phone-in show we call *Birdline*. Between shows, especially in breeding season, people will often call me at home to tell me what they've seen. The week before we air, people are emailing the CBC asking when the show will be on next. On the day of the show, the board lights up five or ten minutes before air time and stays that way for most of the hour.

"And now we have Arnie from Yellowgrass. What are you seeing in Yellowgrass?"

"Hello. Yeah, my wife and I were picking chokecherries last week and we saw somethin' we couldn't figure out. We were picking berries there, in the coulee, and walking deeper into the middle of the bush—it was real thick—and right there at my feet was a dead mudhen, just a little chick. But it's weird, 'cause the thing is we were nowheres near water. Nearest slough must've been, I dunno, fifteen or twenty rods away."

At this point it is my job to respond with a rational explanation. The mudhen chick, or American coot, was very likely dropped by a predator, possibly a northern harrier, carrying it to its nest or to a plucking site.

At the other end of the line I often sense a note of disappointment in the caller's voice, as though I had reduced their story to the mundane. It's the same when people call in to report seeing an all-white crow, robin, or duck. They start off excited by what they have seen, and then I deflate them with my explanation of the genetic incidence of albinism.

Once a man called in and described a very large bird, much larger than any eagle he had ever seen. He gave the kind of carefully observed details that I've come to expect from farm people, but he began to sound a little hesitant as he skirted nearer what he had called in to say. Finally, after a pause, he said, "This is going to sound strange, but it looked like a . . . er . . . thunderbird."

"You mean, like *the* thunderbird of . . . the one people see in visions?"

"Um, yeah. I guess so. I'm just wondering, have you ever heard of someone seeing a thunderbird lately?"

I have learned not to discount any reports out of hand, but there are moments in the studio when I stare at the microphone and grope for the right words. Sometimes it seems that, rather than simply having a bird named, the caller wants to have their *experience* named by someone who likewise has been moved in the presence of birds. A feathered creature comes forward into your day from its usual place in the anonymous backdrop behind human doings, and you feel a tug of memory if not from your own consciousness then from intimacies somehow recollected in the flesh. Such an awakening deserves to be recognized, even honoured, but the last thing it needs is explanation. Between *Birdline* and the calls I receive at home, I get to hear a lot of stories from people who notice birds. I think of it as reportage from the front lines where wild things are making some headway in their long, patient effort to bring us to our senses. In a land whose flesh has been scarred from a century of flaying, how can it be anything but a privilege to receive these dispatches of hopefulness?

Then there are times when the reports reveal a whole movement of birds. The dickcissel (pronounced *dik-sissil*) call from Don of Mossbank was not the first I'd received, merely the northernmost in a flurry of sightings this summer. What does it mean when a grassland bird like the dickcissel comes across the border in greater numbers than ever before? Having never seen the bird myself, the little understanding I can manage comes from reference books.

Most field guides have about as much confidence in declaring the boundaries of the dickcissel's range as they do in declaring its placement in the taxonomic order. It looks superficially like the introduced house sparrow, but at one time it was lumped in with blackbirds, orioles, and meadowlarks. Now taxonomists argue its nearest relatives are the tropical seedeaters, placing it in the same family as cardinals and buntings. Meanwhile, no one can say precisely where to mark the northwestern limit of its breeding range, partly because it is such a wanderer. A species that nests in the tallest grasses, it may have been tied to the dynamic ebb and flow of tallgrass prairie, whose historical boundaries are equally indeterminate. The miracle of the dickcissel is that it has adapted enough to survive the loss of the prairie it loved best and has figured out how to use other kinds of grass, native and introduced.

Perhaps more than any other bird, the dickcissel testifies to the liberty at the heart of grassland ecology. Many prairie birds come and go from year to year, including the lark bunting and the grasshopper and Baird's sparrows, but the dickcissel is the freest of the free. "Extremely sporadic," Godfrey's *Birds of Canada* pegs it. My oldest field guide, published in 1946 when dickcissels were still abundant, provides more detail: "Most birds have a strong attachment for the place where they first bred, returning, if not to the same nest site, at least to the same general area. Dickcissels seem to lack this attachment and often shift breeding grounds from year to year in a most erratic manner. One year they may be abundant, the next absent."[1]

When fire and bison were still choreographing the dance, dickcissels may have arrived here on the northern plains in years when drought, grazing, or fire in the core of their range south of the forty-ninth parallel forced them to wander in search of taller grass. After settlement, the first decade of serious drought, the 1930s, brought a small invasion of dickcissels into southern Saskatchewan and Manitoba, in a zone that reached north of the presumed range of tallgrass. There can't have been much grass in Saskatchewan those years either, but a small colony of dickcissels set up on the edge of a golf course near the Regina RCMP barracks in 1933 and 1934. A few years later, in 1939, a very young and beardless Farley Mowat spotted a dickcissel in a garden on a farm outside Regina.[2]

Those are the first official breeding records for dickcissel in Saskatchewan and among the first on the books for Canada. Since then there have been one or two sightings per decade, and one other breeding record from 1953. And now this year, in the summer of 2006, the biggest dickcissel invasion in a century is underway, with thirty or more sightings in June, mostly clustered in the southeastern portion of Saskatchewan, where heavy spring rains produced thigh-high alfalfa.

Even more strange, birders just across the border in North Dakota recently sighted another songbird that is tied to tallgrass prairie, the increasingly rare Henslow's sparrow. A male was found on a reserve north and east of Minot, singing from a high stand of thatched native grass.

What are these birds trying to tell us? With many species thinning out and disappearing from apparently suitable habitat across the northern plains, believing in the restorative powers of prairie requires an act of faith that is getting more difficult to make as the years go by. Then we get a summer full of dickcissels, prairie evangelists canvassing for believers. From June to August, I watched the alfalfa fields on the east side of our property and listened wishfully for the *chis-chis-chis* of a bird that is doing its best to show us that the dance is not over yet.

Grasshopper Sparrow

The first time you find a grasshopper sparrow you wonder how many you have passed by over the years without knowing. You watch it sing and realize that you have probably been ignoring its thin, buzzing sounds as part of the aural backdrop of a sun-warmed pasture. Unlike most birds, both male and female grasshopper sparrows sing their primary song, which consists of a couple of introductory *tics* followed by a hissing trill that trails off weakly as though swallowed by the wind. The male also sings a second song that is entirely different—a rapid jumble of squeaky and buzzy notes usually given in flight.

Just as easily overlooked as its songs is the beauty of the grasshopper sparrow. From a distance, even through binoculars, it is a beige bird with a ragged little tail and an oversize head. In the hand, you see what another grasshopper sparrow sees: soft, warm tones on the face and breast, a bit of gold above the eye, burnt umber and chestnut on the scapulars, and a shimmer of iridescent chartreuse on the shoulder. The way it perches up on a wild rose bush to sing then flutters weakly over the pasture and dives into the grass gives it an indescribable gestalt that is similar to but not quite the same as that of its cousin, the Baird's sparrow, which can often be found singing nearby. Their genus, *Ammodramus*, seems to have created sparrows designed to exasperate birdwatchers with stingy views, but in truth it's their ecological niche that makes them difficult to see. You will never see a grasshopper sparrow out in the open scratching for seeds like a white-throated sparrow. It nests on the ground and finds its food on or near the ground among the forest of grass stems, coming to the surface now and then to sing or chase off another male. Fittingly, the grasshopper sparrow simply slips away unnoticed at the end of its breeding season. As soon as it stops singing in July, bird observers lose track of it, so no one has been able to figure out exactly when it leaves for its wintering grounds.

The grasshopper sparrow comes and goes in small colonies, nesting in an area for a while and then moving on. Though it is nowhere near as sporadic as the dickcissel, some years it can be hard to find. During the first twenty-five years of recording birds on the Wascana plains, Saskatchewan Museum of Natural History staff never found a single grasshopper sparrow. By 1933, though, the same year the dickcissels showed up, the province's chief game guardian, Fred Bradshaw, was finding grasshopper sparrows in vacant lots on the west edge of Regina; he estimated that at least fifty pairs were in the area. Although the grasshopper sparrow has adapted to disturbed grasslands, bird surveys indicate it is declining by 3.7 percent per year across its range, and since 1980 in Canada it has declined by more than 6 percent per year.

Chapter Five

OF THE AIR

Last night we discovered that the porch I built on the front of our cabin is a giant harmonica. Earlier in the day the radio announced that a forty-mile-per-hour wind was coming. By midnight I was listening to it moan and whistle through the six cedar posts that hold up the porch roof. I tried consoling myself with lofty thoughts about Aeolian harps and then reached for the earplugs.

I'm always impressed when weather forecasters predict a big wind and get it right. How do they know when something that can't be seen is going to start moving faster, and then predict its speed to within a few miles per hour? At breakfast, in the machine shed we've converted into a shared kitchen, I asked Rob, the scientist in our little community of urban refugees. A plant ecologist who reads everything from math texts to the Dhammapada, and freely admits to knowing more about most things than most people know about anything, he had an answer.

"Wind is air moving from a high-pressure zone into a low-pressure zone," he said. "I imagine they can measure the differential between adjacent zones and then make a prediction."

That made sense to me. Nature abhors a vacuum and all that. Lord knows, out here we've got a lot of vacuum to be abhorred. No wonder it's so windy on the plains. Nope, Rob said, we probably get more wind because the land can heat up and cool down rapidly in a continental, semi-arid, and open landscape. Okay, no oceans, mountains, or forests to help moderate air temperatures, so high-pressure zones can arise quickly right next to low-pressure zones, which means we get sudden winds and tuneful porches.

As we talked about the wind, seventy-five to one hundred swallows of three different species were playing in air that was bending aspen trees down toward the lakeside. Everything here—the hump backed contour of the hills, the architecture of grass stems, the swivel of poplar leaves—has been formed in the presence of rushing air.

When the wind arrives overnight or in the middle of a calm morning, it brings with it a sense of the distance it has travelled from other landscapes. Last week it was the smoke from forest fires all the way from the Athabasca delta on the edge of the Northwest Territories. Other days in spring, it gathers pollen from spruce and fir trees as it stirs northern bogs like cauldrons and combs through woodlands before spilling onto the plains. To stand in such a wind is to know the freedom it rides upon as it comes out of the trees—a freedom you can taste, hear, smell, feel perhaps, but to *see* it, to behold it with the faculty that dominates human witnessing of the world, you need to look for something with wings.

An odd creaking and rushing sound passes over the cabin as I sit on the porch. I lift my head to have a look. Another cormorant on its way to the water. The wings of some birds make distinctive noises, and in quiet places like this you can learn to identify them. The whistle of canvasback ducks is at a different pitch from that of buffleheads. Canada geese have their own pinion-rattle and creak. The pelicans, when they come low over the cabin, make a funny *whoof*-ing sound with their wings. Flickers sound like cloth snapping on a line. Hummingbirds sound like souped-up bumblebees.

The barn, tree, and bank swallows make no sound with their wings that I can hear from this distance, but they are among the aerial masters of the bird world. Swallows spend far more time in the air than most other birds—hours on the wing either playing or grazing their way through airborne plankton, the invisible matter that enlivens the air. A cubic yard of air, I once read, can contain thousands of living things: bacteria, protozoa, small insects, fungal spores, pollens, algae, lichen. Most of it, the invisible or barely visible flotsam and jetsam of the atmosphere, completely escapes our awareness.

Becoming aware of life that moves in the invisible realm of air may be the very exercise that led to human consciousness. This thought comes from David Abram's groundbreaking book of eco-philosophy, *The Spell of the Sensuous.*[1] As the harmonica-porch began playing its first mournful strains last night, language from a chapter called "The Forgetting and Remembering of the Air" came to mind. Abram opens the chapter by describing the Lakota and Navajo understanding of the air as the continuous and material flow that enters our bodies and consciousness in breath and thought, thereby connecting us to everything else in Creation. Though it is articulated here in fresh prose, this kind of philosophy is what we expect from the Aboriginal peoples who came into their identity within the open, airy landscapes of the west. The surprise in Abram's account comes when he goes on to demonstrate that deep in our own religious traditions there is a similar reverence for the air, though lately it has been reduced to the symbolic or merely metaphorical. Using the roots of several words—*spirit, psyche, soul, anima,* and *atmosphere*—Abram argues that for Western civilization too, the air, in breath and holy wind, has been the very medium of our interconnectedness and the source of our awareness.

Whether it is Navajo, Lakota, Christian, Jewish, Islamic, or Buddhist, much of human spirituality, at least on the mystical side of things, aspires to bring awareness or consciousness to a deeper level.

Through a practice of paying attention, getting rid of attachments, and surrendering to what is here and now, the mystic empties the self and comes to see and trust a communion that was there all along, as common and everyday as the breath of Creation within and around us, anchoring all living things to the present moment.

Is it possible that we first became aware of that communion by seeing it manifest in the creatures that live in the air and give it a voice?

From the dove of peace to winged angels, from the spirit hovering over the deep to Dante's starlings and Gerard Manley Hopkins' kingfishers and kestrels, birds are in our religious art, fables, proverbs, parables, poetry, and myths, illustrating at least the possibility of a human way in the world that rises above mindlessness, ego, hatred, and destruction. If they have failed us in this role, the fault is our own, arising from the very shallowness of our regard for them as nothing more than symbols of our ideas, just as the air is now regarded as merely a metaphor for spirit.

We are fascinated by birds, hold them in our esteem, because they put flesh upon, incarnate the soul of the land they inhabit, bringing it to our senses in ways that mammals, insects, or reptiles cannot match. Remove the forest's warblers, thrushes, and owls, and the truth of what a forest is, and the wisdom it offers, is rendered insensible. In the presence of birds, something in Creation keeps us back from the brink, mindful of a spirit that is ascendant and yet available to our ears and eyes. What happens to a civilization that loses contact with birds? Will we forget what we ever meant by soul and mindfulness?

Abram says that our language and culture are rooted in the knowledge that air is the matrix of spirit and awareness, but his larger thesis argues that language and culture arose from our sensuous immersion in the "more-than-human" world of nature. Somewhere along the way we extracted ourselves from nature and forgot that the air is "the very mystery of the living present." Somewhere along the way we convinced ourselves that the air is lifeless and empty, at best a metaphor; that awareness is entirely contained within the human mind.

Applying Abram's philosophy to birds, I've begun to wonder if our ancestors learned reverence for air by living in proximity to the sparrows and finches that dwell in dry, open landscapes. The religions he considers each developed in grassland or desert places—the geography of the spirit where the *spirit* of the geography is embodied in creatures who fly and sing in perfect liberty. In an era when most people have little contact with nature, it seems naïve and impossibly optimistic to believe that we might once again come to know the consciousness and spirit that move in and around us by paying attention to birds, listening to their song, and watching them fly, soar, and glide. Yet it may be the best way available for us to reawaken to the holiness in which we live, move, and have our being.

Flight is one thing. I can watch the swallows tossed by gusts of wind over our cabin or the turkey vultures effortlessly riding updrafts above the hills, and tell myself that a bird moving freely in air traces the arc of spiritual liberty sought by desert mystics, but my doubts dismiss it as metaphor, imagery.

Flight*song*—the spiralling notes of a pipit three hundred feet into the sky, the rapid windchimes of longspurs fluttering above their brooding mates—is something else. Like all music, it bypasses our reasoned categories and comparisons and plays directly to the heart, where desire and imagination offer the deeper witness that makes us human.

The airborne song over the plains of Galilee may have been what inspired Jesus to use birds in warning his followers against too much sowing and reaping. Advising them to live in the faith of God's care and not worry about tomorrow, he told them to "consider the birds of the air. They neither sow nor reap, and yet your heavenly Father feeds them." It is a message we need today more than ever, when we have taken sowing and reaping to new extremes. Set aside your need to plan, build, and control; live joyfully today. No bird exemplifies this surrender to God's grace more than one that sings as it rides the air currents. We call this flightsong or "skylarking," and it is found almost exclusively in songbirds that live in open, untreed landscapes.

All around Jesus as he travelled the grassy plains and valleys of the Galilean countryside, the air would have been filled with the flightsong of grassland birds. Birds like the fantailed warbler. Mediterranean field guides say it flies in undulating arcs, flashing its tail and singing at the top of each wave. A bird that sings aloft is claiming nothing but the liberty that resides in its spirit, which is *of the air*. To experience it first-hand is to discover why the birds of the air are worth our considering.

The first time I stood in the middle of a pasture full of skylarking birds I was doing what birders do—looking for a bird I'd never seen before. I'd driven south of the city to a large community pasture where a birder friend said I'd find lark buntings. It was a June morning, just after sunrise. I got out of the car and stepped over the barbed wire and into the grass. Spotting two pronghorns grazing on a ridge nearby, I crouched low to see if they would stay. Within seconds birds that I had disturbed returned to their flightsong. Lark buntings and chestnut-collared longspurs began lifting from the grass around me to sing as they floated on set wings. Beneath them the trills of Baird's sparrows and the fluting of meadowlarks filled the air nearest the ground. But above all of this, the swirling song of Sprague's pipits fell to the earth in streams. I lay in the grass beneath a sky that was inhaling and exhaling song. The pronghorns stayed and I stayed— immersed in sound more than hearing it, powerless to name the truth it bore.

Consider the birds of the air. They fly over the prairie, bearing messages to the Creator, and promises to all creatures below. Just now, their voices hang briefly on the wind, each song a passing testimony to the sacramental presence that rises and falls in every living thing. Should we ever set aside our sowing and reaping long enough to listen, might we remember that we too share in the spirit that animates all of life? And, what is more, that we are bound by its daily promises?

LARK BUNTING

The lark bunting is another vagabond prairie bird that will suddenly take a notion to nest in an area for a couple of years and then move on. One of the most gregarious of grassland songbirds, it roves southern Texas and northern Mexico in massive winter flocks looking for grasslands that have received enough moisture to support their numbers. Coming north in spring, the flocks separate into smaller colonies, setting up to breed on sage prairie, shrubby grassland, or even cultivated fields.

Severe drought at the heart of the lark bunting range in the northern states, southwestern Saskatchewan, and southeastern Alberta sometimes pushes the colonies northward in search of moister conditions. During the droughts of the early 1930s, early 1950s, 1964, and 1985–86, numbers of lark buntings came as far north as the Regina plains to breed. Range maps show the large geographical zone that encompasses all the places where they have been known to show up to breed now and then. However, in most years lark buntings are rarely found outside the core of their range.

The lark bunting is an oddity among North American birds. It is the only member of its genus and, unlike any other sparrow on the continent, the male changes its dress from a black-and-white tuxedo in summer (ranchers on the northern plains call it the "white-winged blackbird") to a drabber suit of browns and greys the rest of the year. And unlike many grassland birds, lark buntings are out in the open, demanding attention. People see them along roadsides, flying above crops and pastures at mid-day, drinking from the cattle trough, perching on fence posts. Like mobs of teenagers, they seem to do everything as a group. The males sing in communal songflight, rising in unison and then falling with their wings held above horizontal as they let out their bizarre choral arrangement of low whistles, toots, and percussive trills and buzzes. It has a chanting cadence that belongs to scrubby sagebrush prairie, and hearing it is, as Frank Roy wrote in *Birds of the Elbow*, "a memorable auditory experience, perhaps without parallel in the prairie bird world."[2]

The lark bunting's nomadic habits make it one of the toughest birds for population researchers to nail down, but all states and provinces except Montana have shown a steady decline, which has been confirmed by Christmas Bird Count data from the southern states.[3]

Chapter Six

THE SPARROW'S FALL

Some time just before dawn this morning, I was awoken by coyotes. They were making weird tremolo calls that sounded like loons, and by the time I figured out it was coyotes I was fully awake.

Then I realized that the harmonica-porch was silent. The wind had fallen. After two days and nights of wind it was dead calm. I'd been waiting for a windless morning to take my bicycle out onto the community pasture. I'm not much of a cyclist, but I brought one of our old clunkers out to the cabin, thinking it might allow me to explore farther out onto the grassland south of our property. On foot, I can only get so far in a morning before the birdsong fades in the heat of the sun, and it is time to head back. I'd never reached the middle of the pipit fields, and I thought a bike might get me there.

Unable to sleep anyway, I jumped into some shorts, put my binoculars around my neck, and headed out the door at 5:10, carrying some fruit, trail mix, and a bottle of water. I took one last look at the map we keep in the machine shed, planned a route, and straddled my bike. It is a bare-bones mountain bike that needs a tune-up and has never been off the pavement. Not really suited to off-roading, but neither are my legs, so we make a good match. My drumsticks are less than Grade A, but I thought a long ride up and down prairie hills might be just the kind of workout they needed.

Later in the morning, as I began rationing my food and water and fantasizing about a helicopter rescue, I realized I'd overdone it, gone too far into the pasture. On the return trip, I got to see some new places since I couldn't find the cow trail that got me there, and along the way I dispelled the quicksand myth that local farmers have been propagating. Not that there aren't some hellacious mudholes that will hold you down for a good spell. The myth I was able to disprove is the one that says you should never panic in quicksand because you'll get stuck worse than ever. Quite the contrary, I found that arm-flailing, wide-eyed panic, even with a bike overhead and no bottom underfoot, served me well enough.

I rode back the last half mile uphill, pedalling hard in case Karen was watching from the porch. As I rounded the bend into the yard, my thighs screaming, I decided I should try a fancy dismount to punctuate my triumphant return as extreme prairie biker. Coasting to the front of the cabin, I swung off the bike and stuck a flawless Olga Korbut landing. The spasms locked onto my legs the moment my heels hit the ground. I think double charley horse is the technical term. My knees would not bend, so I fell over and rolled on the gravel a couple times to see if that would help, and that was how Karen found me: covered in mud and cramped from the hips down, writhing and yelling beside my fallen bike.

People who live on prairie farms and pay attention to birds don't go for 5 a.m. bike tours with binoculars dangling from their necks. They don't wear Tilley hats and Rockports. They don't talk about rarities and compare life lists. They are a dead loss to ecotourism, never go on field trips because they live in the field already. They just notice things—walking to the quonset, sitting on the tractor seat, driving into town. And the drama they see in the comings and goings of birds, their annual striving to bring something to life in the land, runs parallel to their own work raising crops, livestock, and children.

What's more, a few of them manage to communicate with the birds. Some with gestures and kindness; some with words. Every family has a story about a grandfather or aunt who taught a crow to count or a magpie to speak; about dad feeding partridge in the yard during a storm; breaking the crust on a snowbank to let the snow buntings out; moving the horned lark nest from the furrow; leaving grass on the road allowance for the meadowlarks and sparrows.

These are the folks who bring to mind Wallace Stegner's famous lines about prairie dwellers: "It is a country to breed mystical people . . . perhaps poetic people. . . . It was not prairie dwellers who invented the indifferent universe or impotent man. Puny you may feel there, and vulnerable, but not unnoticed. This is a land to mark the sparrow's fall."[1]

With people noticing the sparrows and the sparrows sometimes noticing the people, a kind of mutuality between the human and the other-than-human becomes possible. If prairie people consider the birds more than city dwellers or people who live near mountains or forests, it's because they experience more of that vulnerability beneath skies that bring both blessed rain and deluge, zephyr and plough wind, sun and drought, snow cover and blizzard.

Sometimes when they notice the birds, I hear about it, either on the air during *Birdline*, or at home by phone or letter.

A PHONE CALL FROM A MAN
WITH PRAIRIE CHICKENS IN HIS FLOWER BED

His voice cracks in places, can't quite contain the mix of enthusiasm and concern. The message says his name is Lloyd and he has a question about prairie chickens—sharp-tailed grouse, that is. He's got a mother prairie chicken nesting in his flower bed. One of the chicks is out by itself and the mother is ignoring it. He wants to do the right thing but isn't sure what that is. Do they catch it and put it in a box to protect it, or do they just let it fend for itself?

A NINETY-TWO-YEAR-OLD MAN FROM CENTRAL BUTTE WRITES ABOUT THE BIRDS OF LAST MOUNTAIN

A handwritten letter: small, round, and neat cursive on unlined stationery. The address is Central Butte and it is signed, "Yours truly, Edgar." There's a picture enclosed—an overexposed shot of a brown thrasher standing on a stairway where seeds are strewn. You can see the frame of the window through which it was taken. After asking for help in identifying the bird in the photo, he says that he started watching birds in 1923 at the age of nine when his family moved to Last Mountain—a bird paradise. In the spring of '24 a farmer gave him a dollar for driving his four horses on the harrow for a day. He took that dollar and bought Taverner's *Birds of Western Canada*. After that he and his brother collected a single egg from thirty-seven different species.

In the fall of '26 he got to know some chickadees on the property. One was cheekier than the rest, brave enough to come to his outstretched hand and get bread crumbs. Within a week he had five chickadees all over his head and shoulders. They'd ride to the barn with him and in the morning when he went out to do chores he'd give a whistle, imitating their song, and they would come to greet him.

The birds disappeared for a spell, but the next fall he was out with a friend hunting rabbits and the friend said, "Edgar, there's a bird riding on your gun barrel." Edgar gave the whistle and four more chickadees came out of the bush to join the one on his rifle. He hadn't seen them for months and he was a half mile away from the yard where he'd been feeding them, but they still knew Edgar, and responded to his call.

A MAN REMEMBERS THE CLIFF SWALLOWS OF HAFFORD

He heard the Hafford cliff swallows mentioned so he had to call in. They used to nest beneath the eaves of their buildings on the farm. You'd see ten or twelve of them working together on one mud nest until it was done. Then they'd get started on the next one and the next until they had a bunch of them. Amazing to see them working together—like the original prairie socialists. Never had any trouble with bugs in the yard as long as the swallows were around. Some people didn't like the droppings they leave so they'd chase them off with guns. Then they'd be going out to buy a bug zapper soon after that. Hardly see swallows in the Hafford area since they put the power lines underground.

A WOMAN SPEAKS TO THE BIRD WITH ORANGE UNDER ITS WINGS

She can't see very well anymore, but she can see that when it flies out of the nest hole there is a gorgeous flash of orange. She watches it through her bedroom window, an arm's length from the tree it nests in. She knows it is the mother, and she has been speaking to it every morning for several weeks. At first it was scared of her voice, but now it seems to like the sound. After her partner flies off for a bit, the mother comes out to listen for her voice. "Good morning, birdy," she says, "Sun's up. Good morning."

A MAN FROM HORIZON
WHO TALKED TO LARKS AND LONGSPURS

He grew up on a mixed farm a few miles from a place called Horizon but it's not there anymore. That was in the forties and fifties. Ranched there himself until 1975 when his arms and shoulders gave out. Couldn't do the heavy ranch work anymore. Through the

fifties and sixties he had two shelters on the outskirts of the yard—
one for the cows and one for the weaned calves. The horned larks
usually would come back in the first week of February. If he didn't
see them by Groundhog Day he'd get worried. By late March they'd
be scraping out a nest close to the cowshed. The hen would sit on
the eggs even when there was a blizzard and somehow she never
got covered—maybe the snow bounced off the wall of the shed or
something. One little horned lark would let him stay right beside
and talk to her. If the cattle came too close she'd rise up, spread her
wings, and almost hiss at them. They'd jump and get out of the way.
If something happened and the eggs didn't hatch, well, no matter,
they would start all over again.

When he was young he hunted and trapped, but then he got to
the stage where he didn't want to kill birds anymore. He just wanted
to admire them. In a lot of ways they're more intelligent than people
are—the way they learn to take care of one another. The way they
learn to trust you. Eat right out of your hand, sing right over your
head, stay on the nest and never move because they know you, your
voice, your clothes.

Even as a boy he always paid attention to birds, couldn't hear a
song without stopping to listen. His dad didn't approve, swore at him
for wasting his time with birds. Sundays were the days he was free to
walk the pasture and visit the birds. Along the south side there was a
ridge, an outcrop of rocks that stretches all the way from Estevan to
Maple Creek, and in some places it goes underground. Around the
rock, there would be some grass growing here and there in between.
That's where the longspurs were. Chestnut-collared. It was nothing
at all in the spring of the year to find a dozen pair in a quarter-mile
length of that outcrop and they'd nest right there between the rocks.
They felt safe there because the cattle would not try to step among
the rocks. Once he found a nest he'd take careful note of where it

was, and then he'd come back every day, talk to the birds a little bit, quietly. They'd get used to him till he could sit down within five feet of a longspur on the nest and she wouldn't get up. The male would come, a little bit concerned, and he'd sit on a rock and sing and sing and sing.

They get to know you if you talk in the same low tones all the time, say the same words over and over again. He'd talk to them for a while, and they just seemed to take it all in—fluff up their feathers and preen themselves and put on a show. That's how he talks to all the birds—still does even now.

He misses the music of the longspurs, the songflights of lark buntings, and the way the burrowing owls once flew in to land on fence posts near him. Other people own the land now, and he would like to go back sometime and see if there is any trace of burrowing owls where they used to be. He's afraid the grasshopper spray got rid of most of them, but he'd like to see if they're still there.

Nowadays he talks to the barn swallows in his shop, where he repairs farm equipment. For thirty years, since he and his wife moved to begin a grain farm farther north, barn swallows have been nesting in his workshop. For the last four or five years, there's been a male who comes in through the west window where a small pane is missing. In spring, before any swallows have arrived, he's had the shop door closed and been working at his bench when that male has arrived for the summer. It comes right in through the hole in the window. The bird goes right to its favourite perch on the stovepipe over the workbench and it begins to chatter at him. He answers back, "So you're back again for another year." Two or three days later, a female will come by, and the male shows her around the nesting spots. She is usually nervous for a while, but he gentles her down, and pretty soon she's almost as tame as he is. That bird will sit within ten feet of him, even when he's pounding or grinding something or the air compressor is going. He does not care one little bit. But if a stranger comes and he doesn't like the stranger's voice, he will give an alarm cry and dive at him.

Another time he saw a male swallow lose its partner when it had five flightless young still in the nest. The widowed male somehow communicated the situation to another pair of swallows nearby and the three adults together raised ten nestlings that summer, helping one another out at the two nests.

If the birds disappeared he'd miss their friendship. They are true friends, he always says. Human beings you can trust to a point; birds you can always trust. They're always going to be the same. If they like you and think they're your friend, they'll keep showing it until the day they die.

In the middle of my extreme biking safari, and before the exhaustion, the mud, and the double charley horse, I did manage to get to the centre of the pipit fields. It was late summer and the pasture was quiet. A couple of vesper sparrows flitted here and there. Two mule deer bucks grazed in higher grass, their velveted antlers glowing with the tawny light of morning. I sat down to eat my apple and orange in a weedy field that had been "improved" by scarifying or scratching the sod to a shallow depth and then seeding it with alfalfa and crested wheat grass. Both are introduced species, but the wheat grass is a pernicious invader that contributes to grassland bird decline.

I remembered a biologist telling me that when you scarify and reseed a pasture to wheat grass, the food for birds decreases dramatically. Early-season grasshoppers, he said, are important for longspurs and Sprague's pipits in particular, but he has collected data that show these insects virtually disappearing from pastures improved with crested wheat grass. The brown-spotted range grasshopper, known to be important for songbird nestling survival, is abundant on unimproved pasture but next to impossible to locate wherever crested wheat grass has been introduced.

I looked on the ground underneath the introduced grasses and found the hidden disfiguration of pasture "improvement." A vital layer of life was entirely gone. On healthy native grassland, below and between the taller vegetation, a richly textured understorey forms a dense pelt of ground lichens, algae, fungi, and club mosses. This "cryptogamic" layer is a galaxy unto itself, delicate and spangled with the bright growth of things that hug the earth. Any improvement that breaks the living crust will destroy it. Grassland biologists don't know what losing the cryptogamic understorey will do to native grassland, its soils, plant, and animal ecology, over the long term, but one thing is known: once it is gone, it is all but impossible to restore. Grasses and forbs can be seeded, but the cryptogamic layer is too complex a mystery for artificial propagation to duplicate.

There is something so disheartening in the simplified pattern of disturbed pasture. The texture is close enough to real grassland to remind you of what is missing, and so it seems almost worse than the obliterating monotony of a grain field. It always makes me think of the choice someone made, and of the power of one machine-wielding person to alter permanently an ecosystem that has stood for thousands of years.

Ironically, though, having some non-native grass allows ranchers to protect their native range from being damaged by grazing too early in spring. The most beaten-down and weedy native pastures in our valley are those where the farmer merely releases his cattle into the pasture in May and then takes them out again in October. Range-management theory for northern grassland maintains that it is better to delay putting livestock on native grass for several weeks in spring because the natives are slow to get started and vulnerable to overgraz-ing during that phase. That means that most ranchers—as opposed to farmers who keep cattle—will have some land where they grow non-native grass that greens up quickly after snowmelt and provides feed during periods when their native range is being rested.

But the land I was on is not the private property of a single rancher; it is a provincially owned community pasture where local stockmen are allowed to graze their animals in summer. It may not have the federal funding of larger community pastures on the northern plains, but one would expect a certain amount of vision and stewardship even on a provincial pasture. Grassland biologists on both sides of the international border would love to have governments mandate a no-exceptions policy against breaking and scarifying any more native grass on government-owned pasture, including the millions of acres of leased land. Unfortunately, the myth of the independent cowboy entitled to graze public land without government interference still holds enough power to keep such common sense at bay.

I stood and strained to listen for distant birdsong, but there were no birds moving or singing, aside from a family of magpies yakking to one another in a distant bluff, and two Swainson's hawks sitting on a large stone pile a mile to the southeast. The horizon was dominated by evidence of the ultimate improvement for land classified as unproductive: gravel quarries. A mile-long ridge of stockpiled gravel loomed over the east side of the pipit fields.

A jet passed by in a sky without song. This is what it will be like, I thought, when the last birds disappear from this pasture. In my lifetime I could witness the mixed-grass prairie and its birds receding from here, like the tide going out for the last time, a long, slow wave drawing back into a sea that exists only in memory.

It would be so easy to give up on these birds, write them off as the collateral damage of our civilization's blitzkrieg advance. Each spring I am amazed that the birds themselves have not given up. They come back, set up on a patch of grassland, sing, court, build nests, lay eggs — even if the grass is all wrong, the grasshoppers are scarce, and there isn't the right kind of cover to protect nestlings from predators. They fail, re-nest, fail again, then leave for the winter.

I sat in the cricket-song quiet for a good spell before a bird finally spoke up. The softest, fading trill floated upward from the pasture, letting me know that there was still at least one Baird's sparrow remaining in the grass. How did it fare this year? The breeding season was all but over and its song was a faint shadow of its spring exultation, but it was unmistakably that of a Baird's. *Next year, next year. There is always next year.*

Farmers call this "next-year country" because they have the same tenacity—never giving up no matter how bad things get. For the birds it is more than tenacity, though. It is survival by passing on traits that until recently have allowed them to thrive in this particular place. We see it as fidelity, an unwarranted faithfulness not necessarily to one patch of land but to a matrix of soil, vegetation, and climate, to a life on the land.

The summer-ending song of a bird that very likely failed to raise any young this year cries out to a more perfect fidelity dwelling in this land that marks the sparrow's fall. In the gospel of Stegner's allusion, Jesus tells the peasants of Galilee that not a single sparrow falls to the ground without God's knowing and caring. Our ancestors came to this land with that gospel and many others consoling them as they stripped the prairie of its sod, and fought against drought, grasshoppers, and early frosts. The power of Stegner's adaptation is in the shift it makes from God to land. Not only God, but the *land* itself keeps watch, keeps faith—for in prairie we sense an abiding awareness and attention that may be more obscure in other landscapes. God knows the sparrow. The land knows the sparrow. The trick of remaining here is to become a people who know the sparrow too, who will not give up on creatures who ask only for a place in the grass.

Baird's Sparrow

"During one of our Buffalo hunts, on the 26th July, 1843, we happened to pass along several wet places, closely over-grown by a kind of slender rush-like grass, from which we heard the notes of this species, and which we thought were produced by Marsh Wrens (*Troglodytes palustris*), and my friends [Edward] Harris and John G. Bell immediately went in search of the birds. Mr. Bell soon discovered that the notes of Baird's Bunting were softer and more prolonged than those of the Marsh Wren. They had much difficulty in raising them from the close and rather long grass, to which this species appears to confine itself; several times Mr. Bell nearly trod on some of them, before the birds would take to wing, and they almost instantaneously re-alighted within a few steps, and then ran like mice through the grass. After awhile, however, two were shot on the wing, and both fortunately were found, and proved to be an adult male and female. We found this species abundant in all such situations as I have mentioned above, and doubtless it breeds in them."[2]

This is John James Audubon telling the story of the first scientific record of Baird's sparrow near old Fort Union in today's North Dakota.

It was to be the last species Audubon would discover. Returning home to civilization, he named the bird for the young ornithologist Spencer Fullerton Baird. Almost forgotten after that, the Baird's sparrow was not seen for three decades. A single bird was shot in Colorado and then, as the North American Joint Boundary Commission passed through North Dakota in 1873, ornithologist Elliott Coues found them breeding in abundance once again.

The Cornell Laboratory of Ornithology's online version of its multi-volume *Birds of North America* has the following to say of the Baird's sparrow's habitat needs: "Baird's Sparrow is considered a defining feature of summer bird life for mixed-grass and fescue prairies of the northern Great Plains of North America. . . . Areas of potentially suitable prairie can become unsuitable when overgrown with woody or exotic vegetation because natural patterns of fire and grazing are lacking." The report goes on to say that the Baird's sparrow was until recently thought to be entirely dependent on native grassland, but it has been found nesting in "formerly cultivated lands with structural components resembling native prairie, and in agricultural use such as hayfields or pastures with strong incursions or plantings of non-native grasses. Baird's sparrows also attempt to nest in land currently under cultivation and this habit is likely part of the reason it has been declining."[3]

With its nomadic habits, moving to find suitable nesting grounds from year to year, the Baird's sparrow is another grassland bird that biologists have difficulty assessing accurately. Even so, the retraction of its already small range and studies indicating a general decline led the Committee on the Status of Endangered Wildlife in Canada (COSEWIC) to list it as threatened in 1989. A few years later that decision was overturned on the basis of new research including a large-scale population study in Saskatchewan. Prairie naturalists who have watched the rapid dwindling of this species in recent decades over and above local and temporary fluctuations have criticized the decision.

Part Two

LIFTING THE VEIL

Chapter Seven

A BITTER GLIMPSE AHEAD

I wasn't thinking about grassland birds the first time I put my kayak, a nine-foot-long hunk of blue plastic, into the south end of the lake that begins a half mile north of our land. Cherry Lake is flanked by two other small lakes that form the headwaters of Indian Head Creek. Deep Lake is the largest of the three, and perhaps the deepest, if its name means anything. I had seen a lot of water birds flying in that direction from Cherry Lake, so I wanted to learn exactly which species were there in breeding season and to listen for songbirds in the woods that cover the hills. Within ten minutes of crossing the beaver dam that marks the outlet of Indian Head Creek into the lake, I'd found red-necked grebes, two loons, and a foursome of female hooded mergansers. From the wooded slopes on the west side, I heard red-eyed vireos, rose-breasted grosbeaks, veeries, least flycatchers, and American redstarts—a typical assemblage for coulees and valleys in the parkland zone. The ravines at the south end of the lake are filled with green ash, aspen and balsam poplar, and Manitoba maple. The shoreline is rocky, and the woods above it are made impenetrable by thickets of hazel. The lake is long and narrow, running on a north-south axis, and after the first mile or so the hills recede and the water opens up on pasture land, most of it seeded to non-native grass. At this point, the wooded lake begins to look like a large prairie slough. A dogleg bend marks the shift with a sand spit that cuts into the middle of the lake, almost pinching it in two.

There are always gulls, terns, pelicans, and cormorants on the spit, so I paddled near its base to view them without putting them to flight. As I drifted in the kayak with my binoculars on a group of Forster's terns, a song wafted over the lake from the direction of the shore. It took me a minute to recognize the voice but it was a Baird's sparrow. With loons and grosbeaks singing just behind me, I hadn't followed the sudden shift to grassland and so I couldn't place the song. I strained to extend my hearing out over the land. There were two Baird's in the grass and a Sprague's pipit singing from above. A loon called again from the south end of the lake, and the mingling of its yodel with the swirling notes of the pipit made for a peculiar combination of birdsong. This might be one of very few places where such a mix can be heard, I thought—I'll have to mention it to Stuart.

Long before we met, Stuart Houston was teaching me about the natural history of the plains. The fall after I began to pay attention to grassland birds I was at a used books sale and found a complete set of *The Blue Jay*, the quarterly journal of prairie natural history published by Nature Saskatchewan. For the next two years I spent my winter evenings reading through every back issue starting in the late 1940s and making my way forward to the current issues I had begun to collect as a subscriber. The articles that interested me most gave a historical baseline for bird life on the plains: "Changing Patterns of Corvidae on the Prairie," or "Four Rancher-Naturalists of the Cypress Hills," or "The Spread of the Western Kingbird across the Prairies." There were dozens of these notes and articles, and almost all of them had C. Stuart Houston, and sometimes Mary Houston, at the top of the page.

Though several years passed before I met the Houstons, I was hearing about them all the time: Stuart, a medical doctor and professor of radiology at the University of Saskatchewan, one of the most accomplished bird banders on the continent, author of several books and a couple of hundred articles about birds and human history on the northern Great Plains; Mary, former teacher, author, and co-author, with her own reputation as a bird bander and amateur ornithologist.

Meanwhile, I was continually meeting people who had been introduced to bird banding, ornithology, and natural history by the Houstons, many of whom were actively banding or working as biologists across Canada. As young students helping the Houstons out on banding trips, they scrambled up trees or over cliffs to get at raptor nests. Back on the ground they went on to become conservationists, doctors, and scientists as graduates of Stuart's ongoing mission to mentor.

That word, *mentor*, particularly as a verb, still makes me cringe a little. It's not merely the oily sheen such a word picks up from passing over the lips of too many motivational speakers. It's that having a mentor means you are good at asking for help and taking advice. I am good at neither of these, and so there has always been something in me that does not want to be "mentored."

The first time we spoke I was working on my book about the Qu'Appelle River. I phoned him, reluctantly, to ask a question or two but then ended up agreeing to have him review several chapters. That seemed innocent enough, but a few months later, as I walked away from the podium at a reading in Saskatoon, there he was in the flesh and with something on his mind, both hands on the handle of his cane, drumming his fingers.

"You need some work on your elocution," he said. "Your words were lost because you weren't speaking clearly." I smiled politely and changed the subject. Later, as we left for the evening, I asked Karen what she thought of Stuart's remarks.

"I think you are being mentored."

Over time I got used to the idea, and realized that I'd been learning from Stuart for years. It was in reading his books and journal
articles that I began to see how questions in natural history are often
answered by digging into human history. A loon singing on Deep
Lake might be a modern aberration explained by the advance of
woodland out onto the plains after we suppressed fire and removed
the buffalo. On the other hand, loons did nest on some prairie lakes
before settlement. Stuart would know if they were here a century
ago or could at least tell me how to find the answer by looking in the
accounts of early naturalists and of bird and egg collectors.

We talked on the phone the night after my kayak trip. I asked
Stuart about old William Spreadborough, who studied the birds
around our land when he stayed north of here at the settlement of
Indian Head in the spring and early summer of 1892. Spreadborough,
he said, came regularly to Deep Lake during his visit and recorded
many of the same birds I saw there—but not loons. More important,
he saw some birds that are now gone. In May 1892 he found several
piping plovers, a small prairie shorebird that is now an endangered
species. They were on the sand spit where I had been watching gulls
and pelicans and listening to the pipit and Baird's sparrows.

Spreadborough shot three of the plovers that day as specimens,
and later he returned to record the first nest for the province. The
piping plover has been declining for decades and has not been seen
on Deep Lake since 1968.

I told Stuart that I'd been feeling smug about my growing bird list
for the area (150 species in under two years) until I read his account
of Spreadborough, who tallied 154 species in the same area in less
than three months.

"Yes, quite remarkable isn't it? And he didn't have your Japanese
optics or modern field guides, or a car to drive around."

I had first learned about Spreadborough during a car trip with
Stuart and Mary. It was the summer of 2005 and we were following

the 1880 trail of naturalist-explorer John Macoun on the 125th anniversary. A self-taught Irish-Canadian botanist, Macoun was sent out from Ottawa and into the Northwest on four separate overland expeditions between 1872 and 1880. In 1880, he and Spreadborough went farther south onto the true open plains, keeping notes on the vegetation and birds of the region and collecting specimens. Their assignment was to determine once and for all whether the grasslands between the forty-ninth parallel and what was then known as "the fertile belt" (a band running south of the forest roughly from the North Saskatchewan River in Alberta down to what is today southwestern Manitoba) were suitable for farming and settlement. A new transcontinental railway would soon be coming west, and there was some disagreement as to whether it should pass through the fertile belt or the more open plains to the south.

By 1880, however, John A. Macdonald's Conservative government in Ottawa, and the private investors who would soon form the Canadian Pacific Railway, were determined to build the railway as near as possible to the forty-ninth parallel. If Macoun's expedition returned with news of fertile land along the southern route, the investors would be happy, because keeping the railroad near the border would save money and prevent American companies from encroaching on the market. For the Macdonald government, a southern route across the plains with farmers settling the land would help bring the west into Confederation and form a bulwark against potential American expansion northward.

Following Macoun's historic trail was Stuart's idea. He had written me a letter saying he had always wanted to write a magazine article or a book that would trace Macoun's 1880 route across the plains, but he was getting too old. He wondered if I'd give it a shot during the anniversary year. I replied, suggesting we do it as a radio documentary for CBC's *Ideas*. We could travel together, discussing Macoun and the landscapes and birds he found, and comparing his observations with what we found 125 years later. We decided to make three trips together throughout the summer, doing our best to arrive in the same places as Macoun on the same dates. In between, I would travel alone to grassland areas to interview biologists, farmers, and ranchers about the birds.

At first I was excited by the prospect of following a historic trail and surveying changes to landscape and bird life in the company of a naturalist whose memory reaches halfway back to Macoun's era. By the time the summer was underway, however, a more personal motivation began to take over.

That year, 2005, was also our first at Cherry Lake, and so come June I headed out to the native and tame pastures south of our land, the place I now call the pipit fields—several thousand acres of grass virtually on my doorstep. I was sure that a patch that size would still be holding onto a relatively healthy bird community. After three mornings of good weather for birdsong, though, I had to face the truth: the pastures had a few Baird's, savannah, and grasshopper sparrows; two or three pair of upland sandpipers; some meadowlarks and horned larks; and a handful of Sprague's pipits. Not a single longspur, no burrowing owls, long-billed curlews, or shrikes. Once again, the birds that I depended on for a sense of home were losing their grip on the land. Chasing the edges of their breeding ranges southward might take me to grasslands where there were better numbers, but I wanted to know why these ones were suffering.

On the trail of Macoun there would be the past, with its abundance and the irrevocable decision to hand the prairie over to ploughmen. But there would also be the present: human and ecological communities damaged by our engagement with the land, and farmers and biologists trying to make sense of it all. Looming over every fragment of wild grass, there would be a future no one talks about, a prairie where no birds sing.

◆

In the near silence of those first June mornings on the pipit fields, the few remaining birds shone in the sun like the shards of Eden tossed into a fallen world. They were as dear and blameless as abandoned children. I saw myself coming back breeding season after breeding season for the rest of my life to listen to a diminishing set of voices. It was a bitter glimpse ahead and I wanted to know why it had to be so, who was responsible, and what, if anything, might be done to save them.

Piping Plover

On the rolling pastures of Saskatchewan's Missouri Coteau, where the song of Sprague's pipits falls to the earth like rain, you will sometimes hear another sky song, especially if you are near the stony beach of a saline slough. Though not a songbird, it calls out to its mate as it flutters like an elaborate flying toy over the nesting grounds using slow, ponderous wingbeats, and tilting from side to side. The piping plover, like most prairie birds, knows that the air is the place to be seen and heard.

The size of a thrush, the piping plover is one of the smallest and most endangered shorebirds to nest on the Great Plains. A sandy-coloured dollop of energy propped up on short orange stilts, it skitters along the water's edge only to dissolve into the background when it halts among pebbles and sand that match its plumage. The trick of disappearing on an open beach despite bright orange legs and bill is managed by strategically placed bars of black on the tail, brow, and breast that break up its general pattern of sandy brown above, white below.

There are three populations of the species: one on the Atlantic coast, a tiny Great Lakes population now showing tentative signs of recovery, and the Great Plains population, which is by far the largest. The Great Plains birds winter on the Gulf Coast, where they are losing beach habitat to dream homes, resorts, and recreational vehicles. Within a few weeks of arriving on their northern prairie breeding grounds in May, each male scrapes a shallow nest on the beach of a shallow lake or slough, lining it with small pebbles and other bits of stuff. If all goes well, his mate will lay four buff-coloured, black-speckled eggs that look much like large pebbles. A day or two after hatching, the young are up and running. They fly before the end of their first month.

During the 1940s, the piping plover began to decline all across its range. By 1978, it was officially listed as a threatened species in Canada. That status was upgraded to endangered in 1985, and in the United States the Great Lakes population is listed as endangered and the Great Plains population is listed as threatened. For all piping plovers, a primary cause of decline is human disturbance of beach habitat on wintering grounds, but the prairie population faces its own set of problems. Settlement has brought great numbers of gulls, crows, black-billed magpies, great horned owls, foxes, and raccoons out on the plains. Some of these predators are new to the prairie, and some have merely increased in numbers, but they are eating more piping plovers, as adults, eggs, and nestlings, than the population can afford to lose. Other factors in their decline include habitat destruction from cattle coming to drink at plover nesting sites, and nesting zones flooded when water managers raise water levels on reservoirs such as Saskatchewan's Diefenbaker Lake, where large numbers of Great Plains piping plovers nest each spring.

An international census of piping plovers is held every five years. The most recent, in 2006, had some good news for the species in Saskatchewan, where between 30 and 40 percent of the Great Plains population nests each year. The survey results showed the highest number of adults in the province since the survey began in 1991, representing a 22 percent increase over fifteen years, and an overall improvement in totals for the whole plains population.[1] Thanks to the efforts of Canadian and American wildlife agencies, ranchers, water managers, and conservation groups, the prairie piping plover may be on the way to recovery.

Chapter Eight

WAITING FOR THE PIPIT

Although I had seen Sprague's pipits in the distance many times before as they flew above other plains and hilltops, the day I finally saw one at arm's length I almost did not recognize it. I was with poet and naturalist Don McKay in a pasture at the north end of Last Mountain Lake. Don was teaching nearby at St. Peter's Abbey and had agreed to join me for a day of prairie birdwatching. I was getting started on the radio documentary and had arranged for us to visit some bird researchers who were studying the pipit and other grassland birds in the national wildlife sanctuary that surrounds the north end of the lake.

The Sprague's pipit is thought to have been one of the most abundant songbirds of the northern plains in pre-settlement days. The remaining population is estimated at roughly one million birds nesting all over the larger native pastures of Saskatchewan, Alberta, eastern Montana, and western North Dakota, yet it goes virtually unknown and undetected by people who live in its midst for a life-time. Even the keenest of birders count themselves lucky to glimpse it as a distant silhouette, and ornithologists have been able to learn very little of its breeding biology.

On the other hand, if you walk through a big piece of native grass in this region during summer you are almost always near a Sprague's pipit. The trick is to actually see one. They do not perch on fence posts or vegetation, but when the male sings, and he will sing for hours at a time, he chooses the highest site available, about five-hundred feet above the grass. Several grassland birds lark, but none so high and so persistently as the Sprague's pipit.

"If you're out walking the prairie and you hear something that sounds like a little UFO landing, you'll know you are in the presence of a pipit," Stephen Davis tells Don and me as he sets up his mist nets to catch the speck in the sky we are craning our necks to view. Davis, a wildlife biologist with the Canadian Wildlife Service, specializes in grassland birds and chairs the national recovery team for the Sprague's pipit.

Later, as we tried to describe the pipit's song to someone who had never heard it, Don called it a "skirling sound." More like the air speaking than a bird, he said. That sounds right—this thin downward spiral of a song, ethereal yet so adapted to its ambience that it seems to be coming from the sun or the sky itself.

So you are out on the prairie, you hear the sound of a small spacecraft landing, and you look up at the clouds. If you find it at all, it will be the merest dot of a bird, and if you can manage to track its trajectory in your binoculars you will see it flutter to gain altitude. Then, if you don't lose the pipit against a patch of blue sky, you may see it reach the top of its climb, set its wings, and glide. This is the precise moment it releases its song, but the bird is so distant that it takes a few seconds for the sound waves to fall to your ears. Then, because it has drifted downward while singing, it climbs silently again to the proper height before repeating the song. This continues—climb, set wings, glide and sing, climb, set wings, glide and sing—as the pipit inscribes a spiral in the sky above the piece of prairie it has chosen for the season.

This aerial rite, a wild ecstasy enacted over little circles of prairie six to ten acres in size all over the remaining grasslands of the northern plains, is remarkable enough, but there is more. Eventually, the male pipit will come down to the ground to feed, investigate an interloper, or interact with its mate and nestlings. Sometimes it comes down for only a moment before returning to its sky perch. The form of its descent in all cases is one of the most easily overlooked spectacles of the prairie, a marvel typical of a landscape that yields its secrets only to a discipline of stillness and attention.

A male pipit comes to earth in a reckless freefall, an all-out wings-folded dive that must be seen to be believed. One moment it is floating near the clouds fifteen stories aloft, and the next it has turned to stone and begun plummeting toward the land in utter surrender to gravity. Accelerating second by second, it is hard to follow with naked eye or binoculars but you find yourself bracing for a crash when, at the last second, the pipit suddenly opens its wings, braking on the air and arcing gracefully to disappear into a tussock of spear grass. From bird to stone to bird again in a long line with a J-hook at the bottom, the pipit in this way stitches heaven to earth, marking ever so lightly its small claim upon sky and grass.

Stephen places the mist nets strategically and then puts a small life-size replica of a pipit in the grass a couple of paces away. Don and I admire the model and ask where he got it from. Eventually and reluctantly, he admits to carving it himself, but dismisses it as a quick and rough piece, nothing worth our attention. Then he tells us, after some prodding, that he is a competitive bird carver.

Next to the decoy pipit, he positions a device that plays a recording of a pipit song in a continuous loop. Once everything is set, he turns the recording on and we all retreat a few steps to watch and wait, while the real pipit continues dropping fresh versions of its song from on high.

•

The song and fall of the pipit have always been part of the prairie at this latitude. The original buffalo-hunting peoples would have had their stories about such an abundant bird, or perhaps about the sound that falls from summer skies. If such lore remains, it would, like any piece of oral tradition, be difficult to locate. And if you were to find someone who kept that knowledge, the act of translating it and transferring it to written text would drain it of meaning and significance anyway, and might well dishonour the relationships that sustained pipits, grass, buffalo, and people for so long in this land.

The earliest explorers of the northern Great Plains did not record the bird. John James Audubon, nearing the end of his career with a trip out onto the Missouri River plains in 1843, was the first non-Aboriginal person to become aware of the pipit, though he might easily have missed it altogether if his party had not finally realized that the ventriloquial song was coming not from the grass but from the sky:

> On several occasions my friend Edward Harris sought for these birds on the ground, deceived by the sound of their music, appearing as if issuing from the prairies which they constantly inhabit; and after having travelled to many distant places on the prairie, we at last looked upwards, and there saw several of these beautiful creatures singing in a continuous manner, and soaring at such an elevation, as to render them more or less difficult to discover with the eye, and at times some of them actually disappearing from our sight, in the clear thin air of that country.[1]

After Audubon collected the first specimen, the pipit was not seen or mentioned again until Thomas Blakiston, naturalist and magnetic observer on Captain John Palliser's expedition, found it in abundance on the northern buffalo plains that now form part of Manitoba, Saskatchewan, and Alberta. He described his first encounter with the bird at Fort Carlton, an hour's drive north of today's city of Saskatoon:

> The Missouri skylark, hitherto looked on as a rare bird,
> is common on the prairies of the Saskatchewan [River]
> during the breeding season. The first occasion on which
> I found it was in the neighbourhood of Fort Carlton, on
> May 6th. When disturbed from the prairie grass which is
> its general haunt, it utters a single chirp, and immediately
> mounts in the air by a circuitous course, with a very undu-
> lating flight, to a great height, where it rests in a peculiar
> manner on its outstretched wings and utters a very striking
> song, which it is difficult to describe, and I can liken to
> nothing I know. . . . I should recognize the note instantly,
> even if I heard it in the depths of a mangrove swamp in
> the tropics. I found it rather difficult of approach and
> hard to shoot. How this bird should have been so long
> overlooked seems marvelous, for I do not know a more
> common bird on the buffalo plains of the Saskatchewan
> during summer.[2]

Old Blakiston must have been a keen eye, because after him several other naturalists would pass through the region collecting and studying birds, and virtually all of them would miss the pipit either entirely or at least in their first summer's study.

A.C. Bent, one of the early twentieth century's most celebrated American field naturalists, travelled through southwestern Saskatchewan in 1905 and 1906 to record the status of its birds. In his report, published in an ornithological journal, he prefaced his findings with a description of the changes already happening upon the Canadian plains. He felt he had to visit the area and see the bird life before settlement brought "marked and rapid changes in the great wild-fowl breeding grounds of northwest Canada."

He goes on to say that between the two years of his study, "the change was so striking as to indicate the passing away within the near future of nearly all the great breeding resorts of this interesting region. . . . The disappearance of the birds is not due to persecution, as they are seldom killed . . . but the prairies are being cultivated . . . and the whole country is being settled up so rapidly that they will soon have no suitable breeding grounds left."[3]

In the species account that follows, however, he admits to being initially blind to one of the most common birds:

> Sprague's Pipit—Entirely overlooked in 1905, probably
> because we did not know where and how to look for it or
> realize the difficulty of seeing it or hearing it. It was really
> fairly common on the prairies of 1906, frequently heard
> and less frequently seen.

Between 1857 and the time of Bent's expedition a century ago, several naturalists had travelled through the area recording birds, and by 1910 a few pioneer naturalists had taken up homesteads in places where pipits were common. Nonetheless, only one or two of these even mention the bird. Most prominent of all who missed the pipit, even as it dropped song after song upon their heads, was John Macoun, the naturalist-explorer whose 1880 expedition Stuart Houston and I followed in the summer of 2005.

Despite many months of travelling on the plains, Macoun and his men did not once identify the bird that provided the background music for much of their passage. To be fair, Macoun was a botanist and his eyes were on soil and vegetation, not the sky. Even so, this is the man who went on to an appointment as Canada's "Dominion

Naturalist," and then published *The Catalogue of Canadian Birds*. In it he admits that neither he nor his bird man, William Spreadborough, noticed the ubiquitous pipit, despite Spreadborough's staying behind one spring to dedicate himself to birds on the plains and valleys around the settlement of Indian Head. From May 1 to July 1 of 1892, he was here, exploring the land just north of our property, and may well have checked our small lakes and pastures for birds. In those two months he recorded 154 species but missed two of the most abundant prairie birds at the time: the Baird's sparrow and Sprague's pipit. It would not be until 1894, when Macoun and Spreadborough came once again onto the Canadian plains, that they finally figured out what that sound was coming from the sky.

All things considered, Macoun's inability to see or hear the pipit is more symbolic than anything else. He was, quite literally, the last naturalist to see the northern prairie as an uninterrupted sea of grass. Upon his return east, his recommendations sealed its fate, bringing the railway to the south and with it the ploughmen who began tearing at the ancient sod.

In my mind, Macoun is forever wandering in that fateful year of 1880. Blissfully naïve, imagining lovely Irish gardens and fields, he makes his way from Brandon across the Pipestone Creek and the Moose Mountains, up onto the Missouri Coteau to Old Wives Lake and then on to the Cypress Hills. From June to September he walks and rides beneath aerial territories of pipits strung together in a chain broken only by the occasional stretch of burnt prairie. The birds do their part, offering their daily psalms as they always have, but the first man to imagine wheat fields in place of the seven-thousand-year-old mixed-grass prairie is utterly deaf to their song.

Now, of course, the "what if" implied in this view of things is mischievous. Had Macoun by some miracle seen the intrinsic value of vast stretches of natural grassland, had he even recommended it be used only as cattle pasture, sooner or later the pressure to grow grain on every arable piece of land would have had its way. Macoun was merely the instrument of a particular moment in history ordained by choices our civilization made long ago in taking up the plough.

Even as he explored and wrote notes on soil fertility and rainfall that summer, the railway was advancing toward the prairie from the east. By September it had made its way past Winnipeg, each new piece like a section on a pontoon bridge heading out to sea. Within five years, the land-hungry masses, lit by an optimism Macoun had kindled, were to begin their rail journeys out onto the plains. The destruction of the primeval grasslands was underway.

Yet agriculture in those days was not the all-consuming enterprise it has become in recent decades. Labour was provided by the farmer and his family with the help of horse and ox. Work animals need pasture, so every farmer had to retain at least twenty to eighty acres of native grass. And even land under cultivation kept some grassy zones at the margins, around sloughs and rock piles—tolerable habitat for an ecological community that thrived in and around farms. Farmers were able to withstand crop failure or low prices by feeding themselves and their local communities with produce from their barns, chicken coops, and gardens. Settlements continued to grow and new homesteaders arrived right through the first fifty years after Macoun, vindicating his optimism. In the wet years of the 1920s, the southern plains of Saskatchewan and Alberta produced well, and even the wild prairie survived in a few large tracts, providing breeding places for the pipit and other birds dependent on native grasses. If the great "wild-fowl breeding grounds of Canada's northwest" were to disappear as A.C. Bent thought they would, it would take more than fifty years.

As we wait for the male pipit to descend, a few drops of rain fall instead. It has been wet for the past two years, strangely so: deep snows in winter, the rains of early summer filling sloughs and creeks.

And in fall farmers talk of sixty-bushel-an-acre crops ruined by rain at harvest and sold as animal feed.

Stephen kneels in the grass with his bird-banding gear next to him in a rucksack. From under his ball-cap brim his eyes follow the pipit circling against the overcast sky. He looks like a boy watching a kite, but something in his posture brings to mind a phrase I read recently in an essay by Jeffrey Lockwood. Lockwood, a grasshopper biologist, talks about the need for reverence in his field research, and says that the prairie brings him to a kind of prayerfulness, in which he is forever petitioning for a question worthy of his life's work. Toward the end of the essay, he tallies the hours he has spent observing grasshoppers over the years and says that such a labour, seeking after the right questions summer after summer, would be insane if it touched only the mind and left the heart and soul alone. He speaks of an "expression of faith in mysteries and lessons," of an "act of receptivity to the world," and then, without a trace of pretence, he says that he has become "a seminarian of the grasslands."[4]

It is a surprising and lovely metaphor, one that only makes sense after you have met a few biologists pursuing questions with great humility in this landscape. Stephen Davis is one of them, and seeing him there in the grass waiting for his pipit to surrender, I recall others I have met, and allow myself to imagine a new order of grassland friars. Like the mendicants of old, their abbey is the open air. They beg questions not food, arming themselves to tend the mysteries of soil and leaf, grasshopper and bird. And each question, if it is worthy, is like a prayer, a respectful inquiry into a unity that will never yield enough answers to be completely possessed in the mind.

"Look," Stephen calls out, pointing at the dot in the sky, "it's coming down. Keep your eyes on it."

Don and I do our best to hold our binoculars on the pipit falling like lightning from the sky. At the last moment, the missile opens its wings and glides into the grass softly. Stephen tells us it should make its way toward the decoy and speaker broadcasting recorded pipit song from the other side of the mist net. Then he spots it moving over a sparsely vegetated patch of ground, and we crouch to watch as it walks directly toward the decoy. At the right moment, Stephen gets up and moves toward the mist net from behind the bird. It flushes and hits the net, dropping softly into one of the pouches of fine nylon netting. Moments later Stephen is next to us, cradling the pipit in his palm.

I've always thought of this bird as the great voice in the sky, the spirit of the plains, so it is a little like unmasking a god to see one in the hand. So strange to see in feather detail a bird that you've only experienced as a distant silhouette. On its wings and back, the centre of each feather is a rich umber. The legs and feet are flesh pink, the tail long with white outer feathers. The face is tawny like little bluestem grass in winter. It has a long, slender bill the colour of horn, dark eyes large and bright, giving it the gestalt of a deer, something free and vulnerable and filled with grace.

Don and I stare as Stephen strokes the pipit's breast with an index finger. He explains what he is doing as he weighs the bird, measures its wing chord, blows on the breast feathers to look for a brood patch, on the vent to see its cloaca and determine its sex. Gently and quickly, he examines each wing and the tail for signs of moult and wear so he can estimate its age. The pipit for its part seems resigned but does not forfeit its wild dignity.

"S7, 8, and 9 have been replaced with a pre-alternate moult." Stephen turns the bird over and extends a wing, examining each feather and dictating to a student assistant who records the assessment on a form. "S2 is broken in half. Tail's in reasonable shape. Greater coverts are uniform." He explains that, with so few specimens in museums and other collections, they are still trying to learn the moult sequence for Sprague's pipit so they can age them accurately. For most birds, say forest wood warblers, this work was done long ago.

"Then we'll be able to go into an area and see what proportion of the birds are hatch year, second year, which ones were born the previous year and returned the next, how many are more than two years old. If you've got an area with mostly older birds then you've got a pretty good population. The birds are not being supplanted by young birds recruiting in from other areas. There should be a good mix. If you have a population that's all second-year birds, then some alarm bells should be going off.

"Then we know the place is what we call a 'sink.' It means the pasture is not producing a lot of young and instead young birds born elsewhere are coming in to try breeding, but for some reason the few birds hatched there are not making it to breeding age themselves."

Stephen plucks a single tail feather from the pipit, places it in a plastic bag, and tells us that it contains a geographical signature that he will use to figure out whether it was grown here at the north end of Last Mountain Lake or somewhere else. By looking at the proportion of stable hydrogen isotopes in a feather and referencing it to a map of hydrogen for North America, biologists can tell where it was grown. The isotopes occur naturally in rainwater. Their ratios vary predictably according to latitude, and the local soil passes on its signature of isotopes through the food web via the tissues of plants and insects, ultimately leaving its mark on the feathers of birds.

Together with banding recaptures (that is, capturing previously banded birds) and all the other information gathered from birds in the hand, isotope signatures allow researchers to develop a fuller picture of the composition of a local breeding population.

As Stephen finishes explaining, I think of the pastures where I've seen longspurs and pipits dwindle to nothing in a few years. These spots, along the rapidly retracting northern edge of the zone where these birds breed, were probably sinks for one reason or another. Many were small, degraded pastures where the landowner had seeded non-native grasses, taking advantage of misguided government incentive programs. Changing the habitat structure and reducing plant diversity can both diminish the food supply and assist predators. Predation in particular can often make the difference between a pasture that sees a good number of its young birds survive to migrate and a pasture that keeps recruiting young birds from outside the population who do not have the experience to rear young successfully.

It seems fair to assume that over the past century the smaller fragments of grassland surrounded by crops have been acting like ecological sinks for grassland birds and other organisms that evolved in landscapes bounded by the larger forces of grazing, fire, soil, and climate. As long as there were some birds present, each fragment seemed to be a functioning facsimile of a native grassland ecosystem. By the mid-1980s, though, researchers had twenty years of data from the North American Breeding Bird Survey (BBS), enough to demonstrate some alarming trends. It took the BBS and its alliance of amateur birdwatchers and statistical analysts to lift the veil, but it would be field biology that would witness the dysfunction and decay at the heart of grassland bird communities.

There is something about a bird in human hands that brings the truth almost too close to bear. The proximity of its innocence calls up a sense of discomfort, responsibility, and shame from which we can no longer look away.

Back home in the city I was halfway up a stepladder mounting a clothesline on the garage when I glanced back toward the house, unconsciously drawn by a flicker of movement on the deck. It was a small bird quivering from distress. It must have hit the upstairs window and fallen to the deck. A cat from the neighbourhood would soon find it, so I walked over, picked it up, and examined it in the hand: a white-throated sparrow, heading north to the boreal forest for the summer. Nothing appeared to be broken, but its left wing drooped and it was having trouble standing on its left leg. Many birds that hit windows die upon impact; others sustain a concussion and recover if you find a safe place for them to sit for an hour or two. But studies show that some of these birds too will die within a couple of days.

I placed the sparrow beneath an overturned laundry basket and kept an eye on it for the evening. At bedtime it was still conscious but breathing rapidly and apparently paralyzed on the left side. I would check it again in the morning and then decide what to do.

The next day nothing had changed. The sparrow lay on its side trembling and conscious but unable to perch or fly. There is no way to rehabilitate such a badly crippled songbird, so I picked it up and held it in the bird bander's grip and pressed my right thumb down firmly against its heart. Its mouth opened and a single note pierced the air; there was some twitching and then it was still.

It's never easy to kill a bird. They want to live as much as anything wants to live. To wring the neck of a grouse you have shot is to stand within a certain shadow of remorse, but something different happens when you have to still the beating heart of a small bird wounded by your car or house. In the silence after the struggle is over, if you don't stuff your ears with rationalizing excuses, you will hear the still, small voice of your own complicity for the millions of birds we sacrifice every year in the New World: in the south, where the coffee and banana plantations destroy millions of acres of rainforest, where slash-and-burn agriculture in the Amazon basin trades in the world's richest avifauna for a few years of cheap beef, where the pampas of Patagonia are ploughed under and poisoned with pesticides long banned in northern nations; and here in Canada and the United States, where we do nothing to halt the commerce that drives destruction in the south, and where we continue to extract energy and resources, build our cities, and grow our food in ways that destroy marshes, grasslands, meadows, and forests.

Sprague's
Pipit

Based on a mistake in Audubon's book, *The Birds of America*, most species accounts say that the type specimen for the Sprague's pipit was shot by Audubon's friend, Isaac Sprague, the botanical illustrator Audubon commemorated in the species' Latin name. Sprague was on the Missouri expedition of 1843 and was the first to find a pipit nest, but the journal of one of Audubon's best gunners tells a different story about the discovery of the first Sprague's pipit—a story corroborated in the journals of both Audubon and Sprague himself. Edward Harris wrote in his journal that he and John G. Bell, another bird collector, raised their guns and shot simultaneously at a single pipit, bringing it down together. The entry for June 19, 1843, in Audubon's journal of his Missouri River expedition says, "Harris and Bell have returned, and to my delight and utter astonishment, have brought two new birds: one, a lark, small and beautiful."[5] Bell already had a vireo named after him and Harris a sparrow, so perhaps Audubon was doing his best to spread the honours around. Regardless, this fact has been buried, along with the bird's first common name, the Missouri skylark—an evocative though unfortunately inaccurate title, since the bird is no lark and it lives well beyond the Missouri drainage.

Thirty years passed before another American ornithologist, Elliott Coues, found a Sprague's pipit singing over the same Missouri plains, stirring him to write, "There is something not of the earth in its melody, coming from above, yet from no visible source. The notes are simply indescribable, but once heard they can never be forgotten."[6]

Studies of Sprague's pipit songflight displays have shown that they often last for more than a half hour. Some individual males have been recorded singing aloft for up to three hours before returning to the ground. No other bird on the planet makes such extravagant flight displays. Hidden in her domed nest shaded by dense grasses, the female somehow watches her mate in flight, and when he falls to the ground she will sometimes fly up to meet him at the last moment. The first pipit nests found by naturalists were located by observing a female leaving her nest and flying up toward her plummeting mate. Although recent studies in Saskatchewan are rapidly filling in the information gaps for the pipit's breeding biology, it remains one of the most obscure songbirds in North America.

Right into the early twentieth century, the Sprague's pipit was one of the most abundant prairie songbirds, but its dependence on large tracts of ungrazed to lightly grazed native grassland has put it on Canada's official list of threatened birds. It is now thought to be declining at 6 percent per year. BirdLife International says that in the United States the Sprague's pipit has declined at a rate of 32 percent per decade since 1970.[7] As an endemic species of the northern Great Plains with a very small breeding range and steadily degrading and fragmented habitat, the Sprague's pipit is an emblem of the plight of grassland songbirds.

Chapter Nine

A CANOPY OF SONG

Yesterday morning I got up early and drove out to the pipit fields to see what I could find. In six miles or so, stopping every quarter to half mile, I heard four pipits. After some effort and neck strain, I managed to find the fourth one floating amidst the specks I see on my retina whenever I look up at the sky. Following it in my binoculars and watching its stout triangular wings pause and hold the air as it sang, I counted off rapid wing flutters between songs—twelve, then fifteen, eleven, sixteen, fifteen, thirteen. I remembered one of Stephen's students telling me that by listening carefully she can sometimes learn to identify individual males by their songs' introductory notes. I decided I would give it a try. I lay down on the road to save my neck and watched the pipit scroll curlicues against the grey of an overcast sky. I listened hard but it sounded like every other pipit I had ever heard, so I shifted my attention to the shapes it made as it flew.

Each time it set its wings it would sail a short distance in one direction, pouring out its song, and then, near the end of the song-flight it would turn rather abruptly. This ninety-degree turn ended the song flight and signalled the resumption of wing-flapping. To regain lost altitude, it would flap its wings in rapid flutters that numbered always between eleven and sixteen. I watched it for several song cycles to see if the pattern would change but it never did. This is pretty cool, I thought. Too bad no one else is here to appreciate my new discovery. I should go wake up Karen—she'd like this. I came to my senses when I remembered previous efforts to show pipits to Karen.

Like many people, Karen gets excited by exotic or colourful birds—an egret or a tanager—but she has yet to discover the joys of rising at dawn to search for tiny, nondescript beige birds that do everything in their power to avoid being seen. We seem to have the worst possible viewing conditions whenever I try to show her grassland birds. It's always too cold or too hot or too windy, and there are a lot of moments that go roughly as follows: "There . . . just follow my finger. You see that dockweed sticking up about fifty paces to the left of that junk pile? No, not *that* dockweed, the one farther out. You got it? Okay. That's where it was singing, but it just dropped down into the grass. . . . Did I mention that this pasture had long-billed curlews only ten years ago?"

Last July, in a moment of weakness or misguided pity for her husband, Karen agreed to come along with me to the pipit fields to make another try. At sunrise we stepped out of the cabin and got into the car to drive around to the south side of the community pasture, where I can usually find birds from the roadside. I wanted to be sure we'd cover enough ground to find the less common species, so hiking would not work.

Right on schedule, a stiff wind came up with the sun, keeping the singers down in the grass. By eight o'clock I managed to find a handful of grasshopper and Baird's sparrows, an upland sandpiper, and a Sprague's pipit, but Karen did not see a single one. They were distant and keeping out of the wind, which dampened their songs, making it hard to distinguish their voices from the swishing of the grass. Karen never complained but by the fourth time I tried to point

out the faint hiss of an invisible sparrow I could see she was longing
for her pillow and warm bed. I regaled her with stories of the pipits I
had seen the day before.

As we drove back, I looked over the steering wheel to the fields
of alfalfa and I thought of John Macoun's bird man again, William
Spreadborough. He could have stayed many places on the northern plains to survey the birds for a summer, but he chose this area.
The night before I had been reading Spreadborough's 1892 records
in Macoun's *Catalogue of Canadian Birds*. It said that the chestnut-
collared longspur was one of the commonest breeding birds on the
prairie in this district. Spreadborough found them in great numbers
and took three specimens, which sit in a museum drawer in Banff.
Today there are no chestnut-collared longspurs on the native grass
pastures near Indian Head. The same goes for McCown's longspur,
which, according to Spreadborough, nested on burnt prairie all
around Indian Head. Now the nearest McCown's are southwest of
here one hundred miles or more away and receding fast. Ferruginous
hawk: Spreadborough found two nests and called them "common."
The species has been gone from the area for several decades and it
is now listed as threatened in Canada. Long-billed curlew: the Banff
Museum has a specimen taken at Indian Head by Spreadborough.
The last sight record for the area was a single bird in 1964 at Strawberry
Lakes, a couple of miles south of our land. Loggerhead shrike: today
it is a threatened species, but in 1892 Spreadborough found several
nests in the Indian Head area. I have not found one in three summers
of searching. Burrowing owl, now an endangered species, was once
common here. In 1934, a local bander put bands on twenty-seven in
a single summer. No one has seen one in these parts for thirty years.
Other more resilient grassland species hang on for the time being:
Baird's sparrow, grasshopper sparrow, Sprague's pipit, Swainson's
hawk, bobolink, short-eared owl, sharp-tailed grouse, horned lark,
western meadowlark, upland sandpiper. I can still find these birds on

the pastures south of Indian Head, but roughly half of the grassland species that were common here in Spreadborough's time have been extirpated from the area.

We may find it hard to imagine the abundance of bird life that greeted prairie naturalists like Spreadborough—the fullness of song reigning over long miles of grass—but we are heading for a day when it will be hard for anyone to imagine that prairie skies were ever anything but silent.

When conservationists talk about the transformation required to reduce the collateral damage of our growth-at-all-costs civilization, the question of hope inevitably arises. *Is there any hope?* people ask, as though it too were a commodity someone might sell them. By "hope" most seem to mean the calculated odds of a particular strategy or program succeeding, as though we need to know whether our efforts will be rewarded before we commit ourselves to anything. This is a tawdry kind of hope masking a wider despair that keeps us mired in the status quo, averting our eyes from the carnage all around, shrugging off responsibility with a sighing, "Well, what can you do?" In opposition to Emily Dickinson's lively dictum—"the thing with feathers that perches in the soul and sings"—hope is reduced to something that struggles in our hands and dies.

There is another kind of hope, though, one that sees things as they are. It bears witness to the complicity encompassing not only the way we feed and house our families, how we travel and make a living, but the whole history of our civilization's engagement with the landscape—sees all of it and then, without knowing outcomes, gets down to the good work of setting things back to right.

In the community of bird conservationists you will sometimes meet people who live out this hope, enacting an altogether unjustifiable faith by lending their labour to study and advocacy that come with no guarantee of success. Over the years of work they become creatures as rare and astonishing as the ones they serve.

Stuart and Mary Houston are two such people. They face the truth of what is happening to birds without being deluded by the temptation to blame or turned aside by the temptation to give up. For sixty-five years Stuart has been holding birds in his hands — thousands of birds of more than two hundred species — looking back at the fierce gaze of the ones we have accused of being in the way. You would think living on the prairie through the period of its greatest ecological decline and researching the previous century and a half of pre-settlement and early settlement history would make a naturalist cranky if not outright misanthropic. Instead, Stuart has nothing but compassion for rural people and their struggle to hold on to a culture that has always been conflicted in its orientation to nature. As for the early naturalists and explorers he writes about, Stuart regards them all with great admiration and gratitude for the testimony they provide, allowing us to understand something of the original character of the prairie.

In his late seventies, with a smile that nearly closes his eyes above ruddy cheeks, a white bristle of hair on his pate, and a set of ears made for gathering sound, Stuart would look like one of the mythic forest people of his Icelandic ancestry were it not for his body. At six feet, two inches tall, he is sparely fleshed and long-limbed, more of a Narnian Marsh-wiggle than a Tomten. On the left breast of the light-coloured dress shirts he wears there is always a pocket protector full of pens, pencils, and a notepad. He likes to walk in shorts in all but midwinter, baring knobby shanks that might almost fit into one of the larger-gauge bands in his kit. He is moving more slowly these days, but something boylike in his gestures and gait remains nonetheless, as though his youth has been taken by surprise.

Not long ago, Stuart was still climbing trees to band ferruginous and Swainson's hawks, but arthritis has grounded him and placed a cane in his hands. Just as important as the bird-distribution knowledge gained from his banding, though, has been his attention to people in their teens and twenties who come along on banding trips. He stays in touch with many of the younger people who have passed through his sphere of influence and, given the slightest opening, will brag shamelessly of their accomplishments—not only those of his own children and grandchildren, but of the countless others he and Mary have blessed with their encouragement. Mentorship, I have learned from Stuart, is a habit as well as an art. No young person passes his way without receiving a gentle nudge in the right direction. Not needing to know which seeds might have hit fertile soil, Stuart just keeps on sowing, for experience has proven that some of them will sprout.

And so the fields of medicine, science, human history, natural history, bird banding, and writing on the Canadian plains continue to bear fruit in the careers and avocations of people Stuart and Mary have encouraged. Dozens of stories could be told; here is a recent one. A couple of years ago they met Jared Clarke, a young birder from Regina in his first year of university, and invited him to come along and help band hawks for a weekend. One weekend led to a few more outings together, and within a short time Jared was banding owls and hawks under Stuart's permit. While studying biology, he has worked as a park naturalist, at the Royal Saskatchewan Museum, and at the Moose Jaw Burrowing Owl Interpretive Centre. Initiating his own studies of Cooper's hawks and ferruginous hawks, publishing notes on his research, and setting up a fall banding station for migrant northern saw-whet owls, Jared has in two years become one of the most active amateur banders on the prairie, banding hundreds of birds each year.

When he isn't banding or travelling to attend conferences, Stuart is researching and writing. With Mary's help transcribing and organizing source materials, he has published countless biographical notes on early naturalists, bird banders, and egg collectors on the plains, several books on topics ranging from the history of medicare to the annotated journals of men on the Franklin expeditions, and an astounding array of papers in ornithological, medical, and natural history journals. This may seem a jumble of subject matter but through all of it there runs a coherent regard for human history and natural history, biography and ecology, as elements of a single interdisciplinary flow of avocation and service.

Ask anyone who knows Stuart and Mary how they managed all of this while raising four children and they will unfailingly nod toward Mary. Unflappable, enduring, resourceful, frugal, and wise, Mary is the anchor point around which Stuart has been able to spin his rich and varied life.

When you travel with the Houstons, sooner or later a couple of tales about Stuart's origins as a naturalist will emerge, and as he tells them Mary will smile with a forbearance that cannot quite cover her affection for the man she has been feeding and tending for a lifetime. He begins with something like, "I broke my leg in grade five and that set off a chain of events . . ."

I got the full story as we followed Macoun across the plains. The chain of events explains how he became a birdwatcher as a boy and then helped put together the publication that organized prairie naturalists into the Saskatchewan Natural History Society. It was the late 1930s in Yorkton, Saskatchewan: Stuart learning to type while his leg healed, a couple years later receiving his first bird guide, Taverner's *Birds of Canada*, identifying birds with it until he saw one in his yard that did not seem to be in the book.

"My father suggested I go see Mrs. Isabel Priestly who wrote the nature column every week for the *Yorkton Enterprise*. So I did. She said, 'Those birds are immature goldfinches and, Stuart, you could have identified them yourself if you'd looked at the non-breeding plumages shown in your book.' Then she added, 'We have a walk every Sunday morning, early, before church. Why don't you come along some Sunday morning?' So I started going on weekly hikes.

"That was 1940 when I met Mrs. Priestly, and by 1942 I had begun keeping my own bird notes. Around then Mrs. Priestly said to me, 'Stuart, you can type. Will you type up a list of all the birds we've been seeing on our hikes?' And when I got that done, she said we'd better extend it to list all the bird observations within thirty miles of Yorkton. I suggested that we could mimeograph it to make copies. One thing led to another and eventually Mrs. Priestly wanted to publish an annual nature bulletin.

"We had no idea what we had begun at the time or where it would lead, but we just kept publishing our bulletins. Then, in 1946, Mrs. Priestly died suddenly of a brain hemmorhage. The week it happened I was at the University of Manitoba writing my final exam in pre-med, competing against servicemen freshly returned from the war. Mother knew how difficult it is to get into medicine so she had Mrs. Wilcox, my landlady, sit and watch for the newspaper and tear out the entire page that had the obituary so I wouldn't discover Mrs. Priestly's death before I wrote my exams."

In the years before her death, though, Stuart, still a teen, and Isabel Priestly had built a network of naturalists and bird enthusiasts all over rural Saskatchewan by distributing their mimeographed publications and soliciting reports from observers posted on farmsteads and in towns across the prairie. That first bulletin Stuart mentions was seven pages with a large stencilled title coloured by hand with blue crayon—*The Blue Jay*, they called it. Within a few years, *The Blue Jay* was to become a respected journal shelved in reference libraries around the world, including the British Museum and Smithsonian libraries. Even more important, *The Blue Jay* and the fledgling Yorkton Natural History Society launched a new grassroots movement for conservation on the northern Great Plains, led by people who observed birds, insects, mammals, and plants from the seat of a tractor or on the way out to check on the calves.

Their proudest moment came in 1958, when the most important bird study organization on the continent, the American Ornithologists Union, agreed to hold their annual convention in Saskatchewan. According to Stuart, that meeting of the AOU was different from any other before or since. The continent's top bird scientists were gathered as usual, but they were shoulder to shoulder with young people and farmers and ranchers—the people who lived amongst the birds on the prairie.

The second story that comes out when you get to know Stuart helps to explain how he became interested in writing the history of the early naturalists on the northern Great Plains. Another important encounter during his formative years, it was the summer he got to know a young man who went on to become Canada's greatest storyteller-naturalist.

"It was 1946. A young serviceman just back from the war showed up on our doorstep looking for me. He said his name was Farley Mowat and he told me he was going to write *The Birds of Saskatchewan*. He had come to Yorkton to tell Mrs. Priestly of his plans, not knowing that she had just died. I was banding ducks at the time for Ducks Unlimited so he came to see me. I was just a kid. He drove up in an army jeep. Mother invited him to stay with us, offered him a bed, but he wanted to sleep in his army cot so we set him up in the basement. He had his meals with us and every evening he skinned the birds he was collecting for the Royal Ontario Museum. They were paying his expenses in return for the birds he would collect.

"Every night the boys of the neighbourhood would come down to the basement, watching Farley skin birds and listening to his stories.

At eight-thirty Mother would come down to the basement and say, 'Farley, I think the younger boys, the eight year-olds, should be going home now,' and of course they'd drag their feet because he was telling marvellous stories and skinning birds!

"At nine-thirty, Mother would come back down and say, 'Farley, I think the twelve-year-old boys should be going now.' Then at ten-thirty she'd be back saying it was time for everyone to be going to bed.

"Before he left that summer, Farley told me that the main reason he wanted to write *The Birds of Saskatchewan* was to give Dr. John Richardson from the overland Franklin expeditions due credit for the new species and subspecies he had named from Fort Carlton and Cumberland House in the 1800s. That got me interested in learning more about him, and years later I found a copy of Richardson's *Fauna Boreali–Americana*. It was Volume Two and they wanted forty-five dollars for it. That was one-third my monthly salary as a resident at the University Hospital in Saskatoon but I bought it anyway. It contained even more excitement than I had imagined. Mary and I began to spend every second weekend travelling to Carlton to see the changes in bird life since Richardson was there in the 1820s."

That was the late 1950s. In the decades to follow, Stuart used Richardson's ornithological records as the historical baseline data for his first book, an account of the birds of the Saskatchewan River from Carlton to Cumberland. Today, Stuart is working hard to finish the eleventh and perhaps most important book of his life, the one Farley never got around to completing: *The Birds of Saskatchewan*. Surgeon-naturalist John Richardson will receive all the credit he is due for locating several bird species and subspecies previously unknown to science: Franklin's gull, Forster's tern, olive-sided flycatcher, grey-crowned rosy finch, clay-coloured sparrow, Smith's longspur, the North American subspecies of the black-billed magpie, and many others.

•

When John Macoun made his passage across the plains, it was sixty years after Richardson and farther south onto the dry, open prairie. In that interval the great bison multitudes had been reduced to a few scattered herds, which were to disappear entirely by 1890. That was the one significant absence that we shared with Macoun as we traced his route. Stuart, Mary, and I never talked about bison, but the loss of the prairie's largest grazing animal, still fresh in Macoun's time, was written in every landscape we passed through.

As we began the trip near the Manitoba border on a weekend in June 2005, Stuart reminisced about the feeling of being out on the plains with the music of longspurs, lark buntings, grassland sparrows and pipits pouring down from the sky. He said it was like standing beneath a "canopy of song." That phrase stayed in my mind for the summer as we travelled from pasture to pasture to look for grassland birds 125 years after Macoun recommended that Canada's prairie be put to the plough. Stuart brought along copies of Macoun's reports and sessional papers, as well as relevant sections from his *Catalogue of Canadian Birds*, published in the 1890s. We read bits of them as we followed segments of Macoun's route in three-day trips during June, July, and August, visiting key locations on the same dates mentioned in his papers.

We began where the Pipestone Creek enters Saskatchewan from Manitoba, on the eastern side of what we now call "Palliser's Triangle"—named for Macoun's forerunner, Captain John Palliser, who travelled the region in 1857 and declared it to be unfarmable land, a northern lobe of the "Great American Desert." Palliser travelled during a dry decade and saw dust storms and cracked soils with sparse, withered grasses. The years Macoun travelled west were uncharacteristically wet, and the easternmost portion of the prairie, where we began our trip, would have been particularly verdant. Farther south and west, Macoun and his men ran out of drinkable water on the clay plains, but he was determined to prove Palliser wrong. Historian Bill Waiser, who wrote a biography of Macoun, calls him "a programmed explorer sent West to substantiate federal policy."[1] He did come across some parched, forbidding places on the high plains, but even then he maintained that the precipitation was adequate and the soil fertile.

As we stood on the edge of the Pipestone, vireos and least fly-catchers sang from the aspen woods. The land was the deep, saturated green that comes with heavy rains. May had been unusually wet, as it has been in recent years. A white-tailed deer fawn broke out of the woods and ran through the ditch toward us. Without pausing or looking to either side, it bounded directly between Stuart and me, an arm's reach away, and then trotted on toward the next aspen bluff. With the sun pouring warm yellow tones into the green valley, birds singing, and deer running by, it was possible to imagine the optimism that Macoun felt as he set off in 1880.

The illusion fell apart when we looked beyond the valley. There on the uplands Macoun saw treeless grassland running to the western horizon. In his papers, he describes a shift in the landscape marked by the Pipestone: "About five miles to the east of [the Pipestone Creek], bluffs of wood begin to appear and these continue to the creek, but do not exist beyond it, as the constant fires have swept them all off."

That demarcation no longer exists. Our view of the uplands was blocked in every direction by large aspen bluffs. In between the woods, any open land was in crop. We retired to our accommodations for the night, a local bed and breakfast. The next morning we would begin our search for the first grassland birds singing from unploughed prairie.

Ferruginous Hawk

This regal hawk—its Latin binomial is *Buteo regalis*—is one of the largest buteo hawks in the world, and has a greater wingspan (up to five feet in females) than some Old World eagle species. To get the full measure of this bird, the signature raptor of the northern Great Plains, consider the structure of its nest in pre-settlement days. During the long millennia before the northern prairie was yoked to agriculture, ferruginous hawks made their nests on the ground by piling bison bones into a flattened heap that they would then line with bison fur and dung. Today, with fewer bovine skeletons and more trees on the prairie, they use dried branches and cow dung. Although they now generally nest in lone trees surrounded by pasture with a good supply of ground squirrels near at hand, they will still nest on the ground occasionally. This might seem to put eggs and nestlings at risk from ground predators, but the male leaves his larger and fiercer mate on the nest, feeding her throughout her month-long incubation. A female ferruginous hawk is a formidable bird and has no qualms about facing down a fox or coyote.

There is no hawk with a stronger bond to native grassland. It will use non-native or disturbed pasture if there is a suitable nesting site and enough ground squirrels, but in areas where most of the land is cultivated, nesting sites, grass, and prey are usually not enough to hold a nesting pair. Those that find a productive nesting location will often remain faithful to the same nest tree for years. One of the nests Stuart and Mary Houston monitored in Saskatchewan's Kindersley-Elna community pasture was occupied for thirty-two consecutive summers, setting a record for the species.

During his 1892 stay at Indian Head, Macoun's bird man, William Spreadborough, found this hawk to be common and recorded two nests. Its breeding range until the 1950s reached much farther north than it does today. As recently as 1939, Farley Mowat recorded seventeen ferruginous hawks as far north as the Fort Carlton area of Saskatchewan.

By 1960, though, according to research by Stuart Houston and Marc Bechard, the species' Saskatchewan population was down to between 10 and 20 percent of its pre-settlement size. It was absent from 40 percent of its original range and another 40 percent was but thinly populated because of grassland fragmentation.[2]

While it is now listed as threatened in Canada, there are signs that the ferruginous hawk is stabilizing in some portions of its range. Conservation efforts, including nest platforms erected in appropriate habitat, have spurred local recoveries and improved nest productivity. In particular, a project in Alberta initiated by Josef Schmutz has shown excellent results. The hawk's complete dependence on the Richardson's ground squirrel (known to prairie people as "the gopher"), however, has made it vulnerable to this rodent's long-term decline, brought on by widespread cultivation and a century of persecution.

Chapter Ten

COUNTING BIRDS

One of the things I like best about driving out from our land to look for grassland birds is the possibility of finding a pasture I've never seen before. I'll check the usual sites east of Deep Lake, the pipit fields of the Strawberry Lakes community pasture, and then if there is time I look south. On a fine, clear morning last summer I stopped on a rise near the Strawberry Lakes and stared at a ridge of hills I'd been wondering about for some time. A softer grey-green tone came through the haze of distance, distinguishing the ridge from the ocean of cultivated fields spreading in all directions from its feet. In getting to know native grass you eventually acquire a search pattern that helps you recognize it miles away. With a couple more hours of birdsong left, I looked for a southbound road and pointed the car toward the ridge. When I got there it looked to be a classic moraine running northwest to southeast. A road drew me up onto its western flank. The old grasses—blue grama and various *stipas*— sparkled in the early light. I rolled down my window and drove slowly to the top, listening. I knew the birds before I heard them: a single pipit exulting right overhead, a meadowlark on the fence line, a willet in the grass. Two mule deer halted in their tracks to see what was coming onto their island.

This kind of place, a small hump of native prairie rising up out of the cultivated plains, is as isolated as any atoll in the sea. Parking at the top I could make out the next island in the archipelago of small ridges that runs in a line pointing the direction of the glacier's retreat twelve thousand years ago, stepping higher and higher toward the Moose Mountains, resting just beyond the southeastern horizon. The next ridge in line looked bigger than the one I was on, large enough to host a few pipits and God knows what else.

Twenty minutes later, I was on a prairie trail that made a wide berth around this larger range of hills, cutting through a tame pasture on its eastern side. With the sun getting higher, there weren't many birds: a couple of Baird's sparrows, some meadowlarks, a Krider's red-tailed hawk, and horned larks. Then I thought I heard something different, a faint tinkling song jumbled up with the horned lark notes, but distinct. My ear was telling me there were chestnut-collared longspurs out there somewhere in the distance, but the sound was faint enough for me to write it off as wishful thinking. I drove another half mile south for one more listen. This time I heard it clearly: a high-pitched, hurried set of notes came east on the breeze proving that somewhere out in that weedy pasture there was at least one long-spur. I scanned with my binoculars until I found one, then two, then three males larking above the grass a few hundred yards away. I could see their black bellies and the flash of white on their tail margins. I counted them again and settled on a total of four males. If there were females to match it could be a colony of at least eight individuals here on an all but forgotten pasture some distance from the core of the species' much retracted range. The nearest remnant known to have chestnut-collared longspurs was fifteen miles south. The numbers here matter. This year there are eight chestnut-collared longspurs on this 320-acre pasture of non-native grass, fifteen miles away from a larger colony of the same species. I'll return later in the summer and then next year to count them again. Not long ago there would have been small colonies of this bird on the community pasture near our land too. When did they disappear? How long will these ones be able to hold on? Based on what I saw happen to the last longspurs on the Regina plains during the 1990s, this colony is living on borrowed time.

When I began birding twenty-five years ago, counting birds meant your tally of species, not individuals. One representative of each species was always enough for the list of birds you recorded during a day, a trip, or a year. No need to count the second, third, or fourth meadowlark, once you'd checked it off the list. Before I knew what was happening, though, it became more difficult, and then impossible, to locate that one representative of certain species. Some you could find by driving farther south; others were gone from the region completely. Conscripted by the disappearance of familiar creatures, I changed to a different kind of counting.

From 1986 to 2003, I helped with a spring survey of Regina birds run by the local natural history society. On the second Saturday of May, beginning at six in the morning, I would drive the back roads of a small slice of the glacial lake bed that gave Regina its characteristic pancake topography and rich clay soils. Not far from the southeastern city limits there were a couple of small pastures where I could find a few of the species that like grazed native grass, including colonies of burrowing owls and chestnut-collared longspurs. Elsewhere, in weedy places on the margins of cultivated fields, I would record loggerhead shrikes, meadowlarks, northern harriers, and grasshopper sparrows. On the cultivated fields themselves, I would find a few McCown's longspurs and dozens of horned larks. Looking back through my notebooks, I found a steady decline year by year, so that by 2002 the same kind of counting trip along the same roads tallied far fewer birds for almost every species. Here are the declines evident in two counts held twelve years apart, in 1990 and 2002: western meadowlark, from 39 to 20; chestnut-collared longspur, from

15 to 0; McCown's longspur, from 11 to 0; savannah sparrow, from 68 to 3; burrowing owl, from 3 to 0; vesper sparrow, from 29 to 11; horned lark, from 174 to 8.

This kind of counting, where the observer records numbers of each species by stopping to listen along the same roads year after year, is a less rigorous version of one of the methods biologists use to look at the status of bird populations. If you want policy-makers to recognize what is happening to the birds, you have to use data gathered according to a standardized protocol with random route selection, data that comes from something like the North American Breeding Bird Survey. For more than forty years now, the BBS has been dispatching skilled amateurs out across the continent each June to record birds on more than three thousand survey routes. The Canadian Wildlife Service works with the United States Geological Survey to select routes randomly, foster volunteers, and gather the data so that they can be analyzed and made available to researchers.

In sparsely populated areas like Saskatchewan, birders with the ear to run a BBS route are in short supply. I held off for a number of years, mostly because the routes available within reasonable driving distance from home did not sample birds in landscapes with native grass. Stuart, of course, has maintained at least one route for the last thirty-four years. In 1999, he took on a second route, but in 2006 he relinquished it, along with hawk banding. "I'm winding things down," he says.

Stuart never once asked why I was shirking my duty in not taking a BBS route, which surprised me because he seldom lets an opportunity for good advice slip away, but once you become acquainted with Mary and Stuart and their monumental contribution to the knowledge of prairie birds, the shame of your own paltry efforts begins to work on your mind. In 2003, a route in the Qu'Appelle Valley became available and, though it would have little to offer in the way of grassland birds, I signed up.

Sleeping at a friend's cabin on Crooked Lake, my son Jon and

I rise a half hour before dawn and drive to the starting point. BBS routes require an observer and a recorder so Jon comes along to write down bird data as I chant names and numbers for three minutes at each of fifty stops spaced one half mile apart along a 24.5-mile-long route. We begin next to the largest fen in the whole valley, with marsh birds such as yellow rail, sharp-tailed sparrow, sedge wren, and American bittern lofting their voices into a chorus dominated by cat-birds, clay-coloured sparrows, and yellow warblers coming from the thickets that line the valley road. We finish on the uplands north of the valley, where aspen bluffs and sloughs host the birdsong amidst land dominated by canola and flax crops. The grassland birds I see on my route are the ones that adapt relatively well to the loss of native prairie: western meadowlarks, bobolinks, Swainson's hawks, savan-nah sparrows, and horned larks. Just the same, when I get home after doing my route and look at the BBS data analysis for these species over the years, the graphs show all of them in decline. There is a page on the BBS website that is dedicated to grassland birds, sum-marizing population trends. A couple of mouse-clicks get you to a "Summary of Geographic Patterns," where the authors say that "the largest number of grassland bird species are found in the northern Great Plains." That's something to be proud of, but the next line on the page, under "Population Trends," delivers a punch to the stom-ach: "Grassland birds show the most consistent decline of any group of birds monitored by the BBS. . . . Declines prevail throughout North America. . . . Most grassland birds have been declining since the BBS was initiated in 1966 and were probably declining during the decades preceding the BBS."

A little more clicking brings up graphs for each species' popula-tion trend. Every one I try shows a line sloping downward from left to right. In the simplifying logic of a graph, any downward slope points toward a future zero, but with certain species that future appears to be shockingly imminent. And the other end of the line, showing 1966 when the BBS began, is pointing backward and upward to an unenumerated past when there were more of every grassland species.

As Stuart, Mary, and I drove west from the Pipestone Creek toward Moose Mountain, I skimmed over Macoun's reports from the 1881 Sessional Papers for the House of Commons. In them he says, "We are making a very fine collection of birds, having obtained 31 skins already." He goes on to mention a sprinkling of birds they found here and there, including a flightless juvenile sandhill crane and a chestnut-collared longspur taken on the plains west of Moose Mountain. Macoun's approach to bird research, typical of his era, was to roam the countryside with a small-gauge bird gun in hand, shooting a bird or two whenever it might prove to be a new species for the trip. Later, he would have an assistant skin and preserve the day's quarry as specimens to be examined and classified in the comfort of his study at some later date. No thought for the relative quantity of each species' population, no attempt to estimate numbers, no effort to follow a random transect sampling species composition and abundance. And why would there be? Certainly, the buffalo were all but gone, but other prairie creatures were so plentiful and the grasslands so vast that nothing of man's doing could ever diminish them.

Macoun made his way south and west, unrestrained by the demands of modern science and data collection, recording whatever struck his interest along the way. Following as best we could on the back roads available, we did likewise.

After splashing along muddy roads atop Moose Mountain and coming upon an elk near where Macoun too had seen one, we rolled downhill off the wooded western slopes to the plains below, still searching for the first patch of native grassland large enough to host some birds. Finally, in a soft rain, we found Tecumseh community pasture, a piece of native grass managed by the federal government's

PFRA (Prairie Farm Rehabilitation Association) to provide local cattle ranchers with somewhere to pasture their animals in summer.
Like the Bureau of Land Management in the United States, the
PFRA manages some of the last well-maintained grasslands on the
continent. Their community pastures are almost always in good condition and Tecumseh was no exception. The June grass and *stipas*
were high and lush, with blossoms of groundsel and blue harebell
floating amidst the waves of green. I jumped from Stuart's truck and
over the four-strand barbed wire fence. Even in the rain, a Sprague's
pipit, a couple of Baird's sparrows, and a grasshopper sparrow sang
out. Not a canopy of song by a long shot, but a few representatives
were on hand, keeping the pasture alive for the present.

Back in the truck, we talked about changes to the rural landscape
Stuart has seen since the 1940s: the shift to mechanized agriculture
eliminating the need for horses and the pastures they cropped short
enough to host burrowing owl colonies; the recent trend of ploughing road allowances, which formerly provided roughly sixty feet
of grass on the margins of most fields; the advent of "zero-tillage"
methods, where the farmer uses herbicides instead of mechanized
cultivation to control weeds and crop continuously, thereby eliminating the tilled summerfallow that once supported horned larks and
McCown's longspurs. But Stuart is always careful to point out the
progress we've made in conserving some birds, hawks and owls in
particular, which rural people were shooting in great numbers until
the 1970s. He bears the gains in mind, not to gloss over the general
destruction, but to keep despair at bay, which is simply another kind
of lie, with its own form of retreat. For a naturalist faced with the
diminishing beauty of a beloved world, the job of seeing does not
end with counting one bird instead of twenty. Seeing means opening
your eyes to witness the mechanism behind the horror; lifting the
veil of our myths—from blaming to denial to despair—long enough
to glimpse the disfigurement and decay for what it is.

Chestnut-collared Longspur

In the summer of 1965, two Regina naturalists conducted a survey of grassland birds nesting in a small piece of native grass that remained within the city limits. There were a few scraps of unploughed prairie on the edge of Regina at the time, but they chose to focus on one forty-acre horse pasture sandwiched between Wascana Creek and the Canadian National rail line where it leaves the western edge of the city. As they walked or stood in the grass they were surrounded by male chestnut-collared longspurs performing their courtship songflight. At times, four or five males in the colony would rise up simultaneously from the grass and sing together in chorus as they circled ten feet above the prairie. The high-pitched, rapid tinkling sounded like western meadowlark song, only quieter, less fluty. As the longspurs floated on the wind, the surveyors could see the sunlight shining through the white edgings of their tails, spread to show off a bold triangle of black. And sometimes, when the birds tilted just right, the chestnut of their napes became visible.

The longspur nests they found were recessed into the earth, nestled up against a stone or a pile of dung and carefully lined with hair from horse tails. Each had three to five greenish eggs speckled with lavender and brown. That summer they located thirty-eight longspur nests—a remarkable total for a colony on such a small pasture. But this was the mid-1960s and no one was sounding alarms yet about grassland birds. Little was known about the status of most North American birds, and prairie birds were among the least well known.

It would be the next year, 1966, that wildlife authorities in the United States and Canada launched the Breeding Bird Survey. For the first time, biologists would have access to reliable, standardized data on bird populations along survey routes run by volunteers all across the continental United States and southern Canada. A quick visit to the BBS website today shows that the chestnut-collared longspur has declined by an average of 2.9 percent every year since 1966 all across its range. In parts of its range it has declined by as much as 18 percent per year, and during the last twenty-five years the general decline across its range has accelerated to 4.7 percent per year.

While the Regina naturalists watched longspurs on that horse pasture in 1965, they were joined by city crews doing a different kind of survey work. One by one during the next decade, the pasture and others like it on the edge of Regina disappeared beneath sidewalks, lawns, and bungalows. The forty-acre horse pasture is now covered by a subdivision and part of a park, with its alien grass and planted trees. No longspurs have bred within city limits in thirty years, and the last chestnut-collared longspurs anywhere near Regina vanished in the late 1990s.

Chapter Eleven

DEATH BY A THOUSAND CUTS

The next time I took my kayak out onto Deep Lake was later in the summer of 2005, on a day when I was not travelling with Stuart and Mary or talking to biologists about the birds. There were very few water birds on the lake, so I checked every distant blob with my binoculars. Directly across from me, against the shore nearest the pastures where I hear pipits and grassland sparrows, I saw an unusual shape coming my way over the water: a V-form in front of a long, shallow hump. It's always fun to watch a deer swimming, but as I raised my binoculars I was hoping to see the large ears of a mule deer. The shadow of disappointment upon realizing that it was a white-tailed deer is part of being a prairie naturalist. Later that morning the same feeling would tinge the excitement of discovering a wood thrush singing from a ravine on the west side of the lake. Probably the first record for the area—there are fewer than ten breeding season records for the entire province—but the wood thrush is a bird that, like the white-tailed deer, belongs in the eastern hardwood forests, not out here on the Great Plains. For the most part, I can accept the advance of forest creatures from the east—it is hard not to love a cardinal or an eastern bluebird—but the white-tailed deer is an invader I'd be happy to send back home across the one-hundredth meridian.

Ticks and the spectre of Lyme disease would be enough to make this ungulate unwelcome, but a study released by the Northern Prairie Wildlife Center in Jamestown, North Dakota, suggests that white-tailed deer are eating the nestlings of ground-nesting birds on remnant grasslands. Bizarre as it sounds, they caught on video several deer munching on the flightless young of grassland birds. For all I know, that deer I saw coming across the lake had just downed a brood of grasshopper sparrows for breakfast.

Of course, in the primeval grassland, predators and prey lived together in a dynamic balance for thousands of years and any periodic increase in predation had no lasting effect on the bird population. Today, with native grass fragments engulfed by habitat that fosters barn cats, raccoons, and other alien predators, fewer birds are surviving past the nestling phase.

That night I listened to my my interview with Stephen Davis, recorded right after he finished banding the male pipit. As he crimped the band around the bird's leg, questions ran through my mind. *Why do we have to handle the birds so much to study them? Doesn't banding stress the birds? And the nest monitoring—doesn't it lead predators to the nests? Why not leave them alone and simply monitor the populations with regular surveys?* A light shower blew in so we retreated to Stephen's truck where I was able to ask him these questions.

"If you're not thinking about the effect you are having on the birds then you shouldn't be doing the research. Not to say that we aren't having any influence—we probably are in some way—but we try to minimize it as much as we can. With the radio telemetry work we do, we never put the transmitters on females during laying or early incubation because it may cause them to abandon. When we put them on young birds we wait until they are big enough. The transmitter is about 3 percent of the body weight, and studies have shown that it's quite a reasonable load for the birds to handle. Everything we do requires animal care approval. Our projects are reviewed by committees that involve a variety of professionals including veterinarians and scientists. Everyone, including the applicants, has the best interest of the animal in mind so it's looked at closely.

"A lot of people wonder if we are creating visual or olfactory trails for predators to follow, and the short answer is, 'I don't know for sure, but I don't think so.' Studies done in other areas on these methods we use show absolutely no effect. Out in pastures like this, the cattle are making all kinds of trails and creating this incredible patchwork. Our footsteps and signs probably can't be used reliably by predators because we are also walking throughout the pastures doing other things that have nothing to do with nest monitoring. But it is something you worry about so when we go to nests we always check the area for predators first. We minimize visits and try not to create a trail that leads directly up to the nest. I've monitored probably more than three thousand nests and my feeling—and it's just a feeling—is that we are not allowing predators to find nests."

If someone has to be handling the birds, sampling feathers, finding their nests, banding them, tagging them with transmitters, we could do no better than the likes of Stephen Davis. As he speaks about the decline of the pipit and other grassland birds, beneath the references to data and methods of research I hear a deep and natural affection for the birds. Even so, I asked if we couldn't figure out how to help grassland birds simply by monitoring their numbers from one kind of habitat to another and then creating more of the right habitat. That sounds logical, Stephen said, but unless you determine the productivity and level of recruitment from each habitat—all of which means nest monitoring and banding—you increase the chances that you are promoting the conservation and creation of sink habitats.

"When you count birds, as in the BBS and other point surveys, you get an idea of the relative abundance of birds in an area. You know that there are birds there and they are singing. Probably holding territories, but you can't be sure. What you *don't* know is the composition of the population or their success in breeding and recruiting new adults from within.

"Studies show that you can have a high density in an area, but it may be very poor in terms of productivity and survival. Maybe there are a lot of inexperienced birds, birds that are out-competed by others that are forced to nest in these sub-optimal habitats. Imagine a situation where productive natural habitats and landscapes have been recently altered by humans, say in the last hundred years. And now these habitats, which might be hayfields, have become population sinks. However, natural selection cannot keep pace with the rapid changes caused by humans and the birds are now forced to use habitat selection cues that no longer result in the selection of suitable habitats. So the mere presence of the species in good numbers is a poor indicator of habitat quality."

When I asked about population trends for the pipit and other grassland birds, Stephen said that the BBS data from 1980 to the present show steeper declines for many birds and a greater percentage of species in clear decline compared to the data from 1966 to 1979.

"Today about 80 percent of the birds are showing declines, so the situation isn't getting any better for grassland birds. . . . A lot of the habitat loss occurred before the BBS began. We continued to have some land conversion [ploughing native grassland] in the seventies and eighties, but not enough to account for the changes in bird population we're seeing. Like anything else in ecology, it's probably a number of interrelated factors contributing to the decline."

For the rest of the summer I heard the same message again and again from other bird researchers I interviewed: bird decline is accelerating even though habitat loss has slowed down. No single factor is responsible. It's a combination of the original habitat loss, abetted by improper grazing and management, including fire suppression, which brings on invasive plant species and shrubby growth. Then you can throw into the mix a few other factors: toxins in the environment, West Nile disease, urban sprawl, damage caused by energy-extraction industries, and the compounding effect of drought brought on by global climate change. Most if not all of these destructive forces are also present where grassland birds winter in the southern states, Mexico, and the South American grasslands.

At Grasslands National Park in southern Saskatchewan, referring to the burrowing owl, park biologist Pat Fargey told me about something he calls "short stopping." As the birds in a reduced population come north in the spring they tend to fill up available habitat as they go, and if there is enough for the entire population in the southern parts of their range, areas in the north that were once necessary for a larger population become vacant.

From Rob Scissons, another Parks Canada biologist at Grasslands Park, I heard about an insect that was a source of food and grazing pressure in drought years before it mysteriously went extinct in the late 1800s. The Rocky Mountain locust was a large grasshopper that once blocked out the sun as it flew in apocalyptic hordes to graze drought-stricken prairies down to the dirt.[1] At the Grasshopper Glacier in Montana, you can see a thin pinkish-brown horizon in the layers of ice: the sediment of locust bodies marking a flight year centuries ago. Like the buffalo and like fire, the locust provided intermittent and random disturbances that renewed the grassland and maintained its patchy, shifting mosaic of habitats over the long term. We will never know how important the Rocky Mountain locust may have been for birds like the burrowing owl that prefer heavily grazed pastures and depend on larger grasshoppers for food.

Travelling with John Carlson, a grassland biologist with the Bureau of Land Management just across the border in Montana, I heard the problem of grassland bird decline described as a "death by a thousand cuts" beginning with the original conversion of native prairie to cropland. The steep declines we see now may be ripples echoing from that primary catastrophe. Using David Quammen's analogy of a Persian rug cut into tiny squares, John described a fragile, barely functioning environment that has become unnaturally vulnerable to local and short-term weather events: a late spring snowstorm, drought, flood.

Everything I heard or read about the problem of grassland bird decline seemed to repeat the same messages and ask the same questions. Looking for another angle on things, I started reading about the decline of birds in more heavily studied biomes. Research on eastern forest songbirds, it occurred to me, has been underway for much longer, and has received a great deal more funding and attention from universities and other research institutions. I skimmed some of the literature of eastern forest bird decline, to see what science has learned about the mechanisms by which sink habitats erode local populations of wood warblers.

Then the book review editor for *Canadian Geographic* asked me to review a new book called *Silence of the Songbirds*. In it I came across a theory on the effects of forest habitat fragmentation that might well apply to grassland birds. Bridget Stutchbury, a Canadian ornithologist at York University, spent several summers following hooded warblers and other forest birds around the wooded copses of her summer home in Pennsylvania. She wanted to do more than merely measure the nesting success of the populations she found and to study the way birds behave when they are faced with fragmented habitat. Eventually she began to question some of the established theories that biologists use to explain the effects of cutting up large expanses of habitat into smaller pieces—in particular, the effect of edges. The smaller a fragment is, the more edge it has relative to interior. Many birds pegged as "forest interior" species will generally avoid small woodlands, even when the size of the plot may be equal to or larger than a standard breeding territory for the species.

Before Stutchbury's work, many forest songbirds were thought to avoid fragments for two reasons: one, they prefer forest interior, and two, the edge is a hostile environment for birds. Edges increase vulnerability to predation and brood-parasite species such as the brown-headed cowbird, which lay their eggs in other birds' nests, replacing them with their own. Many studies of woodland birds (and grassland birds) have shown increased rates of both predation and cowbird parasitism when they nest in or near edge habitat. Stutchbury took a second look at the "hostile edge" dictum and discovered that it is not always true. She reviewed the studies and found that some showed little or no difference between rates of breeding success, predation, and cowbird parasitism in forest interiors versus forest edges. By mapping the breeding territories and then radio-tracking species generally thought to be forest interior birds, Stutchbury, her colleagues, and students discovered that many of them actually spend a good deal of their time on the forest edge, singing and foraging and even nesting. At this point, Stutchbury wiped the slate clean and asked the original question anew: why *do* forest birds avoid small fragments? The edge-effect theory applies in some situations but not all. It is not the complete answer to the question.

She began to focus on the sexual habits of certain forest birds, in particular, hooded warblers. She monitored breeding pairs by giving each individual a colour band that linked it to its mate, by radio-tracking the movements of individuals, and by taking DNA samples from adults and young to find out who mated with whom. Before long, her research team was learning that behind the supposed monogamy of the hooded warbler was a soap opera of extramarital liaisons and fighting over access to females. Their DNA fingerprinting showed that approximately 40 percent of nestlings had been fathered by males other than the ones paired with their mothers. Both males and females were observed making dawn forays onto neighbouring territories to obtain "extra-pair copulations."

So, what is the purpose of all this promiscuity? Stutchbury says it is a numbers game in which unfaithfulness is in fact faithful to the health of the species' population over time. Extra-pair copulations allow the females to choose from among a pool of males, thereby increasing chances that at least some of their young will receive higher-quality DNA from experienced males who have proven their ability to survive. For this dynamic to work, however, there has to be a pool. The birds must breed in loose colonies with their territories adjoining one another. This, says Stutchbury, is why small forest fragments large enough to host one or two territories are unattractive to many species. Birds, she argues, are social and prefer to nest in what she calls neighbourhoods, where the females can optimize the DNA of their offspring and successful males can pass on more of their genetic material.

The power of this urge to find extra-pair copulations was confirmed when one of Stutchbury's grad students radio-tagged isolated pairs of hooded warblers who *were* nesting in small forest fragments. He discovered that, in these small fragments, the males would fly up to a mile and a half away from home to obtain extra-pair copulations. Females were disinclined to take the risk of such a flight and had to wait at home for a visiting male. All in all, however, the risk and expenditure of energy implied in such venturing reduced by half the usual rate of nests with more than one father contributing genetic material. Fragments that were too isolated, meanwhile, often contained unmated males, since females are predisposed to select mates in locations where there are chances of extra-pair copulation. For many forest species—for example, ovenbirds, red-eyed vireos, and hooded warblers—up to half of males present in isolated fragments are unable to attract a mate at all.

Now, when I watch male chestnut-collared or McCown's longspurs flying up and down in communal songflight over a prairie hilltop, when I hear four grasshopper sparrows singing near one another while the rest of the pasture is unoccupied, or when I find a lone pipit singing for two weeks above a ten-acre hilltop remnant of prairie, I think about Stutchbury's theories on habitat fragmentation. It would take several summers of monitoring and DNA fingerprinting on larger and smaller fragments to prove anything, but the traditional clustering of many grassland bird territories—from burrowing owls to longspurs to grasshopper sparrows to bobolinks—would suggest the same dynamic at work. These birds, like their woodland relatives, need enough habitat to maintain a neighbourhood and, what's more, they need enough neighbours to provide a functioning community in which pair formation and mate choice can foster a healthy, stable population. A high ratio of edge to interior on a patch of prairie will no doubt give an advantage to predators, but when the local community of longspurs has dwindled down to a lone male singing out to the sky, predation, food supply, disease, climate, and all the other limiting factors that play into population dynamics of grassland birds do not tell the full story. The very suddenness of the collapse may simply be a matter of females giving up on the pasture and moving on to a place with a larger population of males to choose from. "Birds need other birds," Stutchbury says near the end of her book. "As the numbers of migrants continue to fall, this will only disrupt the mating system even more, and in turn the population decline will accelerate."[2]

That may sound bleak, but discovering the reason why birds disappear from seemingly suitable habitat is a vital step toward knowing which fragments are the most important to conserve, as well as what must be done to restore, expand, and maintain the right mix of habitat within and between fragments so that a diversity of bird communities will be able to thrive.

BOBOLINK

One grassland bird whose multiple-partner approach to reproduction has been well documented is the bobolink. Perhaps because its breeding range extends across the northeastern states where much of the ornithological research on North American birds was conducted in the first half of the twentieth century, the bobolink has long been known as a species where males have more than one mate and where nests have more than one father. At some bobolink nests, in fact, there will be three adults tending the young. Sometimes the third bird is a second father; other times it is one of the offspring of one or both of the parents from the previous year's nesting.

Emily Dickinson, who knew her birds, called the bobolink the "Rowdy of the Meadow." One colony in the Qu'Appelle Valley had as many as one hundred nesting pairs some years.[3] Gathering to nest in swales and bottomland where there is enough moisture to grow a lot of grass, bobolinks put on a show each morning. The buff-coloured females perch on the top of dock plants to watch as males take turns flying low over the grass in aerial display. Once aloft, each male flaps slowly, intermittently holding his wings out and gliding, letting the sun light up patches of white and gold on his upper parts and shoulders, which contrast with his otherwise black plumage. Throwing back his head, he unleashes his peculiar song, made of twenty-five to fifty individual bleeps, whirrs, and clanks, sounding for all the world like a Hollywood robot in twitter-pated ecstasy. Some researchers have suggested that females may select sexual partners by the duration of their display. Males in better condition display longer and raise more young than males who display for a shorter time.[4]

Bobolinks arrive on their nesting grounds later than other grassland songbirds, in part because they are coming from farther away. Like the upland sandpiper and Swainson's hawk, they spend the non-breeding season on South American grasslands east of the Andes. Their 12,400-mile round-trip migration each year is thought to be one of the longest of any New World songbird. Originally nesting in tallgrass and mixed-grass prairie of the Midwestern states and southern regions of Canada, the bobolink expanded its range eastward as settlers cleared forests for agriculture. As that habitat grew back to woodland and hay mowing became mechanized and more frequent, the bobolink began to decline and retract its range. At its peak during the early twentieth century, hundreds of thousands of bobolinks were shot as agricultural pests in the rice fields of South Carolina and Georgia. They are still hunted for food as they pass through Jamaica on migration. In Argentina, they are poisoned by pesticides and trapped to be sold as pets. According to the Nature Conservancy, the bobolink has averaged a 3.8 percent decrease between 1980 and 1996, partly owing to haying practices, though low winter survival rates may be the primary cause.[5]

Chapter Twelve

LANDSCAPE PATHOLOGY 101

When Stuart, Mary, and I reconvened to take up the July leg of our journey, we were approaching the Missouri Coteau, south of Moose Jaw. The Coteau has some large, rolling pastures of native grass where we were expecting to see more grassland birds. Macoun's notes for the date of our trip say that he saw lark buntings and that "the commonest bird on the prairie was the Chestnut-collared Bunting."[1] The land we were travelling through still looked like fair chestnut-collared longspur habitat, though perhaps too hilly. As we came up onto the eastern rim of the Coteau at the Cactus Hills, our road became a grassy trail and led us to a gate. Across the barbed wire we could see the trail arcing up and down the hump-backed "kame and kettle" moraine. Thousands of acres of native grass with no trees in sight. We couldn't see to the other side of the pasture but that didn't deter Stuart. It might be our best chance to get a feel for what it was like for Macoun to travel over the wild Coteau hill country. I got out and opened the gate as Stuart drove into the pasture. Our grassy trail quickly faded away and we were wheeling along over trackless hills. As we topped every crest, looking for a road somewhere leading out of the grassland, we would find another gate leading to another set of hills in another pasture. After a while I broke the silence and suggested that we might be lost. Stuart laughed and asked if I'd ever heard what Daniel Boone said about being lost.

"He was out in the wilds of Kentucky and someone asked, 'Were you ever lost, Dan'l?' 'No,' he said, 'but I was mighty confused for two weeks once.'"

We were passing through a great expanse of native grassland but it was too late in the day to hear a lot of birdsong. Still, we should've been flushing more birds as we went along. I estimate that we travelled through twelve miles of virgin prairie that afternoon, but we recorded two Sprague's pipits, a lark bunting, a Baird's sparrow, a chestnut-collared longpspur, and a ferruginous hawk. By the time we found a municipal road on the northwest corner of that block of prairie, I had opened and closed ten gates. The grassland we had driven through was large as remnants go, but a mere particle of the endless hills, plains, and valleys that Macoun saw in 1880. As we came back off the top of the Coteau we took in a sweeping vista of the Moose Jaw River basin, which drains the southernmost reaches of the Qu'Appelle River watershed. From that altitude, five hundred feet above the plains, the land looked like a flayed hide cut into squares. Sometimes, from the window of a plane I can almost see it as the patchwork quilt of picturesque reference, but sooner or later we pass over a curving strip of unploughed land along a creek valley or a moraine ridge and the truth invades. This is the real texture of the prairie, marooned in a landscape utterly subdued, yoked to the quadrangle and its efficiencies of ownership and production. Here is another passage from Macoun, who this time sets his sights on the land I know best:

> Starting from the Qu'Appelle at its mouth as a centre and projecting a line nearly due west to the South Saskatchewan [River], a distance of over 250 miles, and starting at the meridian of Fort Ellice and including only the land south of the Touchwood Hills, a belt, with

an average breadth of 100 miles, extends right up the
Qu'Appelle. Here, we have 25,000 square miles, or over
16,000,000 acres of land lying in one block, that to my own
knowledge, has over 90 per cent [of it] fit for agricultural
or pastoral purposes. The only poor soil in this extensive
tract is that portion between Spy Hill and Fort Ellice, and
two small groups of sand hills lying at the sources of the
Qu'Appelle. . . . . There will be no difficulty in obtaining
first-class wheat crops throughout the greater part of it, as
the soil is generally a rich, black loam.[2]

If Macoun was first to lust over the band of fertile grasslands flanking the Qu'Appelle, he was soon joined by others, including my
mother's father, who came from Scotland in 1906 to get his piece of
it. Macoun's vision of the Qu'Appelle came true, right down to the
details. The only large pieces of unploughed land in that belt of land
are the ones he mentions at Spy Hill and at the river's source. The
rest of it has been ploughed under, except for hillsides in the valley
and its tributaries. We've been growing those "first-class wheat crops"
for a century, and the myths that we've spun to cover up the damage are beginning to wear thin. One of the more recent lies, which
conservationists have helped to foster, is that new agricultural techniques that depend on heavy herbicide use and larger machinery are
"good for wildlife."

These new weed control and seeding techniques, which now
dominate conventional agriculture on the prairie, are having an indirect but very real effect upon a guild of grassland birds that until
recently were thriving on and around cultivated farmland. Here I am
referring to species that have always been more adaptive and therefore able to subsist in the weedy margins of cropland. In this group
I would include some water birds, such as the American bittern,
northern pintail, American wigeon, mallard, and killdeer, as well as

raptors such as the northern harrier and short-eared owl. Songbirds that have traditionally been able to adapt well to breed in farmland include the barn swallow, horned lark, vesper sparrow, savannah sparrow, western meadowlark, and bobolink. The Breeding Bird Survey shows that most of these birds have been declining significantly—some quite precipitously after 1980.[3]

If you access the BBS data broken down by habitat, you find that in the northernmost prairie zone known as Aspen Parkland, which has fertile soils and very high rates of cultivation, many of these classic farmland birds are in trouble. In Aspen Parkland, the rate of annual decline for the northern pintail is 5.6 percent, for the American wigeon it is 3.5 percent, for the horned lark 5.4 percent, for the barn swallow 4.4 percent, and for the western meadowlark 3.8 percent. Other species are showing worrisome but less dramatic rates of annual decline.

As we drove down off the Coteau onto the cultivated plains below, Stuart talked about the changes in farming techniques he has seen during his lifetime—the shift from human-scaled farming to industrialized agribusiness, with the labour of people and animals supplanted entirely by petrochemical-intensive machinery, fertilizer, and insect and weed control. In his mind, there is no question that the economic and technological impetus behind this transformation is driving farmland birds from the prairie.

"Not long ago every farmer respected the sixty-six-foot-wide road allowance along the edge of his fields and left it to grass even if it was weedy. The meadowlarks and other birds had a place to feed and nest. But now, with the cost-price squeeze farmers are under, they need to maximize and seed every inch of land so even the road allowances are under crop. And where there are roads on an allowance, the crop goes right to the edge of the road."

Since the 1980s, a new approach to seeding, weeding, and fertility management has replaced traditional tillage methods. People of my generation remember their uncles and grandfathers out on the tractor in July, raising a cloud of dust on a black, unplanted field. "Summerfallow" was a word we used to describe the dark spaces on the checkerboard landscape, the fields farmers left unseeded on an annual rotation so that all land received a rest now and then to regain its natural fertility. To discourage weeds, they had to cultivate the soil at intervals during the growing season. This sounds virtuous compared to herbicide spraying, but it has severe consequences for the soil. Every time you cultivate soil you release some of it into the air along with valuable nitrogen. As well, soil stripped of vegetation or the residual stubble from a previous crop does not hold snow or spring moisture and will easily erode downstream into local waterways. If weeds could be controlled without tilling the soil so often and crops could be seeded with minimum disturbance to the soil, the farmer and the land would both benefit.

Three technologies came along to make this happen, rapidly redefining farm methods on the northern Great Plains. New seed drills let farmers sow directly into the stubble left over from last year's crop—a method known as "direct seeding." Herbicide companies developed products that help farmers to keep their land virtually weed-free without having to cultivate the soil. Artificial sources of nitrogen, anhydrous ammonia in particular, complete the triad of technologies by allowing farmers to improve the fertility of their land without having to rest it as summerfallow or keep animals for manure.

Farm extension programs, university departments, and government agricultural advisors have embraced the new farm methods made possible by these technologies, creating the jargon of modern grain growers. "Conservation tillage," "chemical sumerfallow," "low-till," "no-till," and "zero-till" are now on the lips of every conventional farmer. "Continuous cropping" is a favourite term, because now farmers can maximize yields and revenues by leaving nothing fallow and seeding all of their land directly into the stubble left from the previous harvest. Conservation agencies in government and the private sector have welcomed zero-till for the erosion control and moisture retention it provides and on the strength of studies showing that the stubble and trash left in fields benefit "wildlife."

These new farming methods have also received the enthusiastic support of Monsanto, the farm chemical and biotechnology conglomerate that manufactures the herbicides used to minimize tillage. Here is a statement that appeared on Monsanto's website, making the same claims that you hear repeated by wildlife agencies and hunting organizations, but placed within the corporation's real message, which is that biotechnology is good for the planet:

BIOTECHNOLOGY CONTRIBUTES TO SIGNIFICANT DECREASE IN PLOWING

Crops developed with agricultural biotechnology reduce the need for tillage or plowing, allowing farmers to adopt conservation or "no-till" farming practices. . . . Since the introduction of biotech crops in 1996, farmers have reduced—and, in some cases, completely stopped—plowing or tilling the soil to eliminate weeds and prepare fields for planting. *The benefits of conservation tillage range from soil erosion control to improved wildlife habitat to a reduction in greenhouse gases and fuel use.*[italics added][4]

There is no denying the soil conservation benefits of zero-till, but sweeping claims about benefits to wildlife deserve a second look. Not surprisingly, an acre of cropland that has stubble or wheat sprouting in spring will host more duck and upland game nests than black summerfallow, but that accounts only for the cropland itself, which at its best is only the most marginal of habitats. What about the more productive habitat in the farm landscape on the margins, around sloughs and bush where our grandfathers did not bother to plough? Answering that question takes us to the economic choices that farmers face in adopting new agricultural practices, making it clear that zero-till and continuous cropping have been a mixed blessing.

Any financial benefit a change in equipment provides to the farmer is directly proportional to the scale of the farm. Someone gearing up with the special seeding and herbicide-spraying equipment to switch to zero-till and continuous cropping has to make a huge investment that can be justified only if it is used to crop several sections of land. The cost-price trade-off for farmers will not allow for any extra labour, and one set of equipment is all many farmers can afford to be running anyway. These constraints mean that thousands of acres that must be seeded in spring, sprayed for weeds, and then harvested in fall within very narrow time frames end up being worked by one or two people using massive machines.

The new air seeders used for direct seeding are sprawling pieces of agricultural ordnance reaching three times the width of the seeders used on prairie farms only twenty years ago. The traction required to pull such behemoths across the land has placed farmers onto fuel-swilling, four-wheel-drive tractors and caterpillars that would not look out of place on a battlefield. The ever-rising costs of fuel, equipment, financing, pesticides, and fertilizer, in the face of a cheap food policy that keeps farm-gate prices artificially low, force more farmers out of business every year and drive those who remain on the land to increase the scale and "efficiency" of their operations. These pressures lead to further changes in farming methods that, taken together with continuous cropping, are creating a landscape that is becoming hostile to any life form that does not contribute directly to the bottom line.

One of these additional changes in method, which is not necessarily part of zero-till or continuous cropping but typically gets integrated into the annual cycle, is known as "straight combining." In the past, farmers would cut their grain with a swather in early fall and allow it to dry in windrows for a few days before returning with the combine, which is a machine that both threshes the swaths of cut grain and separates the grain from the chaff. With larger machinery and more acreage to cover today, farmers can reduce fuel consumption, wear on equipment, and soil compaction by skipping the swathing step and combining the standing grain. Such a practice places even greater time pressures on the farmer, and it also requires him to be a lot "cleaner." In other words, he must use more herbicide to minimize the weeds within his fields *and* along the margins.

Not long ago farmers kept their fields fenced so they could let cattle onto the land after harvest, which would put the stubble, spilled grain, and weeds to use and add much-needed manure to the soil. Today, with fewer farmers fencing their land or keeping livestock, this practice is falling out of use. The loss of stubble grazing is a small thing on its own, but taken together with other changes, it has moved our farmland farther away from the natural cycling of nutrients necessary for the local ecology to support lives other than those strictly required to grow crops.

Meanwhile, a lot of bird habitat on the edges of fields, aspen bluffs, sloughs, and rocky hilltops is being ploughed under in the efficiency compromise that happens when you have to manoeuvre large equipment around obstacles. Conservationists shake their heads when they see a farmer bulldozing bush, filling a slough, or levelling a grassy ridge, but the economics of large-scale grain farming have turned any natural land in the path of machinery into a drain on cash. When seed, fertilizer, and herbicides were cheaper and equipment smaller and more agile, a farmer would happily go around a slough or a hilltop, but now the extra pass or two it takes to pull a large rig around an obstacle means a lot of expensive overlapping of inputs that cost twenty-five dollars or more per acre. Double the seed, fertilizer, and herbicide for a couple of acres as you go around a slough and suddenly you can justify filling it in and bringing it under gainful production. This kind of thinking has gone hand in hand with the zero-till and continuous cropping movements, indirectly making these practices a net loss for wildlife despite the benefits they may bring in soil and water retention and in providing nesting cover for a few ducks. Applied across the whole of the grain-growing regions of the northern Great Plains, these new agricultural practices are eliminating some of the last vestiges of habitat within and around cropland. Instead of a patchy landscape interlacing crops with natural remnants and weedy margins, many farm areas have taken on the machine-perfect grid pattern of land given over entirely to the hegemony of food production.

Although they are not on their own direct causes of the habitat loss, the practices of continuous cropping and zero-till are inadvertently contributing to a form of agriculture that is expunging the leftover bits of wildness in grain-farming landscapes, making it into the land of zero-sloughs, zero-brush, and zero-grass. When I hear people praise these methods as being "good for wildlife" I ask what they mean: for all wildlife, some wildlife, most wildlife? Zero-till is said to be good for wildlife on balance, but who knows enough about what is happening at the foundational level of the ecosystem to make such a pronouncement? When you pump anhydrous ammonia gas into the soil and spray it with herbicides and pesticides, what is happening to the small living things it contains, the microbes that everything else depends upon? And what about the insects and other creatures at the next level up?

Plant physiologists talk about the importance of something called the "rhizosphere," the zone of soil immediately surrounding the roots of plants and populated with bacteria, protozoa, and nematodes. New research from Purdue University in Indiana has shown that the main herbicide used in zero-till, glyphosate (Monsanto's Roundup), is changing rhizosphere microbiology.[5] After it has killed the target weeds, residual glyphosate leaks into the soil's root zone, where it can inhibit enzymes in other plants, reducing their uptake of minerals, especially manganese. Glyphosate is known to be toxic to the nitrogen-fixing bacteria necessary for soil fertility, but this research suggests that it may also be making certain pathogens more virulent while reducing the resistance mechanisms in plants.

By the logic of zero-till, the responsible producer is the one who sprays glyphosate on cropland and its margins to control weeds. North American farmers apply untold gallons of this compound to prairie land every summer, believing that it breaks down rapidly and hurts nothing but the target weed species. Few question its role in "soil conservation" or consider that it may be diminishing the vitality of the soil.

It may be decades before we know what glyphosate and other chemicals are doing to the overall health of the prairie, but I know what I have seen as the land around Regina has been given over to zero-till practices. Yes, it is "merely anecdotal," but where I once saw meadowlarks and vesper sparrows on the edges of every field and McCown's longspurs and horned larks singing above black summer-fallow, the land today is alarmingly empty and silent.

Eighteen years ago, when I first became concerned about grassland birds, I asked an ornithologist working for the provincial government if he knew what was causing them to disappear. His answer was not detailed or particularly illuminating, but it was elegant. There is, he said, "a pathology in the landscape." I knew what he meant but neither of us could name it. Not naming or even describing the pathology in any way keeps the peace in a place where agriculture provides the founding myth of our very entitlement to the land. That foundation spans the moral divide between what farmers want to do (grow food and make a living) and how they do it (with industrial technologies, methods, and marketing systems), convincing them that they have a responsibility to "feed the world," that the land is property to be used as its owner sees fit, and that nature is an obstacle, or at best a fringe benefit of farm life.

Hidden by that founding myth, a malignancy threatens the very wholeness and health of the prairie. Its causes are multiple and masked by a complex interplay that compounds their effect. No one can say conclusively how it operates, and the most insidious factor in the pathology is also the most difficult to bring into the light of day.

Horned Lark

In her first edition of *The Birds of Regina*, Margaret Belcher (Mary Houston's sister) described the horned lark as "a common breeding bird of the open prairie and farmlands where it builds its nest on the ground, sometimes before the snow is gone. Its tinkling song, familiar to every prairie dweller, is greeted as the welcome first sound of spring."[6]

The only true lark native to North America, the horned lark is found on alpine meadows, grassland, and shorelines all around the northern hemisphere. The pale, sun-bleached race we have on the northern Great Plains originally nested on heavily grazed or burnt grassland as well as bare patches of ground. This preference for razed landscape allowed it to adapt and even flourish during the first century of agriculture by nesting in wheat stubble and summerfallow. As woodland was cleared for agriculture, horned larks began to pioneer farther north, expanding their range on the plains. Despite thousands of nests being destroyed during spring seeding and cultivation, it thrived and soon became the most abundant and widespread grassland bird in the region.

Twenty years ago, its status as a ubiquitous farmland bird seemed secure and no one could have predicted the dramatic decline it was about to undergo. When farmers stopped resting land as summerfallow and began to crop land continuously, the numbers of horned larks in heavily cultivated landscapes began to drop suddenly. William Anaka's Breeding Bird Survey at Theodore, for example, shows a drop of horned larks from a mean of 95.3 in the 1970s to 49.8 in the 1980s, when these new agricultural practices first took hold. In the 1990s, the mean dropped to 14.2 larks for the Theodore BBS route. The numbers of horned larks for the route peaked in 1971 at 162; in 2001 there were three. This is only one of dozens of routes on the plains, and therefore not conclusive on its own, but the BBS trend for all routes in Saskatchewan shows a yearly decline of 5.6 percent since 1980. For Manitoba in the same period, the rate of decline is 7.83 percent per year.[7] If the horned lark does not come out of this steep slide within the next decade, a bird we have taken for granted as the prairie's first singer to return in spring will be a candidate for the endangered list.

Part Three

Pastures Unsung

Chapter Thirteen

POISONED LAND

It's early July, 2007, and Karen and I have left Cherry Lake to come back to the city. We are sitting in the waiting room of a clinic in a hospital named for a Plains Cree chief. The room is filled by people our age and older, mostly non-Aboriginal, many of whom would have travelled in from small towns and farms to make their appointments. Women sitting in a circle on one side of the room are laughing. Two of them have bandanas on their heads. This is the cancer clinic that serves all of southern Saskatchewan. The faces across from us are familiar—Slavic and Anglo-Saxon features marked by decades of working in fields and kitchens. Most of them probably grew up on subsistence farmsteads with a full mix of livestock, gardens, and crops, then either left the farm as adults or found some way to live off the avails of modern agribusiness.

If I were to ask any of them about grassland birds, most would mention the meadowlark—the mascot for settler culture on the northern Great Plains. Its song each spring, as reliable as the sun's rising, lets them know that all is well. The price of fuel and fertilizer is through the roof, the school is closing, the neighbours have given up and moved to the city, but at least the meadowlark is back singing on his fence post.

My gaze falls upon a bookcase. Instead of the usual Reader's Digest Condensed Books, it holds a collection of large, hardcover volumes with unabashedly nostalgic titles: *Arrowheads to Wheatfields*, *Our Side of the Hills*, *From Sage to Timber*, *Milestones and Memories*, *A Stake in the West*, *Prairie Trails to Blacktop*. Each is a local history of a small settler community gathered around a prairie town that served as a depot for bringing in supplies and shipping grain to market. Towns with names like Wawota, Sintaluta, Oxbow, Briercrest, and Fir Mountain. Written by the descendants of the original settlers, these books typically begin with a cursory summary of pre-settlement history, adding a bit of colour and folklore in a discussion of place names and landmarks, before diving into the early years of homesteading, breaking the sod, and sowing wheat—the originating acts marking what has become, to non-indigenous people, the real beginning of history in this place.

A substantial overburden of myth obscures the fullness of settler history in such narratives, but these books always contain a few stories that speak to the heartbreak and exhilarating sense of liberty that go with a new life in a new world. I have read more than my share over the years.

I look up again to the creased and tanned faces around us—the children and grandchildren of people named and valorized in these books and their tales of threshing crews and Christmas concerts—and then I remember why we are all gathered here. This new world has lost much of its shine. In farming regions, landscape pathology and the pathology of human disease are beginning to merge—and it will take more than science to bring us back to health.

When Karen was told, two weeks ago, that the lump in her left breast was malignant, disbelief soon gave way to a desire to know the cause. We eat healthy, organic food most of the time; we exercise; we drink filtered water; our furniture is either old or made of materials that don't release toxins; we avoid organochlorines and formaldehyde in household and personal care products; we don't own a microwave; and we never use pesticides of any kind. On the other hand, we grew up in a world that tested nuclear bombs above ground, gave chest X-rays to children, wrapped the built environment in fields of electromagnetic radiation, made plastic toys for babies to chew, chlorinated and fluoridated drinking water, sprayed food and playgrounds with DDT, and filled the air with formaldehyde, benzene, lead, and other toxins from the petrochemicals and chlorinated chemicals we have come to depend upon. Forget about finding a single cause. As for disbelief, the marvel is that any of us make it through life *without* cancer.

The doctors tell us there is no way of proving whether Karen's tumour was triggered by the toxins that accumulate in breast tissue, but the possibility of such a connection, and its very resistance to A-causes-B thinking, made me stop to reconsider my approach to the bird decline question. Taking several weeks off from writing while Karen went through surgery and recovery, I found myself thinking once again about the role that pesticides and other toxins might play.

When I began looking into grassland bird decline, I had expected to find a lot of research into the effects of agricultural chemicals on grassland birds. Reading reports and talking to biologists, I assumed that pesticides would be listed as a primary cause. But instead I found almost no research other than studies conducted to register the pesticides, and none of the experts I spoke with seemed to think that farm chemicals were a major cause. With so many other factors clearly affecting bird populations, and almost no direct spraying of pesticides on grassland habitat in most years, it made sense that biologists would focus on other questions. And if the experts gave toxins little attention, who was I to do anything but follow their lead?

That changed one afternoon as I sat in the waiting room of the breast cancer clinic where Karen went to have further surgery and treatment. While Karen was having a mammogram done, I listened to two farmers who had begun to talk by the window. I heard them say that their wives had been cancer-free for a couple of years, but were back at the clinic for routine checkups. The men quickly got around to comparing their farms—acres under cultivation, crops seeded this year, rainfall in their area. After a few minutes of this, their wives returned from their appointments and joined in the talk. Soon, they had two conversations going and I listened shamelessly to both. The men were talking about some pest that was in their fields and the insecticides they were using to kill it. At the very same time, the women, with their backs to the men, were talking about their breast cancer. One of them began listing all of the farm women she knew who had tumours. The other woman shook her head and then joined in with her own list. "Makes you wonder, doesn't it," the first one said, "all these chemicals we use. They say they're harmless, but I'm not so sure."

I felt like I was watching a badly written docudrama on pesticides and cancer. There were the two sides in front of me: the men who believe the chemicals are harmless and the women who are not so sure. I decided I was not so sure either. I would have to take another look at pesticides, even if exact causes—for the decline of an endangered bird or the carcinoma in the milk duct of a woman's breast—can never be found because they are hidden within a morass of incalculably complex interrelationships and compounded effects from which it is impossible to tease out precise mechanisms of population decay or disease. Even if the best science can do is provide some data showing trends that may point toward possible correlations.

Now I look around waiting rooms filled with other men and their wives, and I wonder how many of them might live in rural areas. In one of Karen's books on breast cancer, I came across a reference to a study published by the Windsor Regional Cancer Centre. It showed that the incidence of breast cancer in women under fifty-five was nine times higher than average for women who lived on farms.[1] Health Canada's Cancer Surveillance Online website has a lot of data on the incidence of breast cancer, including maps that show hot spots in certain provinces. Areas where strong pesticides are used in Manitoba and Prince Edward Island show higher rates of incidence, but other farming areas have only average rates. Some urban areas show higher rates too. As I clicked through the maps that bring up geographical trends for incidence by age group and region, they reminded me of the online bird decline maps on the Breeding Bird Survey website: broad patches of colour on maps that summarize alarming and at times conflicting data gathered over many years, and behind it all two sets of indeterminate causes that may overlap more than we understand.

The day Karen found the lump in her breast I had been talking on the phone to the man who counts birds on the longest-running Breeding Bird Survey route in Canadian grassland. Ian Halliday's route follows back roads on the high plains near Brooks, Alberta. Much of it passes through a large tract of native prairie in excellent condition. Ian signed up for the route in 1968, the year the survey was introduced in western Canada. His BBS partner, William Monro, has been his faithful recorder from the beginning, writing down the data as Ian calls out the names of prairie birds he sees and hears from the roadside in a three-minute span at each of fifty stops.

Ian began by telling me that he and Bill had stopped their survey long enough to celebrate an important anniversary. "We just got back last night. It was our fortieth anniversary doing the survey so at one of our favourite stops we got out and set up a little table and two chairs, opened a bottle of champagne and made a toast.

"After we clinked glasses, William said something about how nice it was to be away from the city and its traffic. How quiet it was

. . . but it was too quiet. The prairie was silent, like it has been for a few years now."

They reminisced about other years when they were hard-pressed to count all the longspurs and horned larks. Then the rancher who owns the native pastures on their route pulled up in his pickup truck to say hello. Ian asked him about the birds he had been seeing lately.

"He agreed with us. He said he just doesn't see the same numbers of prairie birds any more. When Bill and I started doing this route in the sixties we would count two hundred or more chestnut-collared longspurs on the eleven miles of native pasture at the end of our route. This year we had six. Last year it was two! The pasture hasn't changed. The rancher's a good custodian and he's managing it the way he always has, but something's wrong."

He dug out his records and listed off the longspur counts for the first nineteen years: 200, 227, 163, 234, 210, 295, 167, 292, 295, 296, 278, 291, 340, 245, 204, 215, 227, 208, 243. That last year is 1987. When you look at the BBS graph for longspurs on Ian's route, the next ten years of data, from 1988 to 1998, are expressed in a downward arc that starts off slowly and then turns into a freefall, like the trajectory of a high diver jumping from a tower.

"The year we noticed a big drop in longspur numbers I talked to the people at the horticultural station — it's near the beginning of our route," Ian recalled. "The drought was on and they said there had been grasshoppers but there was nothing to eat so they died. That year the prairies were real quiet. We've had a couple of wet years but the grasshoppers and the birds haven't really recovered. What is going on when you go from 250 chestnut-collared longspurs down to six?"

Whatever the mechanism behind the sharp decline in longspurs and other grassland birds that Ian and Bill witnessed from 1987 onward, it was a local expression of a much wider phenomenon. During the same period, grassland and farmland birds began to thin out rapidly all over the northern Great Plains. Thinking back to those days, I cannot say I recall a sudden dropoff after 1987, but when I look back at the BBS data for the prairie regions of Montana, the Dakotas, Wyoming, Alberta, Saskatchewan, and Manitoba, I can see that many birds started to decline more rapidly in that period. By the mid-1980s, prairie naturalists were sounding the alarm for the burrowing owl, sage grouse, and loggerhead shrike, the first grassland birds to make the endangered list. All three of these species were crashing fast even though the rate of virgin prairie being lost to cultivation had slowed to a trickle by then.

It was 1987 before I heard anyone suggest that burrowing owls and perhaps other birds were being hurt by grasshopper sprays that were popular at the time. Burrowing owls, like sage grouse and loggerhead shrikes, eat larger grasshoppers and, in particular, feed their young a lot of grasshoppers. The early 1980s brought severe drought to the prairie, creating ideal conditions for a grasshopper outbreak. It was the worst drought I have seen in my lifetime, and in retrospect perhaps the first glimpse of what climate change will mean for the Great Plains. With no rain, pastures were thin and crops shrivelled in the field. Even before the grasshoppers hit plague levels in the spring of 1985, the grain-farming world was on the verge of collapse. Every time I turned on the radio or opened a newspaper there were more stories of banks calling in loans, farmers going bankrupt and committing suicide, families falling apart, towns withering away. That was when we first began to talk about the "farm crisis," a term that has blown in and out of media headlines with some regularity ever since.

Like most people feeling the turmoil of a social crisis, prairie dwellers will look for a common enemy, a scapegoat whose obliteration will bring about a return of order and harmony. The one to be lynched in the crisis of the mid-1980s was nature itself. In the news and at the coffee shop, everyone agreed: the drought and the grass-hoppers were responsible for the chaos that had come to the prairie world. There was no way to eliminate the drought, but we had the will and the arsenal to annihilate the grasshoppers.

As Karen recovered from her surgery, I began looking back at the record of grasshopper spraying on the Canadian plains during the 1980s. In 1985, prairie governments were introducing rebate programs to help farmers poison their grasshoppers. In Alberta alone, the rebate program for that year allowed landowners to buy more than 400,000 litres of powerful pesticides.[2] A random Google search brought up an excerpt from the proceedings of the Saskatchewan Legislature, where I found an exchange between members of the official opposition and the governing Progressive Conservative party, on May 29, 1985. Addressing the minister of agriculture, one member asks, "When are you going to get your Department of Agriculture to deliver? Farmers want to know: number one, are you going to be providing spray, or yourselves spraying your own property, the property that is adjacent to farmers? Who is supposed to control the grasshoppers there? Are you going to insist that the railways spray their rights-of-way? Are you going to provide spray at a reduced cost to the [rural municipalities] to spray the road allowances?"[3]

The minister's reply reassured the good people of Saskatchewan that almost every inch of public land would be sprayed with grasshopper poison: highway ditches, road allowances in rural municipalities, irrigation canals, railway rights-of-way, all provincially owned lands, and both federal and provincial community pastures. Meanwhile, that year and the next, most private cropland in Saskatchewan was sprayed because farmers were told that their crop insurance would be rendered invalid if they did not. As well, farmers sprayed places that had nothing to do with crop production, because any land that was not bare dirt, concrete, or asphalt was pegged as potential feeding and breeding grounds for grasshoppers. Whether tame or native grass, all pastures were seen as "reservoirs" where grasshoppers could increase and stage an assault upon adjacent crops.

As I read through the history of the grasshopper outbreak and the accounts of pastures being sprayed—some entirely, others only at the margins—I thought about the pipits, sparrows, longspurs, owls, and shrikes using that land and feeding tainted grasshoppers to their nestlings. It was clear that not only cultivated farmland but grassland too was being sprayed with deadly pesticides. The figures speak for themselves. In 1985, somewhere between 9 and 12 million acres of land in Canada's prairie provinces received grasshopper poison. The next summer, in Saskatchewan alone, almost twice that amount of land received spray.[4]

One of the the most popular and powerful grasshopper poisons at the time was carbofuran, a carbamate chemical preferred for its fast "knock-down" qualities. According to the pesticide registration documents I came across on the Agriculture Canada website, carbofuran is a neurotoxin. It works by inhibiting cholinesterase, a critical enzyme for our nervous systems. A quarter teaspoon of the liquid form is enough to kill a human being; a single grain of the granular form will kill a songbird. A neurotoxin. Isn't that what we have been calling the chemicals banned by the United Nations as weapons of mass destruction? Carbofuran is a nerve agent, but in the 1980s our farmers were told to use it on cropland, grassland, easements, ditches, and rights-of-way all over the northern Great Plains.

Reading one research paper, I got a picture of what happens when cholinesterase levels drop far enough. First the poisoned animal begins to convulse and salivate. Paralysis follows and then, sometime later, death by asphyxiation. Birds are known to be particularly vulnerable to cholinesterase inhibitors, and many species are naturally attracted to the granular form of carbofuran because the granules are the same size as the dietary grit they depend upon for digestion.[5]

The document, produced by Agriculture Canada, mentions a single Utah cornfield treated with carbofuran where researchers found 479 dead horned larks. The median number of granules in the birds' gizzards was two.[6] Then comes a report of two thousand Lapland longspurs that died on a Canadian canola field treated with carbofuran in the spring of 1984. That field was merely 160 acres out of the millions of acres of canola on the northern Great Plains treated with carbofuran each year to protect against flea beetles—in addition to the millions of acres treated to kill grasshoppers.

When Canada's Pesticide Management Regulatory Agency (PMRA) finally got around to searching for carcasses on sample fields and extrapolating the results, the estimated annual kill of songbirds on prairie farms was staggering. When I asked, the PMRA would not confirm any numbers, but I dug out an email exchange I had saved from years before when I first started keeping a file on grassland birds. Looking for information on grassland birds and pesticides I had contacted Pierre Mineau, a wildlife toxicologist at the Canadian Wildlife Service's toxic chemicals division. He told me that the bird kill from the granular form of carbofuran alone was somewhere between one hundred thousand and one million birds per year.

At the same time, the liquid form of carbofuran was killing birds and reducing nest success throughout the region. In a 1987 issue of *The Blue Jay*, I found an article by Paul James, a Regina ornithologist, and Glen Fox, a CWS wildlife toxicologist. In the summer of 1986 they observed ninety-nine nesting pairs of burrowing owls in farmland and ranchland to see the effect of grasshopper insecticides. Their results showed that all but twenty-three of the nesting pairs were subjected to at least one spray of pesticide within four hundred yards of their nest burrows. On the Regina study plot—the farmland half of the study—97 percent of burrows were exposed. Roadside spraying by municipalities was responsible for 77 percent of the total exposed. On sites where liquid carbofuran was sprayed within four hundred yards of the burrow, nest productivity (number of young per nest) was 2.44 compared with 3.8 for unsprayed nests, but when nests were sprayed within fifty yards, the results were even more dramatic. Nest productivity dropped to less than half of the productivity level for non-sprayed burrows. Of the five nests that received direct aerial spraying with carbofuran, no adults were ever seen again above ground. All five had complete nest failure. The adults disappeared, making it impossible to determine whether they abandoned their nests, or died away from the nest sites or in the burrows.[7]

After a protracted deregistration process, granular carbofuran was phased out in the 1990s. Eventually, the liquid form was also banned for some but not all applications. I'd like to believe that the carbofuran days are behind us but, banned or not, supplies remain on the shelves of farmers, waiting for the next grasshopper outbreak. Not surprisingly perhaps, there has not been a major outbreak since the 1980s (there was a minor one in the mid-1990s), and grasshoppers have been uncharacteristically scarce even in drought years.

Meanwhile, other highly toxic insecticides remain on the market, registered by the very American and Canadian agencies that originally approved carborfuran despite the manufacturer's own supervised field trials in which at least forty-five species of birds died.[8] Terbufos, another granular insecticide used in canola in place of carbofuran, is exactly half as lethal. This means that while a single grain of carbofuran kills 100 percent of songbirds in a test, only half die after ingesting a single grain of terbufos. Eating two grains of terbufos evens the score, yet until 2004 it remained a registered pesticide legal for use on canola where migrating flocks of longspurs, horned larks, and sparrows congregate to feed in spring.

In addition to the grains of pesticides, songbirds often eat the small canola seed itself, which, until recently, was treated with another powerful chemical, lindane. Lindane is an older, very persistent toxin that has made its way around the globe by travelling in the atmosphere. It can now be found in water in the remotest regions of the Arctic. It occurs in everything from polar bear fat to human breast milk, and has been linked to breast cancer.

The PMRA deregistered lindane for use in treating canola seed in 2001. The manufacturer, Crompton Corporation, called for hearings to demand the deregistration be reversed and threatened Canada with a challenge under the North American Free Trade Agreement. The PMRA invited the Sierra Club to participate in the hearings, but the organization quit because it was concerned that the hearing process could favour Crompton. Using the U.S. Freedom of Information Act, the Sierra Club got hold of some correspondence between Crompton and the American Environmental Protection Agency in which a Crompton representative argues that the EPA should continue supporting lindane as seed treatment because the review process underway "should result in a reinstatement of lindane registration in Canada."[9]

When I read the Sierra Club news release about the correspondence, my first thought was, why is Crompton so sure? From whence does such confidence arise? The manufacturers have staff who work full-time on gaining the favour of the pesticide approval agencies, "building rapport" by whatever means are necessary. Not that there is a great resistance or mistrust coming from the approval agencies. In the original registration process, believe it or not, the PMRA typically relies on studies done by the manufacturer to show that the chemical falls within acceptable safety margins when applied according to instructions—which is another issue on its own.

Once its insecticide or herbicide is registered, the burden of proof in any effort to deregister will undoubtedly fall to the public, a few non-governmental organizations, and underfunded wildlife toxicologists in other government agencies—most of whom barely have the resources to launch a deregistration process, never mind building rapport.

In the case of carbofuran, it took nearly twenty years for American environmental groups and wildlife scientists to get it partially deregistered. The Canadian Wildlife Service's Pierre Mineau helped initiate the process in Canada. By reviewing reports from field tests conducted on American crops, looking at bird carcass counts and then adjusting the numbers with field-proven rates of scavenging and of searchers simply overlooking dead birds, Mineau estimated eight million birds per year were killed by granular carbofuran in American cornfields alone.[10]

Mineau is one scientist who sees what we are doing with insecticides, but what about the other scientists, the ones we have hired to safeguard health, children, wild creatures, and wild places from dangerous chemicals? Are they immoral or merely incompetent, or is the division of labour so diffuse and obscure that they can easily turn away and say, "I'm not responsible, I'm just doing my job"? If it's the latter, the more disturbing truth is that we are all looking away from the destruction. For every scientist who says he is just doing his research, there are hundreds of farmers who will say they are just growing food, and millions of consumers who will say they are just buying and eating it.

As I waded through more documents from Agriculture Canada and the PMRA, I thought again about the risk-benefit trade-off that secures our modern comforts, the gamble we forget but which comes to mind whenever someone is diagnosed with cancer. I began to feel for the first time that the gamble is not mine to make or unmake on my own. In effect, government agencies are quietly rolling the dice on my behalf, justifying the risk of cancer and the killing of birds and other creatures to ensure that high-yield agriculture continues on its inexorable path. In a measured and coldly reasoned cost-benefit analysis, the pesticide review documents look at a chemical's dangers to wildlife and human health and weigh these against its value to agriculture. For approved chemicals the message between the lines is, *Yes, this chemical may kill birds, amphibians, reptiles, mammals and non-target insects of all kinds, and may compromise human health, but look at the benefit it provides to farmers!*

This gets at one of the most cynical and irksome subtexts of every pesticide review document—the suggestion that the PMRA is doing it all for our farmers. If the tractor rallies, protests, and blockades over the loss of farm subsidies in recent decades have shown anything, it's that farmers have little or no political power, even in the prairie states and provinces. Farmers have always been an underclass and, with their numbers declining year by year, they have no hope of influencing public policy on their own. Who does the PMRA have in mind, then, if it isn't farmers? The pesticide companies? They have the lobbying power to influence agricultural policy to be sure, but the trade-off between food production efficiency and the health of the land is not made merely to enrich the moustache-twirling villains we like to imagine at the helm of such companies. The real beneficiaries, sadly enough, are you and me. The entire nation, growers and eaters alike, is being served by Agriculture Canada's efforts "to achieve security of the food system," as its official mandate claims. Pesticides and the other technologies of modern agriculture have been developed with our tacit consent so that per-farmer yields will be high enough to ensure low food prices—low enough to spare the general populace the presumed drudgery of having to grow any of our own food.

This is the moral compromise that since World War II has kept us going to the supermarket and the restaurant instead of to the garden or the cold room. If it has brought us any security, it is the dubious sense of ease that goes with having been liberated from our responsibility for the quality of our engagement with the earth. Any consideration of value or weighing of pros and cons is handled for us by professionals in Agriculture Canada who have mastered the art of writing around consequences that might point toward the rot at the heart of the system.

In the carbofuran discussion document, I came across a section where the reviewers calculated crop losses and additional costs for producers if they were to be forced to switch to alternative pesticides. They set the cost to wheat farmers alone at approximately seventeen million dollars per year under market scenarios considered likeliest by their experts—the manufacturer and its hired consultant.[11] I searched the document carefully, but was not surprised to see that the millions of birds lost each year from a pesticide such as granular carbofuran were not assigned a value of any kind. This weakness in weighing costs and benefits is never mentioned in the report, but by any standard of logic a value would have to be assigned to the creatures killed by the product if the methodology on which these decisions depend is to be taken seriously. By the time I put the report aside, I felt as if I had been fogged by an elaborate smokescreen of reasonability that showed costs and benefits being carefully balanced, but obscured the cold truth no one wants to face: specifically, that human beings receive the benefits by enjoying relatively cheap food grown by a few farmers who do the dirty work on our behalf, while the real costs are borne entirely by the wild creatures we keep out of sight and out of mind.

Reading the document long after the fact, it was hard to believe that granular carbofuran was ever deregistered. I remembered speaking shortly after it happened to two people who sat on the review committee, where they represented provincial and federal wildlife agencies. Each, independently of the other, told me that the Health Canada officer who led the review did a good job in seeing that the bird-kill data were taken into consideration. Each also hinted that he may have done too good a job, because shortly after the deregistration he was moved suddenly from pesticide review to medical device compliance. I wanted to see if he could tell me why he had changed jobs, so I tried calling him several times, leaving him messages. He never returned my calls, but I eventually received the following officially approved statement in an email: "Thank you for your interest in the carbofuran study. However, as I am no longer with the PMRA, I do not feel it appropriate for me to comment on this issue. I have contacted the PMRA, and they have suggested that you contact their Pest Management Information Service for more information."

Not a surprising response, given that three Health Canada scientists were once fired for publicly questioning department policies and blowing the whistle on manufacturers who pressured them into quickly approving agricultural drug products. Initially, the three had denounced the government's approval of growth hormones for cattle, pigs, and chickens. They were reprimanded and threatened with a gag order at the time, but during the mad cow disease outbreak of 2003 they spoke out again, criticizing approval processes. This time, all three were fired.

These are the kind of reports that make it easy to demonize the pesticide review agencies as corrupt servants of the farm chemical industry, assigning to them all of the blame for the toxification of our food, land, bodies, and birds. But the gamble is not that simple, and solid moral footing is hard to come by. Like most North Americans, I depend on industrialized systems to grow, process, package, and deliver much of my food, taking advantage of the big machine that keeps agricultural decision making in the boardrooms and laboratories of people who can legitimately claim to be serving the public interest by ensuring food systems security.

Beyond the smokescreen of pesticide review, we all have to answer for the agriculture that is destroying the grasslands of this continent and contaminating our food. The moment you take part in the economy—purchase something, sell something, put money in a bank—you are ensnared in a morally compromising web of commerce, investment, and exchange, the very expansion and productivity of which would be completely impossible were it not for steadily increasing per-farmer food yields. Economic development, rising standards of living, and associated population growth and urbanization are driven by modern high-yield agriculture. Take away the fertilizer, fossil fuels, and chemicals from agriculture and a lot more people would have to be willing to leave the city to grow food.[12]

The day we got confused following Macoun through the Cactus Hills in the summer of 2005, Stuart, Mary, and I got a first-hand look at the legacy of carbofuran in burrowing owl country. Leaving the hills, we made our way through the flat land east of the Coteau, which until recently was the centre of population density for the burrowing owl in Canada. Before the crash in the 1990s, the level plains south of Moose Jaw and southwest of Regina still had good numbers of burrowing owls in colonies ranging from two to twenty-five pairs each. By early evening we had visited twelve colony locations that Stuart had marked on his topographical map. At several sites we saw the yellow signs indicating the landowners' enrolment in "Operation Burrowing Owl," a voluntary, non-binding agreement not to cultivate their burrowing owl colonies. At each place, we stopped to scan the pasture for owls and then tried to find the landowners to hear what had happened to their owls. The story was remarkably consistent: "Yes, we used to have the ground owls. We loved havin' them around. They've been gone for some time. Must've been '99 or 2000, somewhere in there that the last ones went. We never changed the pasture. They just dwindled away and then there were none."

Five out of the first eleven former colonies we visited had been cultivated and planted to crops since the owls disappeared. The very last site we checked looked the most promising. It was much larger than the twenty-acre horse pastures we had been seeing, and the native grass was in good shape though grazed enough to keep burrowing owls happy. There were signs on the road warning motorists to slow down and watch for owls, and at two corners of the pasture we found what Stuart said were antennae for monitoring radio-tagged birds. We scanned the grass with binoculars but never managed to see an owl. Later we found the landowner's son, who told us that they still had a few pairs of owls and that biologists were monitoring them. Carbofuran just about finished them off in the 1980s, he said, but they were able to hang on. Now, instead of spraying the pasture, they just cultivate a buffer zone of summerfallow around it to keep grasshoppers from spreading to cropland. Before we left he said he wanted to protect the pasture somehow so that future landowners can't cultivate it.

It was the voice of the first farmer, though, that lingered in my thoughts as the day ended. It was a small farm near Drinkwater. When we knocked on the back door there was no response. Stuart's rule for finding farmers at home is that if there are two or more vehicles in the yard there is going to be someone in the farmyard even if no one answers the door. There was only one vehicle, but after a couple of loud "halloos" from Stuart, a figure appeared across the yard, carrying a five-gallon pail.

We introduced ourselves, and the farmer, in his early seventies, said his name was Dave. There was gentleness in his smile and voice, and he looked like a man who finds a reason to be outside every day of the year. That day the reason was a couple of hungry pigs. As Stuart told him we were checking up on the "old burrowing owl sites," Dave's face changed. He shook his head slowly. "Oh, yeah, I used to have lots of 'em," he said. "They disappeared four or five years ago, I guess. I put signs up because a couple got hit on the road. We had those boxes for them. People used to come and band the little ones every year . . . and I just don't know. For some reason they just . . . disappeared."

He said he wondered about the badger-proof nest boxes the Operation Burrowing Owl people had given him, whether he should dig them out, clean them up, and install them again.

"Every spring I listen for them, wait to hear that *cuckoo, cuckoo* noise they make. I just really—I just loved those little birds, y'know. I'd be haulin' manure and they'd be there hopping up and down . . . Their heads would turn to follow me and I swear they'd go all the way around. . . . Jeez, it was sad when they didn't show up that year. I wonder why."

He looked up at us, hoping for some kind of explanation, and we just repeated what he already knew: it was the same all over.

Burrowing Owl

Burrowing owls often seem to be able to put up with people and their messy, above-ground habitations. Farmers sometimes reminisce about the pair that roosted on top of the chicken coop or the one that used to fly over the yard just to torment the dog. Several small colonies once thrived within the city limits of Regina and Moose Jaw. In 1978, the last colony on the northwestern edge of Regina disappeared when the city parks department converted a piece of land into a park. Moose Jaw has tried hard to hold onto its last colony of wild burrowing owls, which once nested inside an abandoned horse track on the exhibition grounds. The city cobbled together some private and public funding and built a burrowing owl interpretive centre onsite, where several captive-bred owls are kept to help educate people about the species and its decline. Tourists from the Trans-Canada Highway stop in and see the tame owls up close and then peer through a blind to get a glimpse of wild burrowing owls nesting inside the racetrack. In the spring of 2006, however, the last wild pair failed to return.

As wonderful as it is to have burrowing owls in town or at the edge of the farmyard, the causes of proximity between a wild creature and built environments, as well as the creature's responses to that proximity, can easily be mistaken for tolerance, curiosity, or even affinity, especially in an endearing animal that has certain antic behaviours. The dwindling colonies in prairie towns and cities were attracted to a few scraps of grass with the right conditions for nesting: shorter vegetation on level ground and plenty of burrows from Richardson's ground squirrels and badgers. If the only place they could find those conditions in the sea of cultivated land happened to be a pony pasture next to a farmyard or a school play-ground on the edge of town, that is where they made their last stand. The one bowing to say "howdy" from the chicken coop or backstop was feeling worried about its nestlings a few yards away, and when it "tormented" the dog it was doing its best to drive a predator away.

Without any livestock to keep, most grain farmers in burrowing owl country have found it difficult to leave the old horse paddock uncultivated, even when the soil and the price of grain are both bad. On the fertile clay plains that burrowing owls prefer, the few shreds of pasture that remained into the 1980s eventually became ecological traps, exposing the species to the usual population threats that come with habitat fragmentation: predation from skunks, foxes, and barn cats, poisoning from insecticides and rodenticides used on adjacent cropland, shortages of prey, and reduced genetic diversity.

A spectacular 22 percent annual rate of decline took hold in the 1980s, knocking the Saskatchewan population back by almost 95 percent. Neighbouring states and provinces were losing their burrowing owls too. The descent picked up momentum as the burrowing owl began to follow trends set by human communities in the same landscapes: adults produced fewer young, and those that survived to adulthood chose to go elsewhere to raise their own young—probably to places where there were more of their own kind.[13] Rural Saskatchewan, it turns out, is a net exporter of both young people and burrowing owls: the farm kids heading to Calgary and Vancouver, the owls, biologists speculate, stopping off in the northern United States on their return migrations, to fill in available gaps in suitable habitat and established colonies.

There have been brief spurts of recovery: from 2001 to 2004, the number of owls under Saskatchewan's stewardship program, Operation Burrowing Owl, almost doubled, despite a minor decrease in its human membership, but the general erosion continues both in Canada and in the northern states.[14] With such a rapid range retraction and so many young owls "short-stopping" south of the border, the Canadian population may not be able to pull out of its tailspin.

Chapter Fourteen

LETHAL DOSE

Toward the end of my conversation with Ian Halliday—the man who has been surveying grassland birds on a BBS route for forty years—I asked him if he thought there was a way to bring back the longspurs that had dwindled away on his Brooks, Alberta, route. There was a long pause, and then a careful answer that carried with it the depth of witness of one who has not looked the other way, who has seen what is and then testifies without flinching, without rancour or despair. He said that both he and his BBS partner, William, are retired geologists who worked in the fossil fuel industries. "Geologists take the long view," he said. "The earth has had big extinctions before. This could be another one. No one knows for sure."

I had been hoping for a more encouraging response, but I appreciated his candour. At least he is out there looking and listening. There are naturalists on the prairie who would rather avoid the unpleasantness of grassland bird decline altogether. After a few depressing outings at increasingly silent pastures, birdwatchers just stop going. There's more to see in the city with its artificial woodlands and wetlands.

In 2005, I travelled to the University of Lethbridge and found another Alberta man who has the courage to stand amidst the destruction with eyes wide open. It was early spring and gophers were kicking up their heels all around the long campus building, which spans a major ravine coming off the high plains and plunging down to the cottonwood flats of the Oldman River. The first horned larks flew overhead and, not far away, prairie rattlesnakes waited in their hibernacula for a better angle from the sun.

I had corresponded with Dan Johnson a few years earlier when he was the federal government's top grasshopper scientist—monitoring populations and designing control programs—but here he was at the University of Lethbridge sitting in the Canada Research Chair in Sustainable Grassland Ecosystems.

For the first twenty years of his career, as an Agriculture Canada entomologist at Lethbridge's research station, he would go out to the prairie each spring and summer to assess hopper numbers so that prairie farmers would know what to expect from their number-one insect enemy. When he had spare time he would study the relationship between grasshoppers and other elements in grassland ecology. Some of his work related to grassland birds and demonstrated that longspurs in particular rear their nestlings almost exclusively on the small, early-season varieties of grasshopper. He has unpublished data showing that these particular species of grasshopper virtually disappear when native grass is ploughed and seeded to non-native grasses, such as crested wheat grass. At the same time, some of his work at Agriculture Canada was educational. For most farmers, the only good grasshopper is a dead one, but Dan has tried to show people that many species are utterly harmless and don't eat crops. He devised some simple rules of thumb to help farmers keep an eye out for the ones that cause crop damage and not be alarmed at the ones that don't. He listed them off for me with an alacrity that comes with much repetition: "If it clicks or makes noise of any kind, it's not a pest. If it has coloured wings, not a pest. If it is a large grasshopper alive before June 1, not a pest."

During his tenure at Agriculture Canada, Dan did all he could to help policy-makers shift from seeing grasshoppers as pests that must be annihilated to understanding their central role in healthy, sustainable grassland ecology. He wanted to develop management regimes that would curb certain pest species with a minimum of damage to other insects and to the living communities on and around farmland. He would propose projects to his superiors but the answer was often discouraging: stick to grasshopper forecasting and to figuring out the cheapest way to kill them when they reach pest levels.

"I'm glad to be out of there," he said as we sat in the student cafeteria on campus. "Ag Canada is a very strange place." He said he came to see the department as incapable of taking an ecological perspective on farming, despite rhetoric to the contrary. Their policies are driven by economic imperatives that regard natural systems as obstacles to be overcome. Joining the University of Lethbridge's department of geography has given him the chance to look for ways to make our use of grassland more sustainable over the long term.

Yet, even in a research chair dedicated to sustainability, a scientist is limited by the problem that keeps a lot of good work from seeing daylight: funding. Dan has much more freedom to begin piecing together the story of how healthy grasslands function and how human activities interfere, but like most university scientists he relies upon dollars from industry or federal funding agencies.

"I have all kinds of questions I'd like to study, examining the effects of agricultural practices on our grassland ecosystems, but who is going to fund it? No one will pay you to develop grasshopper management methods that can't be packaged and sold for a profit."

Agribusiness is not interested in studying the effects of farming on grassland ecologies, and Agriculture Canada is reluctant to sponsor any program not endorsed by the industry. He makes regular proposals to the federal funding agency for the natural sciences, known as NSERC (Natural Science and Engineering Research Council of Canada). Most are turned down. In 2002, while still at Agriculture Canada, Dan led a team that proposed a comprehensive research project on sustainable alternatives to grasshopper insecticides. They hoped to get the approval of provincial agencies and other funding bodies. He showed me a copy of the proposal, which features a set of projects that fit together in an overall collaboration of the best research into alternative methods of minimizing crop damage from grasshoppers. With twenty years behind him, studying grasshoppers, detecting concentrations, and learning the life histories of pest species, Dan was ready to take the next step and transform grasshopper control on the northern Great Plains. He had a team of the right people and a plan that included research into new biocontrols and disease agents, edge plantings to discourage grasshoppers, and bait methods to be used in hot spots to destroy local concentrations before they get out of hand. The project was rejected by all funding agencies. Here is one response he showed me: "This proposal is not identified as a priority for funding at this time. There are too many outcomes outside the control of this research, the methodology is weak, and no new solutions are identified as possible outcomes."

Every proposal Dan has made to research safer and improved control of grasshoppers has received this kind of response from the funding agencies. He told me that now that he is at a university he has been able to study the way pesticides affect non-target species, including grassland birds. This got my attention, along with some research he has been doing on the "sublethal" and indirect effects of pesticides.

For many years I have been hearing from the anti-pesticide lobby that one of the great shortcomings of the PMRA and its American counterpart in the Environmental Protection Agency is that when they study the risks of a pesticide, they restrict themselves entirely to direct and lethal effects. If sixty-three sage grouse die in a small Idaho alfalfa field sprayed with dimethoate, as they did in 1986, the kill gets duly noted. Meanwhile, several hundred more sage grouse and other animals in the area may fail to breed successfully; their young may die at unusually high rates before fledging; both young and adults may become more vulnerable to predators for a period; they may experience a serious disruption in their endocrine and immune systems; and all of these effects may be compounded by the chemical's conjunction with other toxins in the environment. Some or all of this may happen, but no one notices. Long-term population decay caused by pesticides is never even considered by the approving agencies, let alone studied.

There are reasons for this omission. Sublethal effects and population decline from pesticide use are notoriously difficult to prove, especially with modern chemicals that break down faster than first-generation organophosphates such as DDT and dieldrin. Dan told me that a bird can die of poisoning but show no trace of the chemical that killed it, unless the carcass is found quickly. Even so, the dose required to kill is many times greater for the modern, fast-degrading poisons used today. (Toxicologists call it LD-50, referring to the acute dose calculated to kill half of the test population to which it is given. They express the rate in milligrams of the poison per kilogram of the victim's body weight.) It seems fair to assume that the cholinesterase inhibitors that remain on the market today have some serious sublethal effects on birds who eat contaminated insects or who are sprayed directly. Summer is short and the life of a prairie bird is unforgiving. One or two days of impairment—the typical dizziness, nausea, blurred vision, and shaking caused by these pesticides—might be enough to give a predator the upper hand or to chill neglected nestlings in cool or wet weather.

Then there is the question of endocrine function and immunology. We have no idea what long-term exposure to agricultural chemicals does to the thyroid, adrenals, and pituitary glands of human beings, never mind other creatures. These chemicals, alone or interacting with one another, may be suppressing the immune systems of birds and other animals and making them vulnerable to disease. No one is studying what happens to the health and reproductivity of birds after officially approved farm chemicals go through their bodies, which are already carrying a load of the same cocktail of DDT, PCBs (polychlorinated biphenyls), lindane, benzene, and other persistent wonders of modern chemistry known to be causing tumours in the one species with access to cancer treatment facilities.

Finally, there are the indirect effects of herbicides and pesticides. Eliminating the insects and weeds that birds use as food and habitat is the most obvious direct effect, but what are farm chemicals doing at the foundation of prairie life, where soil microbes create mysterious webs of interrelationship with invertebrate and plant communities that we cannot begin to comprehend?

All of these sublethal and indirect effects must be considered if we are to choose technologies worthy of our goal of feeding ourselves without passing on undue costs to grassland communities. The results from Dan's studies so far have been inconclusive at best. By the time I left Lethbridge, I could see that it was not merely lack of funding that makes it difficult to come to terms with what pesticides are doing to us and the birds. Even in a world with hundreds of well-funded Dan Johnsons, there are limits to what science can say conclusively about cause and effect within chaotic systems. The bewildering and paradoxical web of ecology into which any given toxin is introduced—whether it is the human body, a spoonful of soil, or a community of interdependent organisms—does not yield readily interpreted results to an instrument as blunt and logarithmic as the scientific method. Science is good at proposing reductive, linear, cause-and-effect scenarios and at making predictions that can be tested under controlled laboratory conditions. You want to find out if a pesticide will kill birds, so you get some pheasant chicks and spray half of them with a set dosage and leave the other half unsprayed. You do it in a lab so you can control all conditions—climate, food supply, other pathogens—and observe the subjects with a minimum of influence. Graph the results. Lab work will prove if the toxin suppressed levels of cholinesterase in the birds that died and in the survivors. More graphing. This is the kind of yes–no question that is popular in boardrooms and courts of law. It gives executives, legislators, and bureaucrats something they can use to back up a policy. Exploiting the public's respect for science, they can then use phrases like "science-based" to legitimize their decisions and play both sides of the line of provability to make science say what they want it to say: the best science available "proves X" or "cannot prove Y."

Yet most scientists know that at some level this is all a charade. The actual, multi-dimensional mystery in which birds live, rear their young, and die is nothing like a laboratory, and the very act of eliminating factors guessed to be extraneous to the question at hand renders the results suspect. Ecosystems are borderless, chaotic, and ultimately unfathomable. Much of what happens in grassland is tied to organisms and processes in the soil that are at best poorly understood. As Josef Schmutz, a biologist from the University of Saskatchewan, once said to me, in grassland it's never A causes B, it's A may cause B in situations where C and D are present and as long as E is not happening, except when it is a year of F.

Many researchers keep their sanity in the midst of such complexity by putting on blinders and focusing on a few simple questions about a single species or relationship. Others working in industry and in government regulatory agencies may never raise their eyes above the near horizon of their work to face its contribution to processes that hurt the life around and within us.

I may feel reassured when government or corporate scientists find the courage to speak out against abuse and corruption in their organizations, but at the same time I know I cannot expect science alone to solve problems that reach well beyond the personal cowardice and ethics of a few technicians. We have already handed over to science—or what we think of as science—far too much of our communal and moral responsibility for the way we treat our bodies and the earth. Technologies developed by science dominate the way we live, travel, work, play, think, heal, entertain ourselves, and tell our stories. Do I want to rely entirely on technology for my wisdom, my judgment, my understanding of what it means to be alive? Should I expect science on its own to regulate the relationships I believe to be holy—between the individual and the community, between the body and the earth, between creatures and the rest of Creation?

Scientists, technologists, and engineers are no more to blame than the rest of us. They are our hirelings and do what we ask—namely, to find any means they can to serve our ends: feed us, make us wealthy and comfortable, entertain us, and prolong our lives. We may drag a scientist with some data into the daylight to explain why we must do what we must do, but the justification process itself, while it may be bad ethics or philosophy, is not science, good or bad. The incongruity between what we want to achieve and how we achieve it runs deep in human civilization, and the Age of Reason has only widened the chasm with some new tools.

The scientists I have been speaking to about birds and the doctors I have been speaking to about Karen's breast cancer want to be regarded as authorities in their respective fields, but I see them shrink from the priestly role, the false agency over life and death, and the task of continually justifying imperfect means by pointing to the ends. While they may believe in their research and methods, and while they may possess an understanding of the problem and a suggested way to treat it, they suffer under the pressure of having to reduce, explain, and solve that which ultimately cannot be reduced, explained, or solved. Eventually, there comes a moment in the conversation when I sense that, in taking the path toward fixing the messes we make, they have been distracted by a kind of pragmatic despair, a resignation to the laziness of humanity that has become their dispirited guide. They know that we want them to do the right thing—heal us, feed us, make us safe and comfortable, save the earth—but they can't recommend the right thing being done the right way because the right way might mean we all have to take more responsibility for the health of our bodies and the earth. A doctor who has seen the bad dietary choices of diabetics and a biologist who has attended "stakeholder" meetings in a land-use conflict know what is considered "realistic." Make us better, feed us, save our wildlife, but only if it doesn't require any change, work, or sacrifice on our part. We don't want to pay higher prices for food, don't want to give up bad food, and certainly don't want to lose our right to consume, purchase, and travel with impunity, so you'd better find us some realistic win-win solutions.

Whether it is biology or medicine, science is showing us that the effort to remake the world in our own image has been costly. Even if the best science cannot link exact cause to effect, even if the costs borne by nature and our own flesh are too hidden and deferred to be precisely identified, by now it should be obvious that the bill is coming due.

Toward the end of our visit, Dan told me a story about his entomology professor being called in to identify a large grasshopper preserved in a time capsule that had been buried beneath Winnipeg's city hall in the 1870s. To his amazement, it was a Rocky Mountain locust, North America's only true locust. The species suddenly and mysteriously went extinct in the early twentieth century, but there it was along with a miscellany of bric-a-brac from early settler life on the Canadian prairie. Given the commonplace nature of everything else in the capsule, it is possible that the locust was something familiar to settlers from the region.

No one laments the loss of a plague locust—some flights across the plains were estimated to have numbered in the trillions—but it may have played a central role, along with fire and the buffalo, in renewing the health of grasslands from time to time. The historic irony of the Rocky Mountain locust is that, while it may have been inadvertently wiped out by farming—entomologists speculate that it bred in the same fertile river-bottom land that settlers put to the plough first—it is the one creature whose sheer magnitude and grazing power might have reined in our agriculture and forced it into a more humble covenant with grassland. Whether we regret its extinction or not, its rapid disappearance long before the age of pesticides should make us consider the vulnerability of insects to changes brought on by agriculture.

According to Dan, the overall species assemblage for grasshoppers has changed entirely in the last seventy years. He discovered the change when he took grasshopper records from the Lethbridge agricultural research station in the 1930s and 1940s and put them on a computer spreadsheet, along with recent records from the same region. When he sorted the data by year and abundance, the species list did a complete flip. Grasshoppers that were most abundant in the 1930s and 1940s are now the least common, and species that were uncommon are now the most numerous. What this inversion might mean for grassland or its birds is anyone's guess. We could dismiss it as part of long-term cycling in grasshopper populations but, given the radical changes the prairie has undergone in the past seven decades as farming shifted from peasant subsistence to agribusiness, we have to at least consider the possibility of human causes and then ask what else such an overturn in the species assemblage might affect. Any other response is to look away yet again for something more pleasant on which to settle our gaze.

Science provides some of the testimony, gathering the evidence of bird decline and examining the mechanisms of decay and dysfunction in a species' population, but if we choose a comfortable blindness over moral courage, the data, no matter how impressive, cannot make us see. Beneath the aspirations of biology, of all science, there is the power of a deeper way of knowing, a knowledge that has intuitive and moral dimensions too important to abandon merely because science is unable to provide incontrovertible evidence. Each of us knows that it is not good to kill creatures wantonly. Each of us knows that it is not good to pour poison on the land that feeds us. Any child can tell you these truths.

We have made this land and ourselves unhealthy, justifying immoral means—pesticides and other abuses of the earth—by pointing to the ends: high-yield agriculture, low-cost food, and the economic growth these offer. Questions worth the intelligence and time of our biologists and ecologists would fall out of the larger moral questions we have been avoiding as we push the prairie toward its own lethal-dose rating. How do we live within the limits of the prairie? What can we do to restore our health and the health of the land that welcomed our ancestors?

One day in July, just after Karen's diagnosis, I was walking from the building we use as a community kitchen at Cherry Lake. It's an old machine shed covered in layers of clapboard and the banana-board panelling people installed in their rumpus rooms in the 1970s. Its virtues, apart from providing space to feed thirty people, are the large garage doors on two different walls that allow us to watch the light change over the lake and hillsides as we prepare meals or wash up afterwards. We leave the doors open all day in pleasant weather, and it has become common for barn swallows, bats, and hummingbirds to fly in one and out the other, pausing on occasion to perch on a bookshelf or light.

As I left the building through one of these doors, two barn swallows shot out ahead of me low over the grass like small escorts, their shoulders shining blue back to the sun. There were three swallow nests on the shed, each bursting with young birds, and below one of them a pair of house wrens flying in and out of a knothole in the clapboard siding to feed nestlings somewhere inside the wall.

There were birds all around me, but they moved vaguely on the other side of the cloud of gloom I was wading through. A knot of fear, sadness, and anger had taken hold of my chest, and the loveliness of the day only made it tighten. Such a day was always the backdrop for my dreams of Karen and me living all summer at Cherry Lake after the kids grow up: tending a small garden, reading on the porch, hosting friends and grandchildren. Now came this reminder that even simple dreams can't be guaranteed. I tried to push away the emotion by watching the birds right there in front of me, vivid and intent on rearing their young. An eastern phoebe carrying a moth in its bill paused atop the goldfinch feeder on its way to a nest under the eaves of another building. On the lake there were small flotillas of canvasback and families of bufflehead. Swinging through the air above the yard were dozens of insect-hawking tree swallows. A Forster's tern was heading back to its nesting lake several miles across the pasture land, carrying a single fish in its mouth. On its way it would pass over grassland sparrows and pipits walking through grass toward their nests, bearing beetles and a few hard-won grasshoppers.

The brief and elegant lives of these beings break in upon our slumber like a gentle tapping on the shoulder. We wake up to wonders in our world just in time to learn that they are disappearing and, what's more, our sleep is to blame. A toxicology report on any one prey item carried by these birds—a fish, a grasshopper, a moth—

would show only the smallest traces of the persistent chemicals we have unleashed upon Creation. A similar breakdown of Karen's breast tissue and the milk she fed our children would list much higher concentrations of the same contaminants: dioxins, PCBs, DDT, benzene, flame retardants, and other endocrine disrupters and estrogen mimics.

All human breast milk contains some or many of these toxins, but the risk assessment logic used to approve their application also determines how to treat the patient whenever someone receives a carcinogenic message from the unintended consequences side of the numbers game. The kind of thinking that got us into this mess is put to work in getting us out, or at least in weighing the costs and benefits of treatment.

The oncologists we met with used a computer model to estimate Karen's risk of "negative outcome" (death or relapse) without chemotherapy and hormone therapy, compared with the benefit (reduced risk) of taking these therapies. They also gave us figures on the risks of side effects from the chemotherapy, which is a kind of regulated poisoning of the body. The doctors were always gracious and meant to reassure us, but each time they pointed at a graph or referred to the statistical risk-benefit models, I could not help thinking of the same mathematics being used to justify dangerous substances without really accounting for how they will behave and react within the full interchange of life cycling from one organism to another.

Doing science, whether you are fighting cancer, increasing farm yields, or figuring out bird decline, is so often about controlling nature, which of course is the very fountain of all that resists control. Any control we exert is illusory and brief. Eventually, the pine forest builds up enough fuel and the fire is far bigger than it would've been if we had allowed natural fire; the levee gives out in a hurricane, the plutonium builds up in someone's bones, the bacteria outsmart the antibiotics, and the soil becomes exhausted. Even the science of conservation, in its efforts to "manage" land, operates under an assumption that people control nature. I have heard environmentalists say that it is time we face up to the fact that wilderness is all but gone, and virtually all ecosystems are now under human management. To say that all ecosystems suffer under human influence is one thing; to argue that the earth is now under human control is quite another. Control implies a degree of skill, a mastery of technique to produce a desired effect. The record of Western civilization's orientation toward nature has shown all the control of a muddy-fingered child facing a white wall.

We know just enough about the way nature works to foster the belief that we can manage it by messing around with genes and sub-atomic particles, by raising dams, inventing pharmaceuticals, vaccines, and pesticides. In a person, outlandish delusions of control arise from too much faith in one's own understanding, wilfulness, and ability to influence the world outside one's self. The control freak mentality that dominates government and corporate decision-making likewise places too much faith in the powers of the human mind, in reasoned self-interest unconstrained by any submission to, reverence for, or reciprocity with the numinous mystery behind Creation.

If we can't turn to science alone to heal our bodies, save the birds, spare us from global climate change and every other ecological calamity, where can we turn? That we have to ask ourselves this question at all defines just how far we have given ourselves over to the idols of rationalism. From inside the cult, we can't conceive of an alternative to the technological, data-driven way of life, even though we are discovering that it is a way of death.

I am as subdued by the dictatorship of reason as the next person. The alternative therapies that people have recommended for Karen instead of chemotherapy and radiation seem like a regression to a faith for which I am ill-equipped. Karen, struggling to make her own way through the expectations and fears of those who love her, has chosen to take the poison and the radiation—the numbers are just compelling enough—but she has also decided to follow a path that will complement conventional cancer treatment with acupuncture, herbalism, homeopathics, and changes to her diet. Perhaps even more important, she has opened up everything in her life in a renewal that is sometimes gentle and prayerful, sometimes angry and tearful. She's trying to unearth lost or hidden dreams, to be still enough to hear the voice of God in each day, and to see where, beyond fear and self-preservation, the spirit is calling her.

As I watched the swallows and terns, the late-afternoon patrol of nine turkey vultures drifted by on updrafts rising from the far hills. Other birds are declining but this one is returning in numbers not seen since the bison were erased from the plains. Stuart is delighted with the comeback and has started Canada's first turkey vulture wing-tagging and migration-tracking project. He tells me it's the availability of food and an adaptation to new nesting sites that have made the difference. With white-tailed deer everywhere, there are always plenty of carcasses around, but the interesting thing about turkey vultures is their sudden shift in nesting sites. Instead of laying their eggs in caves and brush piles, they have recently taken to nesting in the upper stories and attics of abandoned farm buildings. Stuart, inclined to smile at whatever prairie life produces, sees the return of the vulture as a sign of nature's surprising capacity for recovery and healing. I want to see it that way too, but I have trouble getting past the symbolism of scavengers lurking in the broken windows of houses where farm children once played. They perch there and on the gables of leaning barns like sentinels waiting for the demise of this land and of the extractive culture we have mythologized and blamed by turns.

Later that afternoon, Karen came back from visiting Sister Theresa, an Ursuline nun who runs a holistic healing centre in the valley and has helped many people recover from cancer. She told

Karen that cancer is an invitation to wake up and come to wholeness. Our bodies can usually heal themselves, she said, when we stop
taking in unhealthy things and begin nourishing them with healthy
things. We hear such simple wisdom from time to time but we ignore
it because it is easier to sleepwalk through life, eat badly, and live
inside the poisonous environments we have made. Then, if we are
lucky, the message in disease awakens us in time to hear the truth of
a healer anew and it triggers something in the heart. Our lives, and
all the lives of this land, depend on just such a change of heart.

Loggerhead Shrike

A long way from water, on the top wire of a barbed wire fence there hangs a frog, skewered on a hook like meat in a cold locker. Forty years ago, a farm kid on the way to school would have known the cause. The "butcher bird" or loggerhead shrike is somewhere nearby—a masked songbird smaller than a robin but with the hooked bill and habits of a raptor. Shrikes are songbirds with a taste for the flesh of their fellow vertebrates, though they will eat larger insects too. The prairie loggerhead shrike hunts from fence and utility lines and from low treetops, pouncing like a small hawk on its prey: birds, rodents, amphibians, and insects. It was once a common sight in grasslands from Texas and eastern New Mexico north through Montana and Wyoming into the Canadian plains. Today there are fewer shrikes all across that summer range. They winter in the southern states and northern Mexico, migrating north in April and May to set up for the summer in pastures or agricultural land with some, but not too many, small trees and thorny bushes.

Pearly grey, with a black Zorro mask, the loggerhead shrike has black wings with white patches at the base of its primaries (the flight feathers toward the tip of the wing). Its rapid, stiff-flapping flight has the buzzy quality of a giant insect, and the resulting blur of black and white wings makes a flicker like an old film running out at the end of a show. With the small, weak feet of any songbird, a shrike uses thorns and barbs not merely for storing food, but to anchor its prey as it tears off bite-sized pieces.

Frank Roy, author of *Birds of the Elbow*, says he first noticed loggerhead shrikes beginning to thin out in the early 1960s.[1] Manley Callin, reporting on his patch of the prairie in the lower Qu'Appelle watershed, marks the beginning of the decline at 1957.[2] During those years, farmers were using organochlorine pesticides, including DDT, at unprecedented levels. By 1959, the use of DDT peaked at 80 million pounds per year in the United States.[3] Canadian farmers were using great quantities of these pesticides as well. It was the 1970s before DDT was banned in Canada and the States, but by then the long-lasting toxins had begun to accumulate in the food web within the flesh of predators. Peregrine falcons and bald eagles were the most spectacular examples, their numbers falling as they struggled to fledge young from thin-shelled eggs. Since then, focused recovery programs have brought these species back from endangered status, but the loggerhead shrike has continued to decline, perhaps because organochlorine pesticides were only the start of its troubles. The carbofuran era of the 1980s and early 1990s may have delivered a further blow, as farmers on the northern Great Plains doused the land to control grasshoppers. Prey shortages caused by pesticides and other toxins may also play a role in the shrike's shrinking numbers. Finally, habitat loss has hurt the loggerhead shrike, though large stretches of apparently suitable habitat remain unoccupied summer after summer. Whatever the mix of causes behind its rapid fall, the prairie loggerhead shrike population has dropped by 80 percent over the last thirty-five years.[4]

Chapter Fifteen

VIGIL

After leaving the old burrowing owl plains on a July weekend of 2005, Stuart, Mary, and I took a detour off Macoun's 1880 trail to visit a landscape he visited a few years later—the plateaus, sage flats, and badlands south of Wood Mountain in what is now the east block of Grasslands National Park. The park and the ranch land that surrounds and crosses over the border into Montana make up one of the largest contiguous pieces of native grassland remaining on the continent. From there we'd be able to stand and look out to horizons of wild grass in all directions. If any place still offered a canopy of song it would be there in the land that drains into the Frenchman River.

Stuart had his own reason for making the detour. The first time he saw sage grouse he was in the Frenchman River Valley long before the park was established. Macoun's visit was in June of 1895, Stuart said. At the time he was beginning to gain some expertise in ornithology and, in his capacity as Dominion Naturalist, was working on his *Catalogue of Canadian Birds*. His account in the catalogue says that he found sage grouse nesting south of Wood Mountain in "the badlands."

We were standing on the rim of those badlands, which are named for the killdeer, a common plover that is now showing signs of decline in prairie regions. There were pipits singing overhead and scolding us from nearby, Baird's sparrows trilling from taller grass and chestnut-collared longspurs all around—easily the most impressive array of birdsong we had come across so far.

In front of us, the terrain fell away into chasms of the remotest land on the northern plains. The sediment of ancient seabeds made light and dark stripes on every eroded landform. Buttresses of soft, grey mudstone arched upward from the valley floor at the base of cliffs and buttes. Sandstone and ironstone capped outcroppings with a dab of rust colour above the fluting of vertical grooves worn into the softer bedrock. Here and there, jutting from the face of a butte or scattered across the bottom of a coulee, we could see harder rocks smoothed by rivers long gone.

Looking to the west of the badlands, we saw vast sage flats covering a broad creek valley with a nap of dusty green. Somewhere in that low forest of sagebrush in the Rock Creek Valley were some of the last sage grouse on the Canadian plains.

Like the smaller and more widespread sharp-tailed grouse, the greater sage grouse enacts an elaborate courtship ritual each spring on ancestral grounds. I had seen sage grouse in other seasons, but knew their mating display only from films and books. Stuart talked about watching them when he was a young man: the males with their sage-green esophageal pouches or neck sacs, white neck ruffs, and fanned-out black tail feathers tipped with white.

"They looked like giants," he said. "You could see them a long way off. And the sound! It travels for miles." With neck sacs full and the surrounding white feathers dangling nearly to the ground in a great ruff, the male approaches a rival on its dancing grounds or "lek" and then suddenly releases the air with a shrugging motion. This makes a loud pop, like a cork being removed from a wide-mouthed bottle.

Stuart opened up Macoun's *Catalogue* and read about the grouse he located in the Frenchman River Valley in 1895:

June 14 we went into the badlands south of Wood Mountain
and had the good fortune to come upon about a dozen
males where there was a little sagebrush. They all escaped
and the whole day was spent trying to find the females but
none were seen. A week later, we reached the valley of the
Whitemud or Frenchman River, a tributary of the Missouri,
where we saw a number of old birds with young under sagebrush and located a nest where the chicks were just emerging from the shell.[1]

In another passage, Macoun mentions the 1874 boundary commission finding sage grouse in the same place twenty years earlier. At
our backs, the length of a football field away, were markers showing
the forty-ninth parallel based on that survey. Following the sage flats
farther south across the border we could see where they continued
into the Bureau of Land Management (BLM) pastures of northern
Montana.

A few weeks earlier, in June, I had been on that side of the border
looking north into Canada and Grasslands National Park. I was travelling with BLM biologist John Carlson, watching grassland birds in
his favourite spot—the upper reaches of Rock Creek. John, who looks
as if he might have been a middle linebacker in college, inherited his
love of birds from his father, Chuck, a naturalist well-known in birdwatching circles. Having grown up on the plains of eastern Montana
and knowing ranch people and ranch country, John is invaluable to
the BLM. Line him up with ranchers and it would be hard to pick
out the biologist. The day we met he was wearing standard ranch
gear: a white Stetson, T-shirt, and jeans with a large belt buckle.

As we bumped along trails in his pickup truck, watching ante-
lope and golden eagles, and talking about his work, I wondered if
his bosses appreciated having a biologist who keeps in touch with
birdwatchers, hunters, ranchers, and scientists to do everything he

can for grassland and its birds. He described a new birding festival he helped launch in the town of Glasgow, to get people excited about prairie birds. When we got to the subject of endangered species, he told me that they've begun to use the status of birds in Canada as an early warning system. Whatever grassland birds the Canadians are worried about today will be the ones American biologists will be working on tomorrow.

When Canada's burrowing owl population crashed in the eighties, biologists south of the border had a hard time believing that they should be concerned about their owls. A decade later, though, the species was in steep decline in northern states. The sage grouse decline has followed a similar pattern, the retraction beginning in Alberta and Saskatchewan and then moving into Montana and Wyoming.

Because the burrowing owl winters in northern Mexico, we've always been able to point beyond the northern plains and suggest that the primary causes are out of our hands. Sage grouse, however, are year-round residents, dispersing relatively short distances but depending on sage flat habitat that has not changed appreciably over the years. Given this simpler set of factors, shouldn't we be able to isolate the primary cause of their rapid decline?

"We know the problem has to be here," John said. "But we're not sure what that is yet. One of the things we worry about is West Nile virus. Sage grouse are extremely susceptible to it. Researchers caught some sage grouse and exposed them to modified viruses of various strengths and every single bird in the trial died. No one has found a live sage grouse with antibodies to West Nile, so that would suggest that every bird that gets it dies."

It seems odd that a mosquito-borne virus would be a problem for a bird that lives in very dry places where stagnant water is rare, but the coal-bed methane industry, which is exploding throughout Wyoming, Montana, and Alberta, has created artificial ponds that are ideal for *Culex tarsalis*, the mosquito that carries the disease. To get at the methane buried beneath the prairie and sage flats, they pump water out of the coal seams and leave it on the surface. The deadly mosquitoes flourish in the artificial ponds, because there are no fish or other predators that might feed on their larvae and pupae.

John speculated on other factors behind the decline. "Sage grouse feed on silver sage, especially in winter. We don't know if the sage is adapted to fire, if the way we've been managing and grazing the landscape has over time altered the ability of silver sage to provide for these birds over winter. There's some evidence to suggest that it's poor chick survival through the summer, but what exactly might be reducing that survival we don't know."

We saw no sage grouse as we moved north along the low hills that drain into Rock Creek, but wherever patches of bare earth showed up on south-facing hillsides we found small groups of McCown's longspurs flushing at roadside. John stopped the truck and we watched some male longspurs in songflight. In ones and twos they rose twenty or thirty feet above a hilltop, giving out a soft rattle as they flapped upward. Through my binoculars I could see a bird open its mouth as it reached the top, spread its wings and tail, and sing its way back down to earth like a small paper kite. There is a sublime clarity to the McCown's exultet that seems exactly right for the high plains, a consummate union of birdsong with the quality of the sunlight and the scrubby grasses that fringe its hills.

The night before I'd found an ink drawing of a McCown's longspur on the desk of John's study where I slept. Like Stephen Davis, John is a biologist who creates images of the creatures he monitors. The drawing showed the longspur at the top of its flight, in that moment we are all afraid of losing—the windblown innocence and joyful purity of impulse that is a bird singing as it hangs in air above miles of grass.

•

Leaving John Carlson that day, I decided I would come back to Rock
Creek the next April, but on the Canadian side of the border, to look
for sage grouse on one of the last remaining leks in Saskatchewan.
Sage grouse are easily disturbed from their dancing grounds so I'd
always thought it best to stay clear, but Pat Fargey, a biologist friend
at the national park, told me of a lek that could be observed from a
hillside more than half a mile away. "But you should go with Chris
Reed," he said. "He's an artist. He comes to the park every spring to
help survey leks. I can set you up."

The name wasn't familiar to me, which was odd because I know
most of the people who help survey birds in this province. "Oh, he's
not from around here. He lives in Toronto, but he's originally from
England."

A few weeks later, I was sitting in the park office listening to a
discussion on how to find a way into the east block of the park when
creeks are running high with meltwater. The map on the table was
a web of dotted and dashed lines, ranchers' trails and creeks that
intersect in places where you can get mired in greasy bentonite mud
twenty miles from the nearest port of call. I might have been nervous,
but leading the discussion was a reassuring voice—British, unassum-
ing, and gentle—blithely stating things like, "No, that trail goes off
this way more. The map doesn't really show it properly at all."

That evening, we drove into the east block from the north, following some of the map's dotted lines. Just before dark our trail disappeared under a creek flowing out of the prairie uplands. Our plan
to come in from the north wasn't going to work. We decided to try
again from the south in the morning. The warden at Poverty Ridge
ranger station would haul Chris and me in to our campsite along
the south side of the Killdeer Badlands and into the east block. For
the night, Chris said we could bunk in an abandoned farmstead that
park employees and visiting researchers sometimes use.

Sitting around a chrome and melamine table in the farmhouse kitchen we ate our boil-in-a-bag dinners, and talked about birdwatching at Toronto's Leslie Street Spit and the tile artwork Chris did for the Friends of Grasslands National Park building in Val Marie.

This is one national park that needs all the friends it can muster. Earlier in the day, I had a hamburger at the café down the street from the gift shop. A man in his sixties, the only other patron, walked into the kitchen and helped himself to the milk. After he sat down at the next table, I talked to him about the park. He said he didn't know much about it; to tell the truth, he said, he'd never been to the park, though he'd lived nearby for most of his life.

Grasslands National Park arose in controversy after years of campaigning by prairie naturalists and biologists who thought it was important to protect one of Canada's last large remnants of native grass. The Saskatchewan Natural History Society, led by Regina botanist George Ledingham, patiently built support for the idea from the late 1950s to the day the park was declared in 1987. A few local ranchers remain hostile to the park—they see it as a waste of good grazing land in a misbegotten scheme imposed by government men controlled by those other urban wastrels, the environmentalists. There is something innately appealing about this perspective and its primary assumption—that ranchers were already looking after the prairie and bringing in outsiders would just put it at risk.

Many, not all, ranchers do a good job of looking after their range, but a grasslands park was necessary for more reasons than protection alone. It has awoken people to the beauty and value of grassland—not local ranchers, farmers, and townspeople, who already knew, but visitors from the prairie region and far beyond. Grasslands National Park will never have the visitation rates and drawing power of a mountain or forest park (and this is one of its many blessings), but the few travellers who take the trouble to place themselves within its austere landscapes usually go home with their understanding of prairie significantly altered. Some, the more contemplative visitors, find a response within themselves that is unmet in other places. In Chris Reed, that response has become a protective care for the park's sage flats, buttes, and stones that seems nearly as proprietary as the attitudes of ranch people who were worried about tourists coming to their world.

As we cleaned our supper dishes in the farmhouse kitchen, I got to hear Chris's story—about a boy from Bristol who now dedicates several weeks each spring to tramp through sagebrush in some of the wildest prairie we have left.

Small-boned, fifty years old or so, with blue-green eyes bracketed by a fair set of laugh lines, Chris speaks with that half-suppressed smile that British people often wear, turning down the corners of the mouth ever so slightly against the upward force of good humour—in a bemusement that qualifies their assertions or observations. In his army surplus jacket, khaki shirt, and plain leather boots, he seemed a bit of an anachronism—not entirely comfortable with the times and culture in which he has found himself. I couldn't help comparing him to other Englishmen who have fallen in love with the prairie—writers like Ernest Thompson Seton and R.D. Symons, and the rancher-naturalists of the Cypress Hills Stuart has told me about.

Yet Chris has none of the cocksure, imperial tone that characterized the first generations of Englishmen enamoured with the west. His self-effacing manner had him discounting the details of his life even as he offered them to explain why he comes to the grasslands each April.

"I was maybe nine years old and my teacher, Mrs. Tyley, was from Winnipeg. She told us about these prairie birds in Canada dancing at dawn, and I was captivated by this idea of the birds, the big wide prairie, and the sun coming up. She had this picture—I can still see it—there was a large grouse and somehow the image really got me. I don't know if it was a sage grouse, but I think it may have been."

At the age of nineteen he moved to Canada's west coast to study at the Vancouver School of Art. Then, in the early 1980s he borrowed a car to drive east with his girlfriend and begin a new life in Toronto. The car broke down on the highway north of the Cypress Hills. Chris remembers the feeling of walking out into a pasture on the other side of the ditch, the sound of the grass in the wind, and birds. By the time the car was repaired and they were on their way again, Chris had already decided to come back to the open prairie.

Over the next few years, returning to Saskatchewan with his girl-friend to visit her mother, he made several trips out to the prairie and began to get to know the grasslands of Cypress Hills and the land slated for the new national park in the Frenchman River Valley. When he first started coming to the park, he would hike for miles through the least accessible sectors and into the adjacent ranchland that would eventually be included within its boundaries. One of the park's first wardens, Mike Wynn, got to know Chris and invited him to help out as a volunteer, surveying raptors and sage grouse in spring.

In those days, a biologist for the provincial government, Wayne Harris, monitored sage grouse leks as well as ferruginous hawk and golden eagle nests in the area. Chris began to travel with Wayne on some of his trips, learning the location of leks and nests in and around the park. They'd survey the raptor nests together and then split up to search for undiscovered sage grouse leks and count birds on known leks. Wayne kept detailed notes on prairie birds, mammals, reptiles, insects, and plants as the spring advanced through April and May. He logged hundreds of miles each year covering not only the southern prairies but the northern regions of the province as well, travelling and spending time in the field, unaffected by the inertia of a bureaucracy that keeps most of its biologists indoors at meet-ings and computer screens. As far as Wayne was concerned, his job was to monitor the non-game wildlife of the province, creatures that received only cursory attention from the hunters and fishermen who ran the department. He rarely took time off, stayed away from the office as much as he could, and scoffed at the notion of hours of work. Wayne Harris was an inspired though workaholic naturalist, driven by his knowledge that almost everything on the prairie is vanishing.

I first met Wayne on a Fort Walsh Christmas Bird Count in the 1980s. He was telling stories to the faithful gathered at a motel in Maple Creek the night before the count. Everyone was laughing but no one more than Wayne, his chest heaving, his eyes shining with tears. I don't remember what was so funny but that was typical of Wayne—whenever we talked, no matter what the subject, he would find something to laugh about. Growing up on a farm near Raymore, Saskatchewan, he was one of Stuart Houston's protégés. He tracked down dozens of great horned owl nests for Stuart and later studied biology at the University of Saskatchewan, becoming a bander himself. As a young biologist with his own consulting firm, and while still running the farm near Raymore, he rapidly gained a reputation as the northern prairie's greatest field naturalist. No one knew the landscapes, roads, ranchers, farmers, and wildlife of Saskatchewan better than Wayne Harris. Unlike most biologists and field naturalists, though, Wayne was a thoroughly rural person. He knew how to sit in a farm kitchen and talk, knew the pressures and worries of farm people, knew what it was like to drive a tractor with hawks following behind to catch the voles stirred up in the furrow. He was a biologist farm people could speak to without feeling rushed or scrutinized in any way. Three years ago, when I received the news that he had been killed in a farm accident during harvest, my first thought was, *Who is going to keep an eye on things now?*

Chris said that Wayne grew more disheartened in his last years as he watched the sage grouse disappear from some of his favourite landscapes. Yet he kept hoping they would find a new lek somewhere. Every spring they would look in new areas of the park to see if the grouse had perhaps moved to a different place.

"I still look for that undiscovered lek. I've been looking for ten years now. It's a bit of a holy grail, this believing there might be a large lek out there somewhere in the miles of sagebrush. It's a big place and I still haven't walked every mile of it. I'm not as young as I was when I started this. These days, just to be safe, the wardens have me radio back to the ranger station each night."

Chris got out a folded piece of paper and opened it up for me to read. It was an email from Wayne in 2001, their last communication. He talks of plans to get together with Chris at "McGowan's"—the farmstead we were bunking in—to check on leks in the spring. He says that of all the old leks in the park only two were active. The others were abandoned. He ended the message on a hopeful note, telling Chris about an encounter the previous spring when he flushed four sage grouse at dawn along a road far from any known lek. He promises to show Chris on the map when they meet at McGowan's in April.

It was late and we had to get up before dawn so Chris packed up his gear: a well-aged camp kitchen, compact but with enough room for a battery-operated espresso whip; a few packets of curried vegetables; maps for a swift-fox release, trapping, and monitoring program he works for these days; and his bedtime reading, *The Life of Samuel Taylor Coleridge*.

In the room where I was to sleep I found the guest book for McGowan's. Flipping back through a few years I came upon Wayne's last entry, a single line: "Looking for undiscovered leks with Chris Reed."

The next morning, Chris and I drove down to the warden station and loaded our gear onto the back of a Parks Canada truck. The east block warden, Archie, drove us out to where we were to set up camp. There was no snow on the ground, but the prairie was frosted white from the cold of a night's cloudless sky. As the sun rose higher the rime would melt, but for the time being the low hills surrounding us sent sharp beams of sunlight back into the crystalline air.

We were about three-quarters of a mile from the lek we had come to observe. It was still early enough for there to be a few birds on the lek and so we listened. First, there came the high *tew* notes of migrating horned larks overhead, and then the unmistakable and peculiar popping noises of distant sage grouse. In my binoculars I could see several males posing like Mr. America contestants near the centre of the lek. Even at a distance, the black fan of tail feathers at the back of each strutting male and the black on their bellies and throats stood out against their white neck ruffs.

After we unloaded and let Archie get back to his station, Chris and I sat down on a hilltop to watch the remainder of the morning's courtship. Chris said that the birds were already winding things down and that we'd see a more intense display at first light the next morning. An hour later, the last hens had flown off the lek to the north and only a couple of persistent males remained. Once they took their leave, Chris and I scanned the flats with his spotting scope to make sure no birds were lingering, and then we hiked down into the valley to look at the dancing grounds.

American researchers were coming in the next week to trap some of the grouse on the lek with cannon nets, and Chris was assigned the task of putting out orange plastic flagging tape to temporarily mark the boundaries and centre. He muttered under his breath as he tied strips of orange to the tops of large sagebrush plants.

"I'm not convinced this is a very good idea. I mean, they're already stressed, the lek is the last large one we have and now they've got to catch them and what? Take blood samples? What for? But what do I know? They're the experts. I suppose they know what they are doing."

He walked me slowly through the axis of the dancing grounds, with the care and light step one might use in a cemetery. He pointed

out trampled vegetation, some tail feathers, piles of sage-green droppings and the strange, black tarry goo the birds also excrete on the
lek. Then he pulled up short.

"What the hell are these doing here?" Chris pointed at a small
pile of rocks. "These aren't supposed to be here. Someone is marking the centre of the lek." The park staff does its best to guard the last
leks, concealing their locations from birders who have been known
to get too close to the grouse. They've caught photographers setting
up blinds on the edge of a lek.

But there is a lot of land for a limited staff to monitor, so Chris
has become an unofficial guardian of the east block. During the
day as he hikes and looks for the holy grail, he returns to favourite
coulees and rock formations, checking in on known hawk and eagle
nests, keeping an eye out for anything out of place. Near our campsite later in the day I found an old 7UP bottle half embedded in the
prairie sod. I reached down, put a finger in its mouth and began
prying it out.

"Oh. Don't do that. Sorry. That's part of the park's human heri-
tage." I could see Chris was only half-kidding. The human history
of settlement and ranch culture is almost as appealing to him as the
natural history. "That bottle was there long before this was a park.
Besides, there's a note in it."

There was a note and I wasn't surprised when Chris admitted
putting it there himself several years ago. He'd already told me about
his first trip to the park, when he scrawled a "sentimental message"
on a two-shilling coin and placed it under a large stone. Every few
years he hikes into the site and checks under the stone to see if it is
still there.

For the remainder of the afternoon we tramped through sage
flats, listening and watching for signs of grouse or leks. We visited the
spot Wayne Harris spoke of in his last email to Chris and saw nothing
to indicate grouse were using the area.

After we returned to our camp just before dark, Chris fired up his backpack stove and we warmed some curried lentils while we chewed on beef jerky. The campsite, on a plain east of the lek with nothing but grass and rocks for cover, was as exposed as a mountaintop bivouac. Here and there, shadows from higher tufts of grass made crescents that looked like wrinkles in the prairie's short-haired hide. My eardrums pressed back against a silence that cupped the air softly against the earth. At dark we walked to the top of a nearby ridge and tried to radio back to Archie at the warden station. No answer, but that seemed right. There was the depth of sky overhead, a gibbous moon slung low over our two small tents, and a prairie that rode off to all horizons. On the ridge holding the radio above his head, Chris was the highest thing in the world, and it felt good to be cut off from the rest of it.

As we turned in, Chris promised that we'd be awoken before daylight by the sounds of dancing grouse. Warming the cold air in my sleeping bag, I worried that something—a sudden blizzard or some other disturbance—might keep the grouse off the lek. Exhaustion took over and I slept until the first percussive pops entered my dreams like a soft pulse coming from inside the earth. It was three-thirty in the morning. I stuck my head out through the tent flaps and saw Chris hunched over his spotting scope. The morning's vigil had begun.

"Can't really see them yet," he said as I settled on the frozen sod next to him.

By five we could see well enough to count birds. We counted and recounted them several times over the passage of the morning. The number peaked at twenty-five, twelve of which were males. Chris was delighted at the small increase from the previous year, and he knew that the numbers would likely build over the coming days. For me, the thrill of seeing the grouse dance was mixed with the sombre truth that this, one of the largest leks remaining in Canada, was small compared to others that have vanished, and that its twenty-five birds represented a significant percentage of the entire Canadian population.

As the sun rose higher, the females walked off the sides of the stage and disappeared into the sagebrush one by one. By eight-thirty, the main group of birds was gone, but three males and one female remained. As long as a female is on or near the lek the males will stay, Chris said. After ten minutes or so, she began walking slowly through the grass to the south, picking her way with short pauses. One male continued displaying and popping his air sacs as he faced the direction of her departure. The other two males simply stood erect in display posture. The active male kept it up, and as the hen got farther away he picked up the pace of his shrugging and popping and scurried to the edge of the lek in her direction. Sixty feet away now, she stopped and looked back to the lek. The active male did his best to engage one of the other two males, to prove himself worthy of her attention. He rushed quickly toward another male and that one reciprocated with the shrug-and-flop move that accompanies the popping sound—though our hearing of it was delayed by distance. The two males faced one another a foot apart and continued shrugging and flopping their neck ruffs. The hen moved farther to the south and, as she vanished into the sage, the third male gave up and flew away. The most active male moved quickly once more in the direction of the hen's departure, even ran a few paces off the edge of the lek, and began displaying in her direction. Then he turned and walked back onto the lek and displayed once more to the only other remaining male. It responded with a perfunctory pop and shrug. Then the two of them stood at ease, lowered their tails and allowed their neck ruffs to settle back into their body feathers. One flew off, then the other. The lek was empty. I took my eye away from the spotting scope to watch the two males flying off to the southwest. A moment later I went back to look at the lek through my binoculars, and then through the scope, but I could not see it. Without the birds, the lek disappeared, as though it never was.

Earlier, Chris had slipped away to check on a second lek nearby that had dwindled down rapidly in recent years. He came back excited. He had found two males where the spring before there was only one.

"You watch a lek decline over the years," he said, "and you wonder how long there have been birds coming to this exact place to dance. And then you think, how long will it be before the last one gives up and never returns?"

Greater Sage Grouse

Sage grouse need large sage flats the way brook trout need streams. They court and nest in sagebrush, live there year-round, and eat sage buds and leaves to survive, especially in winter. Their droppings are the colour of sage, and people who have tasted their flesh say that it tastes strongly of sage.

The northern species of sage grouse is called "greater" because there is a smaller species that lives south of the Colorado River, the Gunnison sage grouse. The greater sage grouse is the largest grouse on the continent, with males weighing in at as much as seven pounds. Early sightings of this bird in Canada indicate that its range originally extended to the sage flats flanking the South Saskatchewan River where it crosses the Alberta–Saskatchewan border and turns eastward. Today, despite the survival of large sage flats in both provinces, the Canadian population is restricted to two small pockets: one in southeastern Alberta and south-western Saskatchewan, and the other in the Grasslands National Park area. Some estimates suggest that by 1970, the continental population had already undergone an 85 percent reduction from a pre-settlement esti-mate of 10 million.[2] Since the mid-1970s, Canada's breeding population of sage grouse has decreased from between six and eight thousand birds to fewer than (some would say much fewer than) one thousand birds. The total number of leks in Canada has fallen by half since 1998, according to the Committee on the Status of Endangered Wildlife in Canada. The U.S Fish and Wildlife Service is monitoring greater sage grouse decline all across its range, and regularly reviews it for inclusion under the federal Endangered Species Act.

As always, the initial loss of habitat from agricultural settlement is the primary cause, but with the amount of sagebrush land remaining fairly stable in the last twenty-five years, biologists believe that something else is hastening the sage grouse's withdrawal from the northern plains. Oil and gas development in sage flats may be a more significant factor than it will be possible to prove outright. West Nile virus mosquitoes breeding in ponds made at shallow gas wells is only part of the problem. Compressor stations, where natural gas from several wells is collected and pressurized into pipelines, make enough noise to drown out the courting sounds of males on leks up to a mile away. Females use the acoustic sounds of males on leks first to locate them and then to choose who they will mate with. Some power lines erected to serve oil and gas facilities cross near nests and leks, giving avian predators an unnatural advantage in an otherwise horizontal habitat with dense ground cover. Roads and well sites destroy sagebrush and introduce weeds, degrading the quality of the habitat and allowing terrestrial predators easier access.[3]

While overgrazing sage flats is not good for sage grouse, the oppo-site—no grazing at all—may be detrimental too. The kind of patchy landscape maintained by wild bison provided sage grouse with lightly grazed places where they could nest in dense cover, as well as more heavily grazed areas where they could forage outside of the nesting season. Greater sage grouse have declined in both grazed and ungrazed sage flats, but it may be worth asking whether the lack of any grazing in the east block of Grasslands National Park has contributed to the decline of its sage grouse population.

The most vexing side of sage grouse decline, however, is the low rate of juvenile survival. Biologists are trying to learn whether it is caused by problems with genetic diversity, predation, disease, or food, but for now all that can be said for certain is that young sage grouse on the northern Great Plains are not making it to breeding age in numbers sufficient to keep the population stable.

Chapter Sixteen

Pathways of Complicity

It was an August weekend in 2005 when Karen and I joined Stuart and Mary to make the final leg of Macoun's 1880 journey. Our turnaround point would be Macoun's own, on the western edge of the Cypress Hills, an outlier of Rocky Mountain foothills ecology surrounded by mixed-grass prairie. Before turning back, Macoun visited Medicine Lodge Coulee, not far from Elkwater, Alberta, where we stayed for our last night.

Macoun's journals tell a story of meeting up with a band of Nakota people who were camping in the coulee. It was a large gathering—he counted 120 tipis—and they had come together to participate in the year's most sacred ceremony, the Sun Dance. For the people of the plains, the Sun Dance is the ritual that places the human, as individual and community, in a full relationship of reciprocity with the rest of Creation. By making prayers and offerings, by fasting and undergoing the physical trials, a person aligns his spirit within the Great Mystery in which we all dwell.

To Macoun, fully a man of his era, the Sun Dance would have been at best an ethnological curiosity of primitive people, at worst a form of devil worship. His journals indicate no particular interest in the ceremony. Approaching the encampment, he and his men found a group of boys shooting arrows at a target. Macoun's men joined the contest and Macoun put up a plug of tobacco as first prize. Viewing it through the lens of all that has happened to the land of the Sun Dance people in the last 125 years, this innocuous encounter between the two cultures feels like a caesura, a pause before the inexorable.

The coordinates of time and space are partly responsible for this reading. This was the Cypress Hills described in Wallace Stegner's *Wolf Willow* as "the last plains frontier." The bison, which sought refuge in the hills and lasted there longer than almost anywhere else, had been gone for ten years. On the eastern side of the hills, Hudson's Bay Company trader Isaac Cowie had shipped 750 grizzly bear skins from his post nine years earlier. A year after that, a band of whisky-fuelled American wolfers came across the border and killed thirty people from the same Nakota nation.

Three years after that, the North West Mounted Police marched west and set up Fort Walsh in the hills to keep order. Part of their assignment was to monitor Sitting Bull and his Lakota warriors, who had crossed the Medicine Line into Canada to seek political sanctuary in the hills.

By the time Macoun and his men were joining the archery contest in Medicine Lodge Coulee, Sitting Bull was east of the hills in Wood Mountain, starving on rations and still hoping to be given a reserve in Canada. (That never happened and he returned across the Medicine Line only to be shot by police a few years later during the Ghost Dance movement.)

Several Cree and Saulteaux bands had already signed treaties and begun the process of moving onto reserves. But here were the Nakota, erstwhile buffalo hunters, in perhaps one of the last great summer gatherings in the Cypress Hills, still the free and self-determined people of the northern plains, survivors of smallpox and starvation, lifting their prayers to the enveloping sky within the prairie's holy circle. Five white men arrive and join in an archery contest. The sun is high, though angling southward now as summer wanes. The pipits overhead sing less frequently, if at all; groups of young longspurs, lark buntings, and meadowlarks move over the grass just beyond the periphery of the lodges' circle. The people gathered there—as their ancestors had and as their descendants surely would—had seen many changes already but could not imagine the even greater upheaval ahead of them. They could not know that the little man who offered a plug of tobacco for the archers would go back east and make reports that in three summers would bring the railway to their world, and with it the hundreds of settlers and the tools that would turn the prairie literally upside down.

Leaving the Cypress Hills on our last day, we skirted south of the Great Sand Hills to see if we could find some of the wetlands Macoun had visited on his return trip. We passed within a few miles of the land my grandfather—the one with the Lee Enfield—homesteaded just before World War I. I thought of a letter Macoun wrote during his expedition. He was writing to his employer, the CPR's Sandford Fleming, to describe a small plot of cultivated land he came across on the prairie—incontrovertible proof that even the poor soils of the dry southwest could be made to grow crops. The farmer was a Métis man with the remarkably prophetic name of Setter:

> Mr. Setter had ploughed up sagebrush and cactus and had sown wheat, barley, and oats and planted potatoes and here on this *Arid* spot were all three quite green—too green for this time of year—and the land which remained unbroken so dry that it was impervious to rain while the cultivated!— it had been ploughed once 2 ½ inches deep—land received the rain and admitted it into the soil. . . . I am now pre-pared to take even *higher flights* than any I have taken before. The matter of soil and rainfall may now be left out of the question.[1]

Macoun may well have drafted that letter once he had himself jumped aboard Fleming's train on his final leg back to Ottawa. Construction of the national railway in the summer of 1880 had reached Poplar Point west of Winnipeg, making its first advances out onto the Great Plains.

Two years later, settlers lit by Macoun's enthusiasm were riding the CPR as far west as Brandon and then travelling by hired wagon out to the homesteads of their dreams. Among them was my great-grandfather, who broke the sod near Souris, Manitoba, and fixed the wagon wheels of Lakota people living nearby. His son, my grandfather, was the one who headed farther west to the Great Sand Hills as a young man to be among the first to try farming in the driest regions of the Canadian plains. Like so many others heading out onto the arid buffalo plains, he had placed his faith in the assessments first made by Macoun. The letter to Fleming shows Macoun's naïve belief—common to botanists of his day—that cultivation worked some kind of magic on a soil, improving its capacity to retain nutrients, receive rain, and support life. This myth survives today in ranchers who "improve" pastures by scratching the surface with a shallow plough. The truth is that when ancient sods are broken, the land's long-accrued store of nitrogen is suddenly released and even light soils will therefore produce a few years of good crops, but the nutrients will be depleted rapidly.

I have a photograph of my grandfather holding sheaves of grain at harvest time in the early 1920s. His smile outshines the sun beating down on his bare head. Right through the decade his quarter section of newly broken land gave him bumper crops. In 1929, things were going so well he made a down payment on a new combine harvester called the "Sunshine Waterloo." The next year the drought hit and his land stopped producing. He never made another payment on the Waterloo and it was repossessed. By 1937, when he realized he was harvesting fewer potatoes than he had seeded in spring, he packed up his wife and five sons, a few cattle, and a team of horses and headed north to bush country.

Meanwhile, on the driest reaches of the prairie, the damage had already been done. No one, not Macoun, not the CPR potentates nor their friends in Ottawa government, could have guessed at the speed and scale of that initial conversion of grassland to cropland from 1883 to the 1930s.

The night before we made the return trip, I dreamed I was standing in a farmyard somewhere in the province's southwest. There were buildings all around me, bare dirt packed from heavy vehicles passing through the yard. I saw a single bird hovering at eye level in the middle of the yard. It was kiting on the wind but completely silent. I looked at its spread tail and saw the extensive white of a McCown's longspur. The back was silvery-grey as it should have been, but the breast didn't have the usual bib of black. Instead, there was a faint mottling there. I stepped closer and saw that in fact the mottling was writing, several words stamped like a brand on the upper breast feathers. It was the name of a land and cattle company. There were other people in the yard and one of them caught the longspur and passed it to me. I held it and read the lettering again. It had changed to a political comment about farm debt and lending institutions. Thinking that the message was significant, something people should know, I looked for paper to write it down but couldn't find any. I let the bird go. Two conservation officers arrived in Smokey the Bear hats. I tried to relate the message to them, but they didn't hear me. I awoke feeling angry at myself for not remembering what was written on the bird, as though having the words might tell me who to blame or what needs to be done.

Finishing the Macoun trip, I felt more confused than ever about whose feet to hold to the fire. I had lost the knack for blaming the "agri-industrial complex" and the comfort that comes with being able to point at something specific and say, "This is what is destroying the land." In its place was the sad confusion of history, imperfectly recollected and interpreted, the inadequacy of science, and a hunger for ways of knowing that are worthy of this land.

Back at Cherry Lake I went for a long walk in the hills and coulees that join our land to the pipit fields. I followed a path that has become familiar enough that I can do it on moonless nights now. Each time I take it, regardless of what shadow might be in my thoughts, I feel an inward turn of something that is hard to name, but "consolation" comes close. I began, as usual, by heading up onto the hills along a trail that the original French settlers used to get out of the valley to the northwest. On the uplands I veered off the trail and circled back toward the lip of the valley where a straight row of stone piles lies hidden in the brush, the boulders encrusted with orange and grey-green lichens. I have been told that burials of this kind are fairly common along the rims of larger valleys, but I stop whenever I pass by, hoping for insight into the lives of those who have lived here longer.

Looking south and east from the burials to the far horizon I could just make out the aspen woods that surround Carry-the-Kettle Indian reserve. The people living there are the descendants of the Nakota Macoun met in Medicine Lodge Coulee. By the time of his visit, the Canadian government was already pressuring the Nakota to accept reserve land away from the Cypress Hills. With no bison to hunt, they were living on handouts from the government, but then Ottawa cut off their rations to force them out of the hills. By 1883, they gave in and moved here to the Indian Head area, eventually settling southeast of town.

The burials at my feet would have predated those events and may well be from the smallpox outbreaks of the early 1800s, when Nakota people died in the thousands. Their bones were scattered on hilltops wherever fever-crazed victims came for the cooling wind and then died. History books say the "Indian Head" in the name of this creek and the prosperous farm settlement north of here refers to a skull on a hilltop, but over time the skull was fleshed out by settler nostalgia and commemorated in an ersatz sculpture with headdress that greets travellers on the Trans-Canada Highway.

The thin whistle of a Swainson's hawk overhead started me walking again. I headed down into the valley and followed another settler trail south to a remote amphitheatre of hills hiding the remains of a homestead where a Belgian family lived for two generations. Arriving in the early 1900s, they piped water from a nearby lake to irrigate market gardens, trucking flowers and vegetables into Indian Head to sell. I walked down a long row of mature white spruce lining the lane that leads to the homestead. Stopping at all the usual places, I stared down into the stone cellar, and into the stone well, checked out the remains of the barn, looked for the old water tower. What nefarious scheme from another era swept these good and industrious souls from their haven? Was it rural electrification? School district consolidation? Surely if I honour the life of these people and decry the processes that ended their stay here, then I will not have to face my own share in those processes.

Nothing worked. The comforts of reaching back to other times and cultures were gone. The burials, this homestead, like so many other monuments around here—the cemetery holding the bones of the French and Belgian settlers, the rusted farm implements dragged up onto the last shreds of unploughed land—have all been tainted by the same myths that have us hailing tourists with roadside replicas of Indians in headdresses.

Seven thousand years of living with the grassland and its creatures has been sacrificed to make way for a civilization that skins the earth alive. Like most people, I can only take small draughts of my anterior responsibility for that founding sacrifice, my ancestral connection to it, and my continuing benefit from it. Having failed to dissolve the truth in the tepid waters of a more honourable agrarian or indigenous past, I turned to go back to the cabin and headed up onto the prairie again.

Minutes later I was on a hillside looking back at our yard. I could see the expanse of brome grass and absinth weeds masking a long rectangular scar where a trailer housed the previous landowners for twenty years. Beside it is the corral where they wintered their cattle. The man and woman who raised three sons in the trailer during those years grew up themselves on local farms. The cattle they kept here were a source of some income and a link to the subsistence farming of their childhoods, but they had off-farm jobs too: he at the local no-till equipment manufacturer, she at the senior care facility in town. Then came the mad cow disease scare of 2003. The United States closed the border to Canadian beef and the price of steers and heifers fell sharply. Small cattle operations on a narrow margin were the first casualties.

I thought of the day we first came out to visit the owners. It seemed like something might be forcing them to sell, but no one said anything and we didn't want the guilt of knowing. The woman was friendly but politely refused to discuss selling. Her husband seemed recently to have talked himself into it. We compensated for our troubled consciences by agreeing to his price without haggling. A few months later we learned that the beef market crash had pushed them toward financial trouble, forcing them to sell the cattle and their land.

That fall, I was out walking in the hills on the south side of our property and stood on this same hillside looking back across Cherry Lake to the yard. We were to take possession in December, but the couple were still living there with their cattle. I saw the woman sitting on the stoop of the trailer with her dog. She stood and began to call the cattle, which I could see a half mile to the east in the valley bottom. Slowly, the cattle stirred and began moving in a line back toward the yard and the corral. She jumped on a quad and drove out to meet them. The memory of her leading the cattle back to the yard that day does not contain the whole story of their twenty-year tenancy on this land, but it came to me as a vivid reminder of my own share in the economic inequities that drive land prices higher and make it harder for rural people to continue farming on a small scale.

I walked back to the cabin and saw as though for the first time our urban-refugee efforts to deflect blame and assert our own innocence. I crossed the yard and passed the sign declaring that our land is now safely under a "Prairie Stewardship" program. The shared kitchen and a new composting toilet, the garbage piles we have trucked to other landfills, and the new fencing we have raised to keep cattle away from the lake and the creek—all of this at one level allows us an illusion of virtue, a false declaration that we are substantially different from others who have owned this land, and that, unlike our cultural forbears, we would never have destroyed the prairie world or pushed its people onto reserves.

Taking in the view across Cherry Lake to the valley that includes our quarter section and the neighbouring land, I felt a familiar desire to lock it all down as though nature could or should be preserved in some static, eternally optimal state where the birds do not dwindle, beavers do not strip a hillside of its trees, lakes do not draw down and become marshes, and pastures stay free of woody growth. The nostalgia of a naturalist is no more helpful than the farmer's fondness for his father's threshing machine. You venerate an earlier, simpler, and less totalitarian engagement with the land, partly because it lets you put on the comforting virtues of that age and shed some of the moral ambivalence of living in a culture that poisons the land and makes it impossible for wildness to thrive.

Thinking back on my summer of looking for grassland birds, interviewing biologists and following Macoun, it all seemed an elaborate way for me to bleed off any residue of ancestral responsibility for what has happened to the great grasslands of this continent. And I began to wonder if you can honour something from the past without denying a complicity hidden in your own descent.

In the end, the trail of our exploring and colonizing testifies that everything in nature that suffers from human agency is a victim of our desire to accuse the other and deflect blame away from ourselves. The first finger we point is at nature itself: too hot, too cold, too dry, too wet, too many gophers, bugs, weeds, deer, geese, mice. Soil comes in for the most detailed accusation: drains too quickly or too slowly; too stony, too hilly, too thin, too heavy. Above all, the land is not enough to give us all the things we need from it. Eventually, we graduate to blaming one another: city people blame farmers for being inefficient, lazy, or dependent on government support; rural people blame the city for not paying the true costs of growing food; environmentalists blame everyone for not eating and growing organic food; First Nations people blame non-Aboriginal people for swindling their land away and destroying their self-reliance.

We are all, at one time or another, the accuser, which is the original meaning of the word "Satan." We are bedevilled by our instinct to point anywhere but at ourselves.

Idealizing the land and the cultures that we have ploughed into the soil as we deflect blame elsewhere is a coping strategy that will not serve us well over the long term. Between 1971 and 1996, the area of land under cropping on the Canadian prairie increased by 28 percent. In just six years, from 1991 to 1996, 1.4 million acres, or approximately 6 percent of the remaining native grassland in Canada, was ploughed under.[2] The sooner we admit that we have all been living off the avails of the original violence done to these plains, the sooner we might begin to accept that we have to learn new ways of drawing life from a land where grass likes to grow.

•

Denying, excusing, looking elsewhere is easy enough until you hold one of the victims in your hand. Once Stephen Davis finished banding the pipit that morning at the Last Mountain Lake bird sanctuary, he asked if Don or I would like to release it. Receiving the bird in both hands, Don looked at it briefly then extended his arms at eye level and opened his fingers. The pipit stayed crouched, as though hands were still holding it in place. It swayed a little, showing no interest in flying. We watched in silence and dread, wondering if it was hurt. Stephen touched it with an index finger—"C'mon. It's okay"—and the pipit took flight, fluttering off weakly a short distance and then diving down into the familiar refuge of the grass.

Later, Don talked about a sense of transgression he felt at that moment, as though we were being clumsy and graceless with a mystery. He spoke of a kind of attention, different from scientific attention, a leaning toward the other without wanting to possess it or turn it into forms of knowledge, a way of listening that might over time deepen our sense of what it means to be in a place.

I have no good reason to believe that great numbers of us will soon be listening to the land, opening our grip and releasing all that we have been holding onto, but there is much in our political and philosophical talk to indicate that we are discovering just how clumsy we have been. At the very least we are beginning to see what suffering we have brought to the prairie by forcing alien and extractive lifeways on its people, places, and wild creatures.

If we were to stop pointing fingers at others, something else might begin to happen. The opposite of accusation, which keeps us scattered, alienated, rivalrous, and deluded, is a humble re-entry into community and creation. There is a healing, gathering force in grassland, and in all natural landscapes, that can bring us together in a circle of shared responsibility for one another and for the health of other beings. Not requiring our management and in fact resistant to our grasp, it asks only that we receive and honour it as an invitation to set aside our orientation toward death so that we might open ourselves to participate in the livelihood of this place. Were we ever to undergo such a transformation, imagine what might be achieved in us, breathed into us, quickened and declared in the life we draw from prairie.

McCown's
Longspur

A female McCown's longspur on her nest can see an intruder coming from a long way off because she is nesting in the most barren of prairie landscapes, where vegetation is down to a few sprigs of grass and rabbit brush. You can walk right past the nest but she will sit tight, relying on stillness and her dull plumage to hide her against the backdrop of a grass tuft, cow-pie, or boulder. Biologists studying McCown's longspurs report having to sometimes lift females off the nest by hand to get a look at the eggs.

McCown's is a grassland songbird that argues for a multiplicity of habitat and management regimes. There are many birds that can nest in taller grasses, but the McCown's prefers thinly grassed pastures and burnt prairie. After a fire or a visit by the trampling multitudes of bison, this bird and the horned lark were both able to move in and nest in a landscape other birds would abandon. Like the horned lark, it survived fire suppression, the transition to domestic grazing, and the cultivation of native grassland by adapting to the nearest thing to its preferred habitat: summerfallow and stubble. Although it is an endemic of the Great Plains and has a very restricted range, it seemed to thrive into the early 1990s on cropland even though farm machinery regularly destroyed its nests.

McCown's once bred as far north as Saskatoon, Saskatchewan, and the north end of Last Mountain Lake. Until 1993 or 1994, it could be found year after year doing its characteristic "butterfly" songflights above the same summerfallow and stubble fields on the flat clay plains surrounding Regina. Then it suddenly vanished from the area. In *The Birds of the Elbow*, Frank Roy reports a similar trend in the Elbow region during the early 1990s. He says that McCown's longspur was locally numerous on certain stubble fields and summerfallow until 1994. His book was published in 1996, but even then there were signs that something was afoot, so Frank commented that "it is possible ... that McCown's are withdrawing from the area."[3] During that decade the species' range retracted rapidly back to the southwest, where small colonies remain on heavily grazed and naturally barren prairie. Although continuous cropping practices have been blamed for this recent range retraction, it may also have been a case of a species breeding in sink habitat for many years, and the last remnant populations crashing as they exported their few surviving young to breed nearer the centre of their range.

Part Four

THE GIFT REMAINS

Chapter Seventeen

LET THERE BE GRASS

Facing east-southeast in a valley bottom, the porch of our little cabin misses every sunset but works just fine for watching the rise of a September full moon. The one time I got to see it I was alone at the cabin for a few days. I had been watching the first sandhill cranes of the fall passing south over the valley as the sun snuck away in the hills without my noticing. The eastern sky had just barely begun to deepen its blue toward black when it lit up again on the edge of the wooded ridge across the lake where a small platoon of pelicans was fishing in the shallows.

It was a pagan glow, like a bonfire lit somewhere just below the horizon. It came up, a great orange beacon, the hallowed harvest moon of farm country, coloured by the dust of tractors and combines rushing to get the year's crop safely into bins. As it hove to the top of the ridge a shimmering wedge of gold unfurled over the far end of the lake. The pelicans, like the farmers working late in their fields, took advantage of the light and kept fishing. They worked the shoals in unison, dipping and swallowing in a moonlit ballet, stirring up wavelets and leaving a stream of glitter behind them receding toward the far shore's indigo.

I raised my binoculars from the pelicans to the moon now sailing westward. Part of the enchantment that first drew me to songbirds was the thought that they migrate at night, navigating by stars and moon. Sometime in the 1980s, I read an article about people who counted migrating songbirds by watching their silhouettes cross the face of the full moon in autumn. I have tried it myself several times, watching the September moon with binoculars or spotting scope, but I've never seen a stream of warbler and thrush shadows fly past. Once a crow; another time a flock of snow geese. Usually, I quit with nothing more to show for the effort than a headache from staring at the optically magnified light of the moon.

From the cabin porch I kept my binoculars trained on the moon and studied its birthmarks while watching for a bird to come into view. Within a minute a small figure made a transit across the white glare, a single bird moving fast to the southwest. As it passed, I heard its contact note, a soft *tew* that I could not be sure of, but which may well have been the flight call of a pipit on its way to the beleaguered pastures of Texas.

As unknowable as the mind of God, a small and delicate being navigates by moonlight across hundreds of miles. In the movement of its shadow, the vibration of its small voice, there was enough for me to imagine praise for the grass that gave it life.

There is an old story of settlement on the Great Plains that is losing its power these days. When I was a child it was still strong and you breathed it in just by living here. No one said it outright or all at once but you pieced it together yourself soon enough: before we came, there was nothing here, just a few wandering Indians chasing buffalo over treeless barrens. Then our people arrived, planted their crops, some trees, and turned a wasteland into the breadbasket of the world.

It is hard to imagine people ever believing that story, but the less convincing it becomes, the more you hear new variations. Where once it was enough for the land to feed the planet, now it should fuel its vehicles too. If grain fails to produce the required wealth and energy, there are other things than fertility to be extracted from the land. Beneath the comforting myth, though, an older story waits for anyone who will listen. A story that can start in soil or plant or animal or air, that can be told by a beetle rolling a ball of dung on a trail the grasshoppers follow, by harvester ants hauling seeds to their storehouse, or by a sparrow hunting on foot that calls out to let his mate know he is near. No matter who tells it, the story comes back always to the abiding providence of grass binding the world together in a weave as mysterious and intricate as the nest where the pipit broods beneath a green roof. Bearing the scent of the grass it pollinates, the wind lifts the story skyward in the breast of a bird and the bird gives it back again in song.

On prairie, grass abides all things, knows all things, feeds all things. It is the answer to every question, the satisfaction of every desire. It is the solace this land longs for, cries out for in voices that have yet to be silenced, from the gentle rattle of the longspur to the lonely notes of the curlew.

Fall has its bounty of reports on how this or that species fared during the breeding season. By Christmas I have a small file with reports from researchers studying certain birds, and Breeding Bird Survey results. The last two or three years have brought some good news to offset the bad.

In 2005, the Saskatchewan BBS results showed a local resurgence of Sprague's pipits, setting a new record for the number of birds reported per route. Although there is not enough data yet to determine statistically significant trends, the index for Sprague's pipit shows a recent and modest increase.

A year later, Stephen Davis had an update for me on that male pipit we had watched him band. Heavy June rains had flooded out most of the nests on his study plots in 2005, but the next summer Stephen found the same male on a pasture a half mile away. This time, instead of trying to breed in a non-native hayfield, it had moved to a piece of sky and grass on native prairie where it might well have a better chance of rearing some young.

In 2006, Manitoba biologist Ken De Smet reported that seven burrowing owls spent the summer on private land near Spruce Woods Provincial Park. Until these birds appeared, the species had been absent from Manitoba for five years and was being considered for official "extirpated" status.

That same year, a single burrowing owl came to a badger hole on the edge of a zero-till field north of Regina, in an area where none have been seen for twenty years. Though it did not stay long, at the time it may well have been the northernmost burrowing owl on the planet. Another Saskatchewan report mentioned a pair of owls that came in spring to a cultivated field near a former colony that has been reseeded back to grass after a period of cropping.

In 2007, a pair of burrowing owls actually managed to rear a family in a field of durum wheat, providing an example of what can happen when farmers make room for grassland birds. Val Thomas, who farms near the village of McTaggart, began sending email dispatches to *Birdline* when her husband Doyle discovered the owls in spring. While he was seeding the field he stopped to do a bit of repair and heard a clicking sound that was familiar but not from recent memory. Looking up he saw a burrowing owl peering out of a badger hole in the middle of his field. That day he made a sweep around the burrow, leaving a circle "the size of a large room" unseeded in hopes that the owls might stay. They reported the sighting to Operation Burrowing Owl, but no one they spoke to held out much hope for a pair of owls trying to nest in such depauperate surroundings. Val and Doyle kept watching and hoping.

By June, with the owls still in residence and the wheat crop greening up around them, biologists came and snaked a video camera down the hole, finding several eggs. Over the next few weeks, the wheat grew high enough to hide the burrow from view. After much pondering, Val and Doyle decided to install three perches made of lathe to allow the birds to see above the crop. This, they felt, would help the owls hunt and watch for predators. A series of remarkable photographs began to arrive in my email, showing the owls roosting on long stakes that hoisted them above the green broadloom of wheat closing them in.

By July 20, four healthy fledglings had emerged from the burrow and were flying back and forth between the perches to catch bugs. For the next three weeks, Val and Doyle watched from the roadside when the owl family came out to feed at dusk. Not long after that, they left the area in ones and twos to begin their fall dispersal and migration. With the crop now ripe, Doyle returned to his field and swathed the wheat.

I want to believe that if enough people are moved by the faithfulness of grassland birds, by the way they continue to follow the promptings in their blood to make more of themselves, we might find ways to lay out a proper reception for them, to spread a banquet of grassland as near as possible to the original bounty prepared by the traditional masters: buffalo, fire, soil, and weather. It would begin with protecting all the different kinds of native grassland we have, restoring them to health, and then making room for a lot more grass, the closer to native the better.

There are signs that such a reception is slowly being arrayed in parts of the northern Great Plains. Old Man on His Back Plateau is a 13,000-acre tract of native grassland in southwestern Saskatchewan ranched by the late Peter Butala (husband of Sharon Butala, author of *The Perfection of Morning: An Apprenticeship in Nature* and many other books) until he turned it over to the Nature Conservancy of Canada. In the early 1990s, Peter showed me around Old Man on His Back while he was still running cattle there. I saw more McCown's longspurs that day than I have seen in the rest of my life. Flocks of longspurs and horned larks rose up from trailside as we trucked over the hills to look at some of the best-managed pasture on the plains. All that was missing was buffalo and now the Nature Conservancy has fixed that by introducing a herd of plains bison.

Not far away, in Grasslands National Park, most of which had not seen grazing since the park opened in the 1980s, biologists released a herd of bison into the west block in the spring of 2006. At the same time, buffalo meat has emerged from its exotic food novelty status to become a popular health food. A recent prairie newspaper article called it the "new red meat," with one-quarter the fat and far more omega-3 fatty acids than beef. Between reintroduction in conservation areas and the growing bison ranch industry, bison numbers have recovered to half a million, half of which are north of the forty-ninth parallel. Although most of these animals are on small properties that are not being managed to create or conserve healthy grassland, it is reassuring to see bison moving over the land again.

Fire is not a popular tool with private ranchers on the northern plains, though it is sometimes used on state-owned conservation land. Up at Last Mountain Lake National Wildlife Area, where Stephen Davis studies the birds, prescribed burning is included in the grassland management cycle, along with grazing. On the remnants of tallgrass prairie from Kansas to Manitoba, regular burning is even more vital in eliminating woody growth and keeping the prairie vigorous and diverse. On the shortgrass plains of Colorado's Pawnee National Grasslands, the United States Forest Service has used fire to provide habitat for the mountain plover, a southwestern grassland bird that is disappearing from its range.

Even more encouraging are the projects that widen the conservation question beyond individual tracts of grassland to ask how we might improve the health of entire landscapes by developing a shared vision for a watershed or a region. The first tentative exchanges of such a conversation are underway with something called the Northern Mixed Grass Transboundary Conservation Initiative. Government land agencies, conservation organizations, and grassland biologists from Montana, southern Saskatchewan, and Alberta—including Stephen Davis, Rob Scissons, Pat Fargey, and John Carlson—have established this network to see what they can do to restore and conserve the ecology of what they describe as "North America's largest remaining tract of native grassland . . . the last, best hope for survival for many imperilled and endemic grassland species."[1] The landscape they have in mind encompasses both Grasslands National Park and Old Man on His Back, along with the surviving ranchland in the larger Milk River, Frenchman River, and Bitter Creek basins on both sides of the border. So far, their work has been to co-operate on regional planning and programming aimed at species recovery, but they are laying down connections that could, given the right support and inspiration, begin to transform the way we manage grassland and lead to a rebirth of the mixed-grass prairie. Prairie animals including the greater sage grouse and pronghorn, in their regional movement across fence lines, jurisdictions, and boundaries, are asking us if we can begin to see the prairie through their eyes.

Properties managed primarily for conservation, though, represent only a small percentage of the remaining native grassland in North America. The rest, whether privately owned or leased from the state, thrive or suffer by the decisions of ranchers—decisions that in turn are influenced by thousands of economic and consumer decisions made in cities. Keeping the prairie grass-side up, and making more of it, comes down to the quality of that hand-off from urban policy-makers and eaters to the men and women who make their living from grass.

Every time a government introduces an agricultural program with incentives, every time prices respond to events on other continents, there is a shift in the ratio between the amount of land used to raise perennial grasses, native or tame, and the amount of land used to raise annual crops. Today, virtually all meat—whether it is lamb, beef, or bison—comes from animals that are fattened on grain in feedlots, some for a few weeks or months at the end of their lives, others from birth to slaughter. To achieve the marbling and fat that consumers prefer, meat producers have tied themselves to the vagaries of the grain industry. Feeding animals grain causes a whole suite of problems, but keeping hundreds of thousands of acres of former grassland under crop to provide feed grain is the one that hurts plains ecology most.[2]

If consumers began to ask butchers and restaurateurs for meat from grass-fed animals that received only a minimal amount of grain, or better yet, no grain at all, the ratio of cropped land to grassed land would shift in the favour of birds. The more meat that makes it to the dinner plate from animals raised primarily or entirely on grass, the more viable it will be to keep land in grass and convert cropland back to grass. Just as "bird-friendly" shade-grown coffee is becoming a way for people to help conserve rainforest habitat for forest birds, grass-fed beef and bison could become a choice for those who want to help protect grassland bird habitat.

Another change that would help sustain healthier grasslands would be to set prices so that consumers would cover more of the costs paid by the ecosystem in creating flesh from grass and water. That way, ranchers could be compensated for the additional costs they incur in raising cattle in ways that foster healthy native grass-land and watersheds. Stocking rates, grazing plans, water use, and fencing would be designed not so much to minimize the rancher's costs as to minimize costs to the land and ensure its long-term health. There might then also be room for programs that expand and restore grassland while increasing biodiversity on existing grassland.

Josef Schmutz, biologist with the University of Saskatchewan's Centre for Studies in Agriculture, Law and the Environment, and Saskatchewan's co-ordinator for the Important Bird Area program, has done some research in this area of biodiversity, consumer choice, and livestock production.[3] He has worked with people in Saskatchewan's Wood River watershed to see if a producer and con-sumer co-operative might be one way to improve the health of the Wood River as it runs through cropland. One of his studies showed that while most people say they want agriculture to do better by the environment, only members of environmental advocacy groups think consumers should have to pay for it. This may sound discour-aging, but the good news is that there is a sector of people who get it. They may not be the majority, but they could be the leaders in the early stages of a movement that has the capacity to bring producers and eaters together to restore health to our food, rural communities, and landscapes. Joe says he believes we live in exciting times because there is a growing interest in grass-fed beef, organic farming, eating local, and the "slow food" movement.

He makes a distinction among at least three kinds of cattle pro-ducers. First, and most valuable to healthy plains ecology, are the traditional ranchers who use mostly native grass, in which rotational grazing maintains a patchy structural diversity to the vegetation that will support a wide range of grassland creatures. They usually culti-vate a small acreage of land to grow winter feed for cattle and horses as well as to grow tame pasture for spring grazing. There are still a good many of these operations on the northern Great Plains, mostly in areas where the ranching tradition, soil profile, and climate have maintained large tracts of native prairie.

The second kind of producer, the farmer with cattle, Joe is inclined to write off as a loss to the goal of ecologically sound livestock management. Here he includes grain farmers who have some cattle but may or may not have any native grass, and the little they do have is often abused. "The mentality is farming not ranching," Joe says, implying that ranchers have in general been kinder to the prairie than their crop-growing counterparts.

Third, there are the "grass farmers" who cultivate large farms of tame grass instead of annual crops and use it to raise their cattle. Grass farmers who finish cattle on grass and avoid grain altogether make a further investment in ecologically sound agriculture. Joe buys grass-finished beef from a grass farmer near Saskatoon. Land seeded to tame grass may never match the biodiversity of a traditional native grass ranch, but a grass farmer can raise livestock on cultivated land seeded to grass and thereby bring back a significant measure of its grassland ecology, preventing soil erosion and providing nesting habitat for a more adaptive suite of birds. Even better, a grass farmer can easily add another level of biodiversity by mixing native forbs into tame grassland instead of using exotic ones. Better still is to use all native grass and forb seed. Over the long term, if agricultural policy were to foster a new generation of ecologically minded grass farmers who were given the economic stimulus and knowledge necessary to raise cattle on grassland restored to native grass and forbs, the prairie's sandier soils that should never have been ploughed in the first place could be placed back on the road to health, offering some grassland birds new habitat into the bargain.

In as little as ten years you can grow a restored prairie that is a fair facsimile of virgin grassland — not as diverse but a net gain over what was on the land before. These places almost always show improved biodiversity over tame grass fields, and support a range of breeding grassland birds. Returning large tracts of prairie to native cover is the single most important step in halting the decline of grassland birds, but we have scarcely begun to talk about it.

Joe believes that one way to pass on a premium to the right livestock producers would be to have non-governmental organizations monitor and certify them so that consumers would know that the higher-priced beef they are purchasing is helping to maintain grassland habitat for birds and other species threatened by agricultural practices that damage or destroy grassland. Joined to the right tax incentives and the participation of private conservation organizations, people could be eating hamburgers and steaks that help protect and foster more grassland habitat. That kind of purchasing power, used to influence livestock production throughout the breeding and winter ranges of this continent's grassland birds, would make a difference, although Joe worries that some species in rapid decline may not have time to wait for such a broad transformation to take hold.

Conventional wisdom says that the interests of wild creatures are either at odds with or incidental to the interests of people who make a living from the prairie. This holds true as long as farmers and ranchers are working in a system that places no value on natural capital, that encourages them to offload costs to the ecosystem and produce unhealthy food for consumers who do not bear their share of accountability for the well-being of the land and waterways that turn grass into flesh. This dysfunctional system is the one we suffer today, and it is spinning out of control, flying apart under the stress of an imbalance that worsens with every attempt to shore it up with more of the same short-sighted technological and political solutions. Dismantle it, replace it with a holistic ecological model that recognizes where real value begins—in the soil and water and health of our ecosystems—that accounts for every withdrawal or cost incurred by the prairie, and that works with the land to produce healthy food for consumers near enough to know that they are also responsible for what happens to a pasture, a field, or a creek, and then, yes, it becomes possible to *share* the interests of wild creatures living on farms and ranches, it becomes possible to see the prairie through their eyes.

Some rural people, cattlemen and -women especially, have shown that they are willing to participate in such a transformation by laying the groundwork in the Prairie Conservation Action Plan, a partnership of ranchers, academics, and conservationists on the Canadian prairie. PCAP, as it is known in prairie conservation circles, has five major goals and every one of them relates to the sustainable use and preservation of native grass. Ranchers active in PCAP often talk about their role as stewards of the "ecological goods and services" that the larger community takes for granted. It may not seem right to commodify a landscape's water, soil, biodiversity, and aesthetics as goods and services, much less to assume that human control is required to "provide" them, but on our overpopulated planet where much of the land base is used and managed to produce food, fibre, or fuel, it makes sense for all of us to value and pay for agricultural practices that serve the long-term health of the land, and its natural and human communities.

I look at this emerging awareness of the link between what we value as prairie people—the long-term health of the land—and what we produce and purchase, and I let myself hope that it will create a transformational space in which a renewed covenant with grassland can occur. For a prairie naturalist, optimism is almost as elusive as the birds in the grass, but if I am patient enough to let them come into the open I can begin to see other forces that could conspire to form that space. One of the most obvious trends is that increasing numbers of prairie people, both rural and urban, are beginning to sense that we have veered away from the moral underpinnings of growing food by abandoning the small family farm with its mix of crops, gardens, and livestock in favour of large-scale, mechanized, and chemical-intensive agribusiness.

Meanwhile, the countryside is emptying, particularly in the drier grassland regions where growing crops has always been a marginal enterprise. In Saskatchewan, the farm population decreased by 15 percent in five years, from 1996 to 2001.[4] Many of those who remain in these places that should never have been ploughed have been seeding their land back to grass and switching to cattle production in response to rising costs for fuel, fertilizer, pesticides, and equipment.

I've already mentioned the renewed interest in bringing bison and fire back to the grassland as management tools. The thought that there are more bison on the prairie right now than there have been for 130 years is on its own a reason to believe that people are opening up to more ecologically suitable ways of making a living from the land. Another factor that creates opportunity for change is consumers' increasing concern for the quality of the food they purchase— both for the sake of their health and for the environmental and social costs embedded in agriculture.

Just as important as any of these factors is that Aboriginal people on the northern Great Plains, after decades of repression and failed assimilation policies from governments, seem to be moving toward a turning point of their own. First Nations and Métis populations are growing faster than the non-Aboriginal population, and even as the passage of time moves them further from their original lifeways and nearer toward a northern mestizo culture, they are finding their own way to be people of the prairie in the twenty-first century. If that way can manage to bring something of the ethics, grounded wisdom, and reverence of their traditions into modern economics and agriculture, it will help us all to discern what kind of prairie we want to leave to our children and grandchildren.

These are some of the forces that may help to ease off our grip on grassland long enough to allow for something new to arise. However, it would be disingenuous not to consider opposing forces, every bit as real, that hold us back from change.

One of the most immediate threats is the recent resurgence of the grain economy. After several decades of stagnation, wheat prices have shot up to their highest levels in fifty years. Low wheat prices are nothing to celebrate, for they have hurt many farm families and spurred the emptying of the countryside, but they have also helped to slow the rate at which native grassland is destroyed and have encouraged people to seed their cultivated land back to grass. During the 1970s, the last decade of relatively high wheat prices, farmers looking to expand their acreage without buying land got rid of their cattle and began ploughing native pasture even on poorer soils so that they could seed more acreage to wheat. Two factors lie behind the rising prices this time: drought caused by global climate change in many other grain-growing regions of the planet, and government decisions to fight climate change by providing incentives for biofuel production. Biofuels have been condemned by eco-agriculture and environmental organizations for their low EROEI (energy return on energy invested) rating; for the habitat loss they cause as subsidies stimulate growers to convert forests, peatland, and grasslands to wheat, corn, or soy crops; and for the water they waste and the additional fertilizer load and soil erosion they cause.[5]

As I mentioned earlier, here on the northern Great Plains, many farmers in areas with light soil were beginning to seed cropland back into grass. Both American and Canadian governments introduced subsidy programs to encourage the process on the poorest soils. But now, with the demand for biofuel, farmers are looking at the higher grain prices and calculating the costs of finishing their cattle on such expensive feed as well as the potential profits to be made if they stick with or go back to growing grain themselves. At best, higher grain prices will impede the conversion of cropland back to grass. If prices stay high or continue to climb, we will see an increase in the net loss of grassland, both tame and native.

Another factor, related to rising grain prices, is the dominant agricultural policy in the United States and Canada, and its alliance with the agribusiness corporations that buy and sell grain and peddle the fertilizer and pesticides that conventional farmers depend upon.[6] No conspiracies are required; the greed driving "agri-food" corporations harmonizes nicely with consumer laziness (it takes work to grow and prepare your own food) and the short-sightedness of our leaders in government and agricultural research under the reign of two unofficial policies that most developed nations have been following since World War II: one, food should cost consumers very little compared to other commodities and, two, the percentage of gross domestic product (GDP) that comes from a nation's agricultural activity should be as low as possible.

No government official will acknowledge that there is such a thing as a cheap-food policy, but meanwhile North Americans have come to believe they are entitled to hassle-free, inexpensive food, as though it were a constitutional right. People complain about rising prices at the supermarket, never considering that the fruit, vegetables, soy, corn, wheat, rice, sugar, coffee, and meat products they eat in a thousand combinations are coming at prices far too low to account for the embodied social costs to local communities and environmental costs absorbed by waterways, soils, and wild ecosystems in and around farmland. Eating more food grown locally and according to ecologically sustainable practices would require discipline and sacrifice from a citizenry that the marketplace and agri-food industry has rendered lazy, overweight, and self-indulgent.

Despite the widespread belief that food is expensive, Statistics Canada figures show that the percentage of disposable income Canadians spend on food has been declining for decades.[7] Relatively cheap food, along with the associated decline in agricultural activity as a percentage of GDP, has become a measure of a nation's "development."[8] In Canada, as in most of the world's leading economies, the products of farming and ranching have been reduced to a tiny percentage of overall GDP. In fact, it is such a small figure now that it is lumped in with fishing, hunting, and forestry, and even then the figure just barely makes 2 percent of our GDP.[9] In Saskatchewan, supposedly the most agricultural of Canadian provinces, agriculture accounts for 7.4 percent of provincial GDP. The commercial real estate sector, which provides Saskatchewan's urban people with shopping malls, apartments, and office buildings, accounts for 12 percent.

Mainstream economics would have us believe that the more advanced a nation is, the less of its energy, intelligence and resources it spends on growing food. Once a nation has reduced the portion of its GDP coming from food production to, say, 10 percent or less, it can hold its head high among the leaders of the world. Instead of the intimate and sacramental entry of the land into our bodies, honoured in the way it is obtained, distributed, and eaten, food becomes at best a form of recreation, at worst a degraded fuel for the labour units that keep more important parts of the economy functioning.

Another obstacle that would have to be addressed is the innate resistance of farmers and ranchers to anything that looks as though it might limit their control over their property. Having been manipulated with bad agricultural policy for fifty years and shunted to the margins of the economy, the few people who still give their labour to growing food have good reason to be wary when others talk about what they should be doing with the land. Perhaps the most unfortunate and vexing manifestation of this attitude is the widespread belief among rural people that if they report a rare species on their land they will be told by government officials what they can and cannot do with the property. The secrecy fostered by such a myth hampers the effectiveness of public awareness campaigns and makes it difficult for biologists to assess populations and monitor wildlife on private land.

Finally, the Aboriginal population on the Canadian plains, like the non-Aboriginal community, does not often follow the wisdom of its elders. Their political leaders can be as misled by short-term thinking as any other group of politicians, and therefore vulnerable to schemes that owe more to the mainstream model of economic development than to their own indigenous values. The culture of poverty, powerlessness, and dependency that many First Nations people live with from day to day has been fostered over decades of colonization. As long as prairie people believe it will be solved with casinos and golf courses on reserves, nothing will bring Aboriginal respect for Creation and concern for future generations into the daily decisions of band councils and, more important, into the policies of our provincial and federal governments.

There are no doubt more obstacles to overcome than the ones I have outlined here, but they illustrate a range of the forces that countervail the trends favouring transformation in the way we use grassland and could close any openings that arise, bringing further industrialization and destruction to the prairie. The two sides, of opportunities on the one side and obstacles on the other, hang in a rough and uneasy balance that may shift in the coming years.

In early fall, on cooler mornings when the wind is down, a fine mist will often move just above the surface of Cherry Lake as it begins the long process of releasing its warmth back to the sky. When the sun lights it up from behind, the air's subtlest stirrings suddenly become visible. A boundary layer holds the turbulence an inch from the mirror surface of the water, but above that, even on calm mornings, the mist dresses the air in gowns that reveal it to the eye. A loose pattern forms in a web of condensed air that dances swiftly over the lake.

Now and then a node of this tracery will produce a swirling pillar of mist that rises up like a small ghost two feet or so above the main, and it will race faster than the rest of the air, spinning at great speed until it has spun away all of the moisture in its column.

I have watched this spectacle over lakes and rivers many times and it always leaves me wondering what I will never have light enough to see. And it reminds me that, like a bird in the grass, I too dwell in realms whose dance is not fully revealed by the sun.

The motion of all that cannot be seen or known completely is a wild card in our use of the world that should make us pause and reorient ourselves with a sense of awe proper to the work and materials over which we find ourselves so often fumbling. In the presence of wild birds or mist racing above water, I can believe what the rest of my life denies: that health and regeneration flow like a great river from the heart of Creation; that sun, seed, soil, and rain do the work of growing without any help from us; that the prairie that runs through the marrow of this continent is a landscape inviting us toward a greater resonance between what we achieve and how we achieve it; and that the land itself must always be the measure of our conduct.

Nature stands on the side of change. As the model and instrument of all healing and wholeness, the earth will eventually fix the messes we make. One day, one way or another, this land will be grass again, and birds of some kind, the ones that adapt and survive, will sing again in abundance above shimmering plains. I believe we have a chance to witness its recovery, that we might even be privileged to join in the restoration, if we come to our senses in time.

There are too many days when I can't be anywhere within earshot of birds, but even then I feel them pulling me toward a time when I will escape the clamour of my life in the city and become quiet

enough to listen. It is the glory in things, the light of the divine moving within Creation, that calls out for our ears and eyes. The prairie
world shines with it: the lightning bolt leaping from sky to earth, the
shiver of a rain-drenched sparrow brooding its young, the arc of a
weasel on the hunt, the minute armies of soil microbes, the riffle of
wind on water. Like it or not, human beings are different. We glow
with a lesser glory, but we have *de*light, something that, within the
conundrum of human will, lets us choose to share in and reflect back
that light or to ignore it.

In grassland, the birds of the air have been pouring their blessings upon our heads for more than a century now, inviting us to
receive the freedom they embody, to be washed clean in the prairie
sun and take on the garment of this new world. Instead, we have
played it safe by handing our lives over to reaping and sowing, gathering into barns. The gift remains, teaching us what it means to place
ourselves in the hands of Creation, to become part of that freedom in
a community that includes people and the other ones whose trusting
ways we would do well to consider. If it disappears and the song goes
silent, we may find ourselves given over completely to the grip of
the marketplace and its empty promises; we may forget what we ever
meant by such a thing as freedom.

Three years ago I was with a busload of prairie naturalists hurtling
down a road coming off the east bench of the Cypress Hills. Our
leader was Heidi, the daughter of the hardest-working grassland con-
servationist I know, Lorne Scott, whom Stuart and Mary brought into
the circle of bird and prairie conservation when he was a farm boy
growing up not far away from Cherry Lake. Halfway down the hill to
the valley bottom, Heidi called out to the driver to stop the bus. She
jumped out the door and walked into the ditch with the rest of us trailing behind like schoolchildren, wondering what the fuss was about.

"It's the K-T boundary," she said. "You can see it right here in the road cut."

She was pointing to a darker stripe of soil low in the cut bank's cross-section of earth history. She explained that it is a layer of ash that marks the end of the Cretaceous period and the beginning of the Tertiary, when dinosaurs went extinct.

A song spiralling down on us from above begged to differ. A Sprague's pipit was holding onto its piece of sky and singing as we looked at the ashes from which birds arose as dinosaurs with feathers. Below the K-T boundary only flightless, non-avian dinosaurs are found. Above it, though, fossils of small flying dinosaurs begin to appear. Many of the best fossils, found in recent years, are known as "theropods," a word that means "terrible claw" for the long claw on their hind toes. In addition to a birdlike foot, their wishbone, feathers, hollow bones, and habit of brooding their eggs have made the origin of birds from theropod dinosaurs one of the great discoveries of evolutionary science.

Although the northern prairie was lowland forest when that K-T ash settled onto the surface, I've dreamed up my own links between grassland birds and the theropods. For one, most of the work of finding theropods and describing them as proto-birds has been done in grassland regions of the world: Patagonia, the Mongolian Steppes and the North American Great Plains.[10] And of all the birds on earth, grassland birds are the ones that often still have the "terrible claw" on the hind toe. You see it on longspurs, horned larks, meadowlarks, pipits, and other birds that need the extra stability of a long hind toe to walk and run through grass.

As we piled back onto the bus, the idea of extinction remained with me. If dinosaurs, the dominant mega-fauna of their day, went through an extinction bottleneck that selected characteristics that would over time give rise to birds in all of their splendour and variety, what will we become one bright day? And what will evolution select out of the grab bag of our traits that will be of use to our more grace-ful descendants millions of years from now?

Will it be our rapacity and greed, our violent striving with one another and the earth, or will it be our capacity for delight, self-sacrifice, forbearance, and wisdom? No one can say for certain whether con-sciousness and human choice have any role to play in the selecting, but faith would have us lend our small weight toward the possibility that living well in a place is our way of passing on to the earth's long dream the best possible version of ourselves.

SWAINSON'S HAWK

Not long ago, on warm, prairie summer afternoons you could not look skyward without seeing at least one hawk circling beneath the clouds. Most of the time it was the Swainson's hawk, the dominant buteo, or broad-winged, hawk of the Great Plains, the one that farmers see following behind their machines and pouncing on rodents and insects stirred up in the furrow.

In 1827 at Fort Carlton, John Richardson's gunner collected the type specimen for the Swainson's hawk, though at the time he misidentified it as the common buzzard of Europe. Seven years earlier he had collected the ground squirrel that now bears his name. Today, only the ferruginous hawk is more dependent on Richardson's ground squirrels. The smaller Swainson's will eat a lot of voles and insects as an adult, but it feeds its young on a steady diet of the Richardson's ground squirrel, which most prairie people have always known as the gopher. When gophers are abundant, hawk nests fledge more young. When gophers are scarce, as they have been in many regions, hawk nests fledge fewer young.[11]

With its long, tapered wings and thinner body, the Swainson's hawk is built for distance travel. In July of 1940, a young bird bander named Hartley Fredeen banded a Swainson's hawk nesting on a farm near Macrorie, Saskatchewan. A year and a half later, someone shot it at another grassland farm six thousand miles away, in Cordoba, Argentina. Fredeen's band recovery proved that the Swainson's hawk migrates south to the pampas of Argentina, making it the second most travelled raptor of the New World. Only the peregrine falcon that breeds in Greenland travels farther.

The Swainson's hawks' annual fall migration, in large flocks that converge as they travel down the funnel of Mexico toward Panama, is thought to be one of the great avian spectacles of the Americas. Even on the northern plains, it is not uncommon to spot gatherings of eighty birds fuelling up on crickets, grasshoppers, and voles before departing in late August, but there are places in Mexico and Central America where you can stand on the right afternoon and watch a river of hawks pass overhead. Swirling cauldrons of Swainson's hawks, often containing other hawks, turn in the sky in formations hawk watchers call "kettles." Some kettles will contain five to ten thousand birds and in a single fall the tally passing over one location can reach as high as 845,000.[12]

Josef Schmutz banded a bird at Hanna, Alberta, that made eighteen trips south and seventeen trips back, travelling 250,000 miles in its lifetime before it was found dead in Argentina at the age of nineteen years six months.[13] Neither its longevity nor the distance it travelled over those years was as remarkable as the cause of its death, for it was one of nearly six thousand Swainson's hawks found dead in Argentina in 1995 and 1996. The massacre might never have been discovered if it had not been for a satellite telemetry project initiated by U.S. biologists trying to locate exact wintering sites for the species. Following satellite signals to roost sites, they came upon hundreds of dead hawks.

Away from their breeding grounds, Swainson's hawks feed primarily on grasshoppers and other large insects. During the mid-1990s, Argentinian farmers concerned about grasshoppers began spraying alfalfa and sunflower fields with the organophosphate insecticides monocrotophos and dimethoate. Hundreds of Swainson's hawks following the applicators and feeding on the grasshoppers were sprayed by the poison. They died quickly. Others that merely ate tainted prey died within a few days. Biologists studying the massacre estimate that the total kill may have been as high as twenty thousand hawks.[14] Since the disaster, the deadlier insecticides have been removed from store shelves in the regions where the hawks winter.

With the poisoning in Argentina, habitat degradation and loss, and poor nest productivity linked to renewed efforts to rid the land of grasshoppers and gophers, the Swainson's hawk may be undergoing a period of general decline not experienced by the species since early settlers began to shoot what they considered to be "chicken hawks." Although it seemed to recover from that initial persecution and adapt to agricultural landscapes, these recent factors have made it another grassland bird that deserves focused monitoring.

Chapter Eighteen

To Make a Prairie

To make a prairie it takes a clover and one bee,–
One clover, and a bee,
And revery.
The revery alone will do
If bees are few.

EMILY DICKINSON

It is the middle of April, 2008. Another winter behind me, I decide to head out to the pipit fields for a first walk of the year. My nine-year-old daughter, Maia, has come along and we are holding hands because she is afraid of cattle. I tell her that it is too early in the season for the animals to be in the pasture yet, but she has seen my cattle promises fail before so she keeps an eye on the horizon.

The snow has been gone for a week or more and now the first crocuses are up, their pale violet blooms jutting out of the ground like plastic posies. Not long ago, flocks of snow buntings and redpolls would have been here rolling over the pasture searching for seed heads uncovered by the wind. The first Sprague's pipits will arrive soon but the horned larks and meadowlarks are already on territory.

As we make our way east from the road, I try to ignore the scruffy state of the pasture, the grass hammered down by hard grazing during last summer's drought, the absence of ground mosses and lichens, and the predominance of sweet clover, absinth, and other weeds. We skirt the stony flats beside a gravel pit with three large cones of sand and gravel, and flush a flock of horned larks. The males sing their bittersweet *tee-sip, ti-ti-ti-iiiiiiiiiiiiiiii* as they fly away. Maia asks why birds never sit still and I say something about songbirds protecting themselves by flying away from larger creatures.

Then a meadowlark leaps from a tussock of grass and sings a full song as it flies ahead of us. I remember the Dakota story of the meadowlark as the Bird of Promise, and try it out on Maia, telling her that the bird flies above us and all creatures to tell the Creator what each of us needs for that day. She replies with the skeptical "really?" of an aspiring preteen, but gives me the benefit of the doubt. We have been spending more time together lately, with her mother away at a month-long meditation retreat. Karen finished the chemotherapy at Christmas and the radiation a month ago. The retreat is her way of punctuating the end of formal medical treatment, shaking the dust from her feet, and moving on in hopefulness and health. The time she has been away has dragged on like a second winter, but Maia and I do our best to console one another. Maia began having nightmares soon after Karen's diagnosis and many nights still comes into our room sweating and tearful. Last night, during one of these episodes, she asked how old Karen and I will be when she is my age. When I told her we'd be around ninety she started to cry, and asked why we had to wait so long to have her.

Up ahead in the pasture we see the stone ruins of an old barn I had not noticed before. In a few minutes we are there, peering through an opening in the wall. Small birds scurry like mice over the rubble: American tree sparrows, early migrants that will move on north to spend their summer where forest gives way to arctic prairies. One

of them pops up on top of the stone wall just above eye level. I give
Maia the binoculars. She holds them up and I watch her eyelashes
flicker as she says, "I guess this bird is protected by its cuteness."

Once the tree sparrows disappear, we sit down on the lee side
of the ruins to get out of the wind for a while. Maia leans against
my chest and we close our eyes to face the sun like crocus blossoms.
In the quiet, with the earthy smell of a prairie spring all around me,
my thoughts quickly tumble toward their default question for this
time of year: if the birds seem so hopeful, why can't I be hopeful for
them too?

Scott Russell Sanders has said that hope is a leaping up in
expectation, for the word shares its origins with *hop*. That sounds
about right. A crocus leaps up from the all-but-dead grasses, a meadowlark leaps up in song, a child leaps forward to her teenage years.
Expectation, yes, but in every hop there is also the experience of
groundlessness, and the inevitable return to earth.

After a long silence, Maia tells me she is imagining buffalo in
tall green grass next to ponds filled with ducks. I tell her I can see
them too, and the image sets my mind leaping toward a dream I have
been pondering for some time, a detailed and ambitious scheme for
restoring the long-suffering prairie in and around this pasture. As
always, it comes to me first as a map showing the remnants of unbro-
ken grassland stitched together by corridors and larger blocks of land
seeded back to native grasses and forbs. With the sun warming my
forehead and the weight of Maia against me, I wonder what it would
be like to walk in such a place years from now, holding the hand of
a grandchild.

In the core area, we would enter a gate into a large pasture recov-
ering from intensive grazing. A sign on the gate showing a bird in songflight tells us that we are on land managed by "Longspur Prairie Bison
and Beef," a co-operative made up of private landowners, consumers,
livestock producers, and the local Indian band at Carry-the-Kettle. On

the other side of the fence a couple of experienced riders from the reserve are showing teens from the inner city how to move a large herd of bison from one grazing zone to another. It is part of a prairie awareness camp run by Nakota elders and grassland naturalists. Carry-the-Kettle reserve forms the aspen parkland flank of the 25,000-acre project, but the band also has used some of its resources to lease some of the parcels being rehabilitated from cropland to native grass.

On our side of the fence there are people from the city reseeding a restoration site that has become weedy, while others put up a ferruginous hawk nesting platform. Their work terms each summer advance them from consumer to "conserver" status on a marketing scale that prices grass-fed beef and bison according to hours of labour committed to the co-op. Some people put in hours helping to market and distribute products to stores and restaurants in local towns and cities. Others participate in the prescribed burns held each spring, collect wild grass seed, maintain fences, restore riparian areas, or work with biologists to survey birds, insects, and plants and control invasive species. A resident range ecologist designs and manages grazing and fire regimes in consultation with participating landowners and livestock producers, while contract biologists monitor the health of ecosystems to ensure that restoration sectors are not merely creating sink habitat.

In one of the wooded coulees, there is a campground, a hostel, and a research station for non-resident members of the project who come to work and study. At the growing edge of the project small parcels of land are being added year by year as the community dips into its land trust fund. The trust leases donated and purchased cropland to young families who want to join the co-op. By letting them lease at prices below market value, the trust brings more people into the circle while they restore more land to grass and develop their skills. When the time is right, their land is added into the grazing and fire rotations and the apprenticing families become full members. As more families with small children come to the area, a small village develops and opens the first new school in the district since 1950.

As far-fetched from the reality of today's grassland agriculture as such a scheme might seem, the technical skills and methods required to make it work are already in hand. Nothing on this scale has been attempted, but not because the tools are lacking. Prescribed burns, intensive grazing that mimics natural patterns, monitoring programs, native grassland restoration, and co-operative interchange between consumers and producers are at work right now either on private ranches or on publicly managed rangeland and conservation areas in North America. If the right group of people interested in the right landscape gathered to ask the question—"What do we hold in common in our dreams for this land?"—they might be able to bring all of these elements together to see their dreams shape the way large tracts of grassland are used.

Opening my eyes to the truth of the abused and weedy prairie all around us, I think again about the leaping up that hope implies. In hoping for a renewed covenant with the prairie, I may be leaving the ground behind, but I have trouble thinking of any other way to start the long process of healing. I often look through the books on cancer recovery Karen brings home. There have been twenty or thirty sitting around the house and, while they may differ in the therapies they recommend, they all seem to agree on one point: hope prepares the body for healing.

To live in honest hope is to live well in your own body, in your family, in your community, and in the land that feeds you. It begins in sensuous contact with the world as you find it—whole and broken, familiar and strange, resilient and imperilled. From there, hope feeds advocacy, the passionate defence of the life beloved, and that experience inevitably leads to an encounter with the forces, inside others and yourself, that threaten to bring you crashing back to earth. A more graceful landing is possible—one where hope survives the flight by joining itself to a wider forgiveness and becoming something more grounded, something we have no better words for than *faith* and *fidelity*. Fidelity, living in good faith, brings the arc of hope back down to earth. If I eat and take from the earth in ways that keep faith with it, I replenish myself and the earth in the same movement. The truth of this harmony eludes us most days but lives within every small gesture of forbearance, generosity, and care, from the decision to eat healthy and local food to the farmer who sets aside his pesticides for the last time.

A tree sparrow has come back to sing the soft notes it will voice in full once it arrives on its northern breeding grounds. The sound blends with the silver bells of horned larks now proclaiming their piece of gravel as Maia and I stand and begin our hike back to the car. I take one last look at a horned lark singing next to a cow-pie and I remember, as much in my body as in my mind, the fidelity of birds I have witnessed. Not merely the faithfulness of a pipit back for the third summer in a row to sing above tame hay too short for a safe nesting, nor the sage grouse returning to dancing grounds occupied for fifty years, but the wider fidelity to the prairie over the long trial of its destruction. I feel it as a pull from the centre of my body down to the grass, the weight of all that birds forgive in us, leaving behind, free of gravity, in the air that receives their songs, the simplest of messages: *Replenish the earth and you shall be replenished as well.*

Taking Maia's small hand in mine, I walk and think of the birds now arriving on remnant grasslands all over the plains. Far above the curled blades of last year's grama grass, with the wind sweeping down from mare's tail skies, the sun calls forth its singers. Over low ridges and level plains they rise on drafts of air to make the dawn offering. Listen. The grass accuses no one, the sky bears no grudge, and the song—forsaken, repudiated, still waiting to be received—is a timeless benediction welcoming us into a freedom, a community, and a landscape that may yet bring us home.

Acknowledgements

This book has placed me in the debt of many fine and generous people. Like most naturalists I am grateful to the "field guides" I have learned from over the years. Some were books but the best were the ones who guided by walking along with me in the field, showing me the sounds and shapes of things, answering questions, and sharing their delight. I am thankful especially for the hours I spent with prairie birders, in particular Bob Luterbach and the late Robert Kreba.

My indebtedness to Stuart Houston as an encouraging voice, thoughtful critic, and emergency reference desk increases every time we speak to one another. Even at the last stages of editing the manuscript, when I was scrambling to nail down the population data on greater sage grouse or trying to relocate a lost passage from John Macoun's records, I called Stuart daily for help. His answers—prompt, thorough, and meticulous—saved me a lot of legwork during a busy time.

A number of friends read drafts of the manuscript and gave me their thoughts on how it might be improved: Peter Bruce, Dave Carpenter, Rob Wright, Sylvie Roy, Bob Luterbach, Mary and Stuart Houston, Allan Safarik, Frank Roy, Michelle Sanche, Stephen Davis, and John Dipple. I owe particular thanks to Sandy Ayer, a prairie birder who is also a librarian and poet. Sandy spent many hours with the manuscript, gently telling me what he liked and did not like, suggesting better words, and correcting my usage and grammar. Then, to my amazement, he went back through the whole thing and repaired my lackadaisical endnotes, in many cases going to the original texts to confirm and correct references.

I am indebted also to the many ranchers, farmers, naturalists, scientists, and academics I spoke to during the research and writing of the book. Among the people who gave generously of their time by letting me interview them in person or answering questions by phone and email were John Carlson, Pat Fargey, Rob Scissons, Stephen Davis, Bill Waiser, Brenda Dale, Sue McAdam, Pierre Mineau, Chris Reed, Ron Mayer, Thelma Poirier, Lynn Grant, Lorne Scott, Dan Johnson, Paule Hjertaas, Don McKay, Josef Schmutz, Ian Halliday, and Val Thomas.

Without grants from the Saskatchewan Arts Board and the Canada Council I would not have had the time to do the initial research and write the first two drafts of the manuscript. Thanks to art collector Mavis Jealous for allowing me to use Fred Lahrman's meadowlark painting on the cover.

I am especially grateful for the work, enthusiasm, and thought my editor, Phyllis Bruce, gave this book, from her initial interest in the proposal to the copy-editing of the final draft. Phyllis's firm hand and cogent reflections on the narrative have made more of a difference than I care to admit. Thanks also to production editor Nita Pronovost, managing editor Noelle Zitzer, book designer Sharon Kish, and copy editor Anne Holloway. To Jackie Kaiser, my agent, I must give all the credit for hooking me up with this fine team of book people.

Karen has always been gracious in giving me time to write, but her insistence that I continue writing during her treatment showed me her generosity has no end, for even then she would often bring me tea or a sandwich as I sat at my desk. If there is anything helpful in this book, it grew from the garden she has made of our family life.

Finally, I want to thank my father, now in his late seventies, for getting me outside, taking me hunting and fishing, teaching me how to paddle a canoe, fillet a fish, skin a goose, and without knowing it, introducing me to the colour, light, and music of a prairie dawn.

Notes

Part One: The Dream of Grassland

Chapter One: Out of the Trees

1 Quoted in C.S. Houston and Maurice George Street, *Birds of the Saskatchewan River: Carlton to Cumberland* (Regina: Saskatchewan Natural History Society, 1959), 75.

Chapter Two: Prairie Dance

1 Paul M. Catling and Brenda Kostiuk, "Tallgrass Prairie in the Whitewood Area of Saskatchewan," *Blue Jay* 64(2) (June 2006): 72–83.

2 C.S. Houston and William Anaka, *The Birds of Yorkton-Duck Mountain* (Regina: Saskatchewan Natural History Society, 2003), 137–38.

Chapter Three: Birds of Promise

1 Melvin R. Gilmore, *Prairie Smoke* (St. Paul: Minnesota Historical Society Press, 1987), 149–50.

2 Sir John Richardson and William Swainson, *Fauna Boreali–Americana, Vol. 2, The Birds* (London: John Murray, 1832).

3 J.R. Sauer, J.E. Hines, and J. Fallon, "The North American Breeding Bird Survey, Results and Analysis, 1966-2005." (Laurel: USGS Patuxent Wildlife Research Center, June 2, 2006). www.mbr-pwrc.usgs.gov/bbs/bbs2005.html.

4 J. Frank Roy, *Birds of the Elbow* (Regina: Saskatchewan Natural History Society, 1996), 273.

Chapter Four: Birdline

1 Richard H. Pough, *Audubon Guides: All the Birds of Eastern and Central North America* (New York: Doubleday & Company, Inc., 1946), 222.

2 Mowat, who spent part of his childhood chasing birds in the parkland prairie near Saskatoon, travelled the province in 1939 and wrote down his sightings in an unpublished manuscript called "A Summer Survey of the Birds in Saskatchewan."

Chapter Five: Of the Air

1 David Abram, *The Spell of the Sensuous: Perception and Language in a More-Than-Human World* (New York: Pantheon Books, 1996).

2 J. Frank Roy, *Birds of the Elbow* (Regina: Saskatchewan Natural History Society, 1996), 255.

3 "Christmas Bird Count Historical Results," National Audubon Society (2008). www.audubon.org/bird/cbc.

Chapter Six: The Sparrow's Fall

1 Wallace Stegner, *Wolf Willow: A History, a Story, and a Memory of the Last Frontier* (New York: Viking, 1955), 8.

2 John James Audubon, *Birds of America, from Drawings Made in the United States and Their Territories*, Octavo ed., vol. 7 (Philadephia: J.B. Chevalier, 1844), 359; cited in M.T. Green et al., "Baird's Sparrow (*Ammodramus bairdii*)," in *The Birds of North America Online*, www.bna. birds.cornell.edu/bna/species/638articles/introduction.

3 Green et al., "Baird's Sparrow."

Part Two: Lifting the Veil

Chapter Seven: A Bitter Glimpse Ahead

1 Personal comment, Paule Hjertaas, coordinator for Saskatchewan's portion of the International Piping Plover Census.

Chapter Eight: Waiting for the Pipit

1 John James Audubon, "Sprague's Missouri Lark," in *Birds of America*, on National Audubon Society website, www.audubon.org/bird/boa/NSc.html.

2 Quoted in C.S. Houston and Maurice George Street, *Birds of the Saskatchewan River: Carlton to Cumberland* (Regina: Saskatchewan Natural History Society, 1959), 148.

3 A.C. Bent, "Summer Birds of Southwestern Saskatchewan," *The Auk* 24: 407.

4 Jeffrey Lockwood, "Prayerful Science," *Earthlight: Journal for Ecological and Spiritual Living* 52 (Winter 2005), 14-19.

5 J.F. McDermott, ed., *Up the Missouri with Audubon: The Journal of Edward Harris* (Norman, OK: University of Oklahoma Press, 1951). Also, for a thorough and convincing discussion of the matter, using Audubon's own records as well as Sprague's journals to prove that Harris and Bell were the true discoverers of the Sprague's pipit, see *The Auk* 68 (July 1951): 379–80.

6 Elliott Coues, *Birds of the Northwest: A Hand-book of the Ornithology of the Region Drained by the Missouri River and Its Tributaries* (Government Printing Office, 1874), 43.

7 Birdlife International's Website, www.birdlife.org, contains profiles of endangered birds from around the globe.

Chapter Nine: A Canopy of Song

1 Bill Waiser, interviewed by the author, "Pastures Unsung" *Ideas*, CBC Radio One, September 19 and 20, 2006.

2 C. Stuart Houston and Marc J. Bechard, "Decline of the Ferruginous Hawk in Saskatchewan," *American Birds* 38 (Mar./Apr. 1984): 166–70.

Chapter Eleven: Death by a Thousand Cuts

1 Grasshopper researcher Jeffrey Lockwood has written an important book on the subject: *Locust: The Devastating Rise and Mysterious Disappearance of the Insect That Shaped the American Frontier* (New York: Basic Books, 2004).

2 Bridget Stutchbury, *Silence of the Songbirds* (Toronto: HarperCollins Publishers Ltd, 2007), 213.

3 Manley Callin, *Birds of the Qu'Appelle* (Regina: Saskatchewan Natural History Society), 134.

4 Monica H. Mather and Raleigh H. Robertson, "Honest Advertisement in Flight Displays of Bobolinks (*Dolichonyx orzivorus*)," *The Auk* 109 no. 4, (1992): 869–73.

5 Nature Conservancy, "Animal Profiles: Birds: Grasslands: Bobolink," www.nature.org/animals/birds/animals/bobolink.html.

Chapter Twelve: Landscape Pathology 101

1 Canada, Department of the Interior, *Annual Report of the Department of the Interior for 1880, Sessional Papers*, 1880–81, vol. 3, no. 3, 24.

2 John Macoun, *Manitoba and the Great North-West* (London: Thomas C. Jack, 1883), 74–75.

3 Some species are declining only in portions of their range; others are suffering right across their range. Some have declined steadily during the entire forty years of the BBS; others more precipitously after 1980. The American bittern appears to be declining at 4.2% per year over the entire set of BBS data. In Saskatchewan, the northern harrier, killdeer, and bobolink have been declining at rates of 3.8%, 5.2%, and 8.3% per year respectively since 1980.

4 Monsanto, "Conversations about Plant Biotechnology," www.monsanto. com/biotech-gmo, Biotechnology Topics: Conservation Tillage.

5 "Residual Glyphosate Can Lurk in Soil" and "Glyphosate Affects Roots," *Western Producer*, January 10, 2008, 60.

6 Margaret Belcher, *The Birds of Regina* (Regina: Saskatchewan Natural History Society, 1961), 48.

7 Sauer et al., "The North American Breeding Bird Survey."

Part Three: Pastures Unsung

Chapter Thirteen: Poisoned Land

1 J.T. Brophy, et al., "Occupational Histories of Cancer Patients in a Canadian Cancer Treatment Centre and the Generated Hypothesis Regarding Breast Cancer and Farming," *International Journal of Occupational and Environmental Health* 8 (October-December 2002): 346–53.

2 D.L. Johnson, O.O. Olfert, M.G. Dolinski, and L. Harris, "G.I.S.-Based Forecasts for Management of Grasshopper Population in Western Canada," in *Proceedings of the UN Food and Agriculture Organization (FAO) Symposium on Agricultural Pest Forecasting and Monitoring* (Quebec City: Reseau d' Avertissement Phytosanitaires du Quebec, 1996); 109–112.

3 Legislative Assembly of Saskatchewan, *Saskatchewan Hansard*, May 29, 1985. www.legassembly.sk.ca/hansard/hansard1984-85-86.htm.

4 Paul James and Glen Fox, "Effects of Some Insecticides on Productivity of Burrowing Owls," *Blue Jay* 45 no. 2 (June 1987): 65–71.

5 Agriculture Canada, Food Production and Inspection Branch, Plant Industry Directorate, "Special Review of Carbofuran Insecticide: Effects on Avian Fauna and Value to Agriculture," Discussion Document D93 02 (Ottawa: Plant Industry Directorate, Agriculture Canada, 1993), 7.

6 Ibid.

7 James and Fox, "Effects of Some Insecticides," 65–71.

8 Agriculture Canada, "Special Review of Carbofuran Insecticide," 8.

9   Sierra Club of Canada, News Release, January 10, 2005, "Environmental
    Group Withdraws from Pesticide Hearings in Protest," www.sierraclub.
    ca/national/media.
10 P. Mineau and M. Whiteside, "Lethal Risk to Birds from Insecticide Use
    in the United States—A spatial and temporal analysis," *Environmental
    Toxicology and Chemistry* 5 (2006): 1214–22.
11 Agriculture Canada, "Special Review of Carbofuran Insecticide," 20.
12 None of this justifies the killing in our fields or the lies we tell ourselves
    as we make a show of weighing a pesticide's costs against its benefits,
    although that is what we often hear from the apologists for the
    agricultural-industrial complex. In a book called *Saving the Planet
    with Pesticides and Plastic: The Environmental Triumph of High-Yield
    Farming*, Dennis Avery—a former agricultural analyst with the U.S.
    State Department who now works for the arch-conservative Hudson
    Institute—argues that environmentalists should embrace pesticides and
    petroleum-based agriculture because they minimize the amount of land
    necessary to grow food and feed the greatest number of people, thereby
    preventing famine. Instead of striving to restore health to the land we
    farm, renew rural community, and transform our agriculture to fit within
    the limits of nature, then, we are to surrender to this most despairing,
    cynical message from the cold heart of the agri-food beast: *Pesticides
    and petrochemicals are good for us, good for the earth.* To embrace such
    a program is to ensure that Malthusian population growth will continue,
    causing even greater need for high-yield agriculture and more land
    under cultivation, and ultimately a spectacular death spiral in a world of
    famine, empty aquifers, and ecological collapse. Several years ago, just
    as organic farming was beginning to get a foothold on the prairies, the
    editor of Canada's biggest farm weekly, *The Western Producer*, latched on
    to Avery's ideas in an editorial that reassured conventional farmers that
    they are doing the right thing and in fact saving both the environment
    and humanity by maximizing yields. That the same tabloid publishes
    editorials lamenting rural depopulation and low farm-gate prices is a
    testimony to the near-sightedness and confusion characterizing what
    passes for informed policy and opinion in the world of agribusiness.
13 M.A. Skeel, J. Keith, and C.S. Palaschuk, "A Population Decline
    Recorded by Operation Burrowing Owl in Saskatchewan." *Journal of
    Raptor Research* 35 (2001), 399-407.
14 "COSEWIC Assessment and Update Status Report on the Burrowing
    Owl *Athene Cunicularia* in Canada." Committee on the Status of
    Endangered Wildlife in Canada. (Ottawa: 2006).

Chapter Fourteen: Lethal Dose

1 J. Frank Roy, *Birds of the Elbow* (Regina: Saskatchewan Natural History Society, 1996), 229.
2 Manley Callin, *Birds of the Qu'Appelle* (Regina: Saskatchewan Natural History Society), 122.
3 United States Environmental Protection Agency, News Release, December 31, 1972, "DDT Ban Takes Effect," www.epa.gov/history/topics/ddt/01.htm.
4 Government of Canada, "Species at Risk Public Registry," www.sararegistry.gc.ca. Loggerhead Shrike.

Chapter Fifteen: Vigil

1 John Macoun and James M. Macoun, *Catalogue of Canadian Birds* (Ottawa: Government Printing Bureau, 1909).
2 Government of Canada, "Species at Risk Public Registry," www.sararegistry.gc.ca. Greater Sage-Grouse.
3 C.E. Braun, O.O. Oedekoven, and C.L. Aldridge, "Oil and Gas Development in Western North America: Effects on Sagebrush Steppe Avifauna with Particular Emphasis on Sage-grouse," *Transactions of the North American Wildlife and Natural Resources Conference* 67 (2002): 337–49.

Chapter Sixteen: Pathways of Complicity

1 Quoted in W.A. Waiser, *The Field Naturalist: John Macoun, the Geological Survey, and Natural Science* (Toronto: University of Toronto Press, 1989), 47.
2 Statistics Canada, *Indicators and Detailed Statistics*, Catalogue Number 16–200- XKE (Ottawa: Government of Canada, 1997).
3 J. Frank Roy, *Birds of the Elbow* (Regina: Saskatchewan Natural History Society, 1996).

Part Four: The Gift Remains

Chapter Seventeen: Let There Be Grass

1 Crossing the Medicine Line Network, "About Us," www.crossingthemedicineline.net/about_us.htm.
2 The Union of Concerned Scientists (UCS), a nonprofit partnership of 200,000 scientists and citizens that uses science to inform policy and advocate practical environmental solutions, would agree. The organization has come out strongly against the grain-fed livestock

industry and in favour of grass-fed beef. In a report by Kate Clancy called *Greener Pastures: How Grass-Fed Beef and Milk Contribute to Healthy Eating*, the UCS declares that grass-fed livestock production is healthier for people to eat (Cambridge, MA: UCS Publications, 2006, available at www.ucsusa.org). Grass-fed beef is much leaner than grain-fed beef, and so it generally contains fewer calories per ounce than meat from a grain-fed cow. Like organic beef, grass-fed beef contains no antibiotics or artificial hormones. Beef from grass-fed animals also contains a healthier ratio of essential omega-3 and omega-6 fatty acids. Because we eat so much grain-based food and very little seafood, most of us take in far too much omega-6 fatty acid in proportion to omega-3. Grass-fed beef is a good source of omega-3 fatty acids and can help restore a healthier balance in these fatty acids. Studies have shown that people with enough omega-3s in their diet are less likely to have high blood pressure or an irregular heartbeat. Without enough omega-3s, the human brain functions poorly. A diet high in omega-3s helps to protect people from depression, a number of mental disorders, and Alzheimer's disease. Put a pastured cow on grain for a few weeks and the omega-3s all but vanish, even if the grain is organic. (D.S. Siscovick et al., "Dietary Intake and Cell Membrane Levels of Long-Chain n-3 Polyunsaturated Fatty Acids and the Risk of Primary Cardiac Arrest," *Journal of the American Medical Association* 274, no. 17 [1995]: 1363-67). Conjugated linoleic acid (CLA) is another fat that is considered to be beneficial. A study in Finland showed that women who had the highest levels of CLA in their diet had a 60 percent lower risk of breast cancer than those with the lowest levels. Switching from grain-fed to grass-fed meat and dairy products was enough to put a woman in the lowest risk category, because meat and dairy products from grass-fed cattle have been shown to contain three to five times more CLA than products from animals fed conventional diets, making them the richest known source of CLA. *See* A. P. Simopoulos and Jo Robinson, *The Omega Diet*. (New York: HarperCollins Publishers Ltd., 1999); S.K. Duckett, D.G. Wagner, et al., "Effects of Time on Feed on Beef Nutrient Composition," *Journal of Animal Science* 71 no. 8 (1993): 2079–88; T.A. Dolecek and G. Grandits, "Dietary Polyunsaturated Fatty Acids and Mortality in the Multiple Risk Factor Intervention Trial (MRFIT)," *World Review of Nutrition and Diet* 66 (1991): 205–16.

3   Ken W. Belcher and Josef K. Schmutz, "Management of the Prairie Landscape Through Strategic Consumer-Producer Co-operatives," *Prairie Forum* 30 (2005): 55–72; Ken W. Belcher, Andrea E. Germann, and Josef K. Schmutz: "Beef with Environmental and Quality Attributes:

Preferences of Environmental Group and General Population
Consumers in Saskatchewan, Canada," *Agriculture and Human Values*
24 (2005): 333–42.

4 Statistics Canada, "Farm Population, by Province (2001 Censuses of
Agriculture and Population, Saskatchewan," http://www.40.statcan.ca/l01/
cst01/agrc42i.htm.

5 Econexus, "Call for an Immediate Moratorium on EU Incentives for
Agrofuels, EU Imports of Agrofuels, and EU Agroenergy Monoculture,"
www.econexus.info/agrofuel_moratorium_call.html. This call for a
moratorium on "agrofuels," drafted by the U.K. science and industry
watchdog non-profit known as Econexus, outlines the main arguments
against biofuels. Here is what the moratorium call says about the
much-vaunted "second generation" biofuels: "It is being suggested
that a 'second generation' of agrofuels can be developed that will solve
some of the problems posed by current agrofuels, such as competition
between food and fuel production. The aim is to find ways (including
genetic engineering and synthetic biology) of modifying plants and trees
to produce less lignin, engineering the lignin and cellulose so that they
break down more easily or in different ways, and engineering microbes
and enzymes to break down plant matter. Such high-risk techniques do
not challenge the pattern of destructive monocultures designed to feed
increasing energy consumption patterns. A moratorium on monoculture
agrofuels is needed now, to prevent further damage being done through
the over-hasty promotion of agrofuel crops. In the meantime, the
promises and potential risks associated with second-generation agrofuels
should be fully examined. Whatever the outcome, such fuels will not
be available for approximately ten years and decisive action to address
climate change is required immediately." See also BirdLife International,
*Fueling the Ecological Crisis: Six Examples of Habitat Destruction
Driven by Biofuels*, www.birdlife.org/eu/pdfs/BirdLife_Biofuels_report.

6 The most profound book on this topic is Wendell Berry's *The Unsettling
of America: Culture and Agriculture* (San Francisco: Sierra Club Books,
1977), though dozens of books written in recent decades provide an
up-to-date critique of the agribusiness industry. Among them are Marc
Lappe and Britt Bailey's *Against The Grain: Biotechnology and the
Corporate Takeover of Your Food* (Monroe, ME: Common Courage
Press, 1998); Anthony Winson's *The Intimate Commodity: Food and
the Development of the Agro-Industrial Complex in Canada* (Toronto:
Garamond Press, 1993), and books by Brewster Kneen, including *From
Land to Mouth: Understanding the Food System* (Toronto: NC Press,

1989) and *Invisible Giant: Cargill and Its Transnational Strategies,* 2nd ed. (Sterling, VA: Pluto Press, 2002).

7 In 1961, Canadian consumers spent 19.1% of their total household expenditures on food and non-alcoholic beverages. By 1997 the figure was 12.5% and eight years later in 2005 it was a mere 9.3%. For Americans, the 1961 figure was 16.9% and by 2001 it had dropped to 10%. This trend has been gathering momentum all over the world, though Canada, the United States, and the United Kingdom have led the way with the lowest figures of all. Agriculture and Agri-food Canada, "Canadian Food Spending Declining," 2007, www4.agr.gc.ca/AAFC-AAC/display-afficher.do?id=1170942402619&lang=e.

8 As others have often pointed out, growth in overall GDP is a poor measure of any community or nation's well-being, because it does not discriminate between healthy and unhealthy economic activity. Whether it is from something as wholesome as growing food or from industrial activity that ruins watersheds, eliminates habitat, and causes cancer, we take any growth in GDP as a sign of economic success.

9 *Canadian Encyclopedia,* www.thecanadianencyclopedia.com. "Gross Domestic Product."

10 A great book on this topic is Wayne Grady's *The Bone Museum: Travels in the Lost Worlds of Dinosaurs and Birds* (Toronto: Viking, 2000), in which he travels to Patagonia, China, and Saskatchewan.

11 C. Stuart Houston and Dan Zazelenchuk, "Swainson's Hawk Productivity in Saskatchewan," *North American Bird Bander* 29 (2004): 174–78.

12 A. Sidney England, Marc J. Bechard, and C. Stuart Houston, "Swainson's Hawk (*Buteo swainsoni*)," in *The Birds of North America,* no. 265, ed. A. Poole and F. Gill (Philadelphia, PA: Academy of Natural Sciences; Washington, DC: American Ornithologists' Union, 1997).

13 C. Stuart Houston, "Swainson's Hawk Longevity, Colour Banding and Natal Dispersal" *Blue Jay* 63 (March 2005): 34.

14 M. I. Goldstein, B. Woodbridge, M. E. Zaccagnini, and S. B. Canavelli, "An Assessment of Mortality of Swainson's Hawks on Wintering Grounds in Argentina," *Raptor Research* 30 (1997): 106–107.

Bird Name Index

Entries in **boldface** indicate profiled birds.